# CAMBRIDGESHIRE AIRFIELDS IN THE SECOND WORLD WAR

Graham Smith

COUNTRYSIDE BOOKS
NEWBURY, BERKSHIRE

First Published 1997
© Graham Smith 1997
Reprinted, with revisions 1999

All rights reserved. No reproduction
permitted without the prior permission
of the publisher:

COUNTRYSIDE BOOKS
3 Catherine Road
Newbury, Berkshire

ISBN 1 85306 456 4

The cover painting is by Colin Doggett and shows
Lancasters of 156 Pathfinder Squadron leaving RAF Warboys, 1943.

Designed by Mon Mohan

Produced through MRM Associates Ltd., Reading
Typeset by Techniset Typesetters, Merseyside
Printed by Woolnough Bookbinding Ltd., Irthlingborough

# CONTENTS

# ACKNOWLEDGEMENTS

I am, once again, deeply indebted to a number of people for assisting me during the preparation of this book: Norman G. Richards of the Archives Division of the National Air and Space Museum at Washington, Terry Holloway of the Marshall Group of Companies, Bronwen Wilken, and the staff of Galleywood library.

During the research and writing of the book, I had the pleasure to meet Harold Hernaman, DFC, an ex-member of No 156 (PFF) squadron and his wife, Gwen. And it is to him and to all his wartime colleagues in the Allied Air Forces that I would humbly dedicate this book.

Graham Smith

# CAMBRIDGESHIRE'S WORLD WAR II AIRFIELDS

## KEY TO MAP

1. Alconbury
2. Bassingbourn
3. Bottisham
4. Bourn
5. Cambridge
6. Castle Camps
7. Caxton Gibbet
8. Duxford
9. Fowlmere
10. Glatton
11. Gransden Lodge
12. Graveley
13. Kimbolton
14. Little Staughton
15. Lord's Bridge
16. Mepal
17. Molesworth
18. Oakington
19. Peterborough
20. Sibson
21. Somersham
22. Snailwell
23. Steeple Morden
24. Upwood
25. Warboys
26. Waterbeach
27. Witchford
28. Wittering
29. Wratting Common
30. Wyton

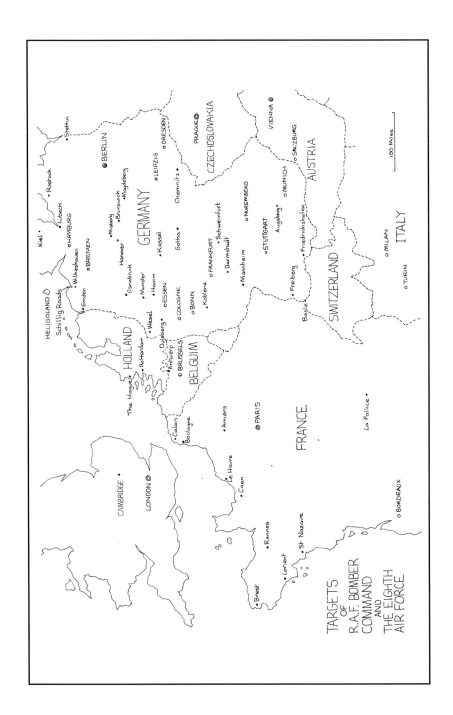

# I
# SETTING
# THE
# SCENE

Just after noon on Sunday, 3rd September 1939 a Blenheim IV (N6215) of 139 Squadron sped down the grass runway at RAF Wyton bound on a secret mission. Few of the airmen who watched the aircraft climb away and disappear into the clear blue sky were aware of its destination or the objective of this first operational sortie of the Second World War. All they knew for certain was that less than 45 minutes earlier they had listened to the Prime Minister's radio broadcast, which had told them that, 'this country is now at war with Germany'.

This dire announcement did not come as much of a surprise; since 25th August the station had been on a 'war footing' and was now operating under Bomber Command War Orders. They had been busy camouflaging the airfield and blackout regulations were being strictly enforced. Families had been evacuated from the married quarters, roads through the station closed, and civilian workers at the airfield screened. Armed guards had appeared at the main gate and patrolled around the airfield, and army personnel now manned the anti-aircraft defences. On 1st September, the day Germany invaded Poland, a general mobilisation of the Royal Air Force was ordered. Everybody on the station was well aware that it was only a matter of time before 'the balloon went up'!

For three days a Blenheim had been placed on constant standby waiting for the arrival of the War Telegram that would activate the first operation. This message was sent from Whitehall a few minutes after

*Record of the first operational sortie of the war, from Wyton on 3rd September 1939. (PRO)*

eleven o'clock on that fateful Sunday morning, and it finally filtered down to Wyton, which also served as the headquarters of No 2 Group of Bomber Command. The Group Commander, Air Vice-Marshal C. T. Maclean, relayed the order to the Station Commander and thus the Royal Air Force went to war.

The Blenheim was piloted by Flying Officer A. McPherson with a naval officer, Commander Thompson, acting as his observer and Corporal V. Arrowsmith as air-gunner. Their orders were to photograph units of the German fleet that were thought to be leaving the naval port of Wilhelmshaven. As the Blenheim flew over the port, the first RAF aircraft to cross the German frontier, McPherson carefully circled the flotilla whilst Commander Thompson took 75 photographs of the vessels moving into the Schillig Roads. As the Blenheim returned home Corporal Arrowsmith tried in vain to radio the vital information back to base, but because of the intense cold experienced at the high altitude (24,000 feet) the radio set had frozen! The aircraft landed safely back at Wyton at ten minutes to five - the first sortie had taken less than five hours.

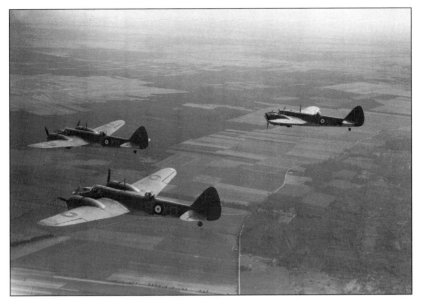

*Blenheim IVs of 139 Squadron. (Imperial War Museum)*

Shortly after eight-thirty on the following morning McPherson and his crew again left Wyton with orders 'to reconnoitre to locate the German fleet off Wilhelmshaven.' The weather was not so favourable, with banks of low cloud forcing McPherson down to almost 300 feet, but with dogged perseverance he managed to track down the German vessels and another batch of successful photographs were obtained. Again, trouble was experienced with the radio but at least this time a message was relayed back, though it was so garbled that no further action could be taken. Once McPherson had landed with further evidence of the current location of the German vessels, Bomber Command decided to mount its first bombing operation.

Five Blenheims of 139 Squadron were despatched, each loaded with four 500 pound bombs, and another ten Blenheims belonging to 107 and 110 Squadrons at Wattisham in Suffolk were also sent. They left in mid-afternoon. All five crews returned to Wyton without locating their targets; they had flown around for several hours in vain before jettisoning their bombs in the North Sea. Flight Lieutenant K. C. Doran, who was leading 110 Squadron, managed to reach the Schillig Roads and four of the crews bombed the German pocket battleship *Admiral von Scheer*, but their bombs bounced harmlessly off the armour plating. Unfortunately, a total of five aircraft failed to return.

The two operations resulted in the award of the first RAF gallantry decorations of the war. On 2nd October the Distinguished Flying Cross was awarded to both Flying Officer A. McPherson and Flight Lieutenant K. C. Doran. Wyton also established another notable first when on 2nd November, HM King George VI visited the station to conduct the first investiture of the war. It was the first to be staged 'in the field' for many a year.

Where Wyton had led the way, the other pre-war stations in the County were a little later into operational action. During 1940 Wyton's satellite airfield, Alconbury, saw its Blenheims and later Wellingtons entering the fray, as did the Blenheims operating from Oakington. The two other pre-war bomber stations, Bassingbourn and Upwood, were largely engaged in training duties, as was the airfield at Cambridge. It was not really until the Battle of Britain that the fighter squadrons at Duxford and its satellite, Fowlmere, came to the fore, as did the small airfield at Castle Camps. Because of its distance from the heavy fighting over London and the South East, Wittering did not see much action until late 1940 when its night-fighter squadrons were engaged in the defence of the Midlands. The airfields at Bottisham and Snailwell, which both opened in 1940, were mainly used by Army Co-operation squadrons.

From 1941 it could be said that Bomber Command held sway in the County, with Wellington and Stirling squadrons operating from Alconbury, Bourn, Kimbolton, Molesworth, Oakington, Waterbeach and Wyton. Perhaps the most momentous event for the County's wartime airfields was the formation of the Pathfinder Force (PFF) in August 1942 with the four original PFF squadrons based at Graveley, Oakington, Warboys and Wyton. Late in 1942 the first Bomb Groups of the USAAF's Eighth Air Force arrived to occupy Alconbury, Bassingbourn, Kimbolton and Molesworth, followed later by another moving into Glatton, and ultimately four Fighter Groups operated from Bottisham, Duxford, Fowlmere and Steeple Morden.

By 1943 three more bomber stations had opened at Mepal, Witchford and Wratting Common, and Bourn and Gransden Lodge joined No 8 Group (PFF), with the airfields at Little Staughton and Upwood being transferred into the Group in the following year. In 1944 the County had 24 operational airfields and the sky was filled with a massive number of aircraft leaving and returning from missions over Germany and the Continent. Few days or nights passed when the countryside did not echo to the heavy throb of aircraft engines - the sky overhead was rarely empty and quiet.

From the first day of the war until VE Day, the County's airfields made a major contribution to the European air war. Many have survived but only a few are still used for their original purpose. It should be noted that although during the war some of these airfields were not in Cambridgeshire, for the purpose of this book all that were, or are now, sited within the County have been included, and to avoid confusion, 'County' or 'Cambridgeshire' are used in their current sense.

# Fighter Command

When the men of Fighter Command faced their sternest test during the summer of 1940, they were serving in an organisation that was barely four years old. Many could remember the time when they were just a minor part of the Air Defence of Great Britain, which then controlled all operations by bombers, fighters, anti-aircraft guns and searchlights. The Command had been formed on 14th July 1936 with Air Marshal Sir Hugh C. T. Dowding as its first Air Officer Commanding-in-Chief. It is to his eternal credit that he managed to develop his meagre and outmoded resources into a force that successfully defended the country against the Luftwaffe - the most powerful air force in the world.

Previously, Dowding had been involved in the service's various research and development programmes and had been instrumental in the early planning of the monoplane fighters - the Hurricane, Defiant and Spitfire - as well as actively supporting the new and revolutionary device, Radio Direction Finding, later known as radar. By mid 1940 there were some 50 RDF stations in operation and 30 were Chain Home Low, specially designed to seek out low-flying aircraft. Allied to these stations were the well-trained Observer Corps, a barrage balloon force and the anti-aircraft batteries, forming an effective Home Defence System which played a vital role in the Battle of Britain.

In August 1939 there were 37 squadrons based in four operational Groups; all but eight were equipped with either Hurricanes or Spitfires. At the outbreak of the war, four Hurricane squadrons were sent to France, followed by another two, and two were effectively lost in the Norway campaign. This depletion of his slim resources caused Dowding grave concern, and he strenuously resisted any further attempts to move his valuable squadrons into France. He considered his main responsibility to be the defence of the Kingdom.

*Hurricane Is practising intercepting a bomber. (Imperial War Museum)*

The air battles over France during May 1940 brought the Command and its pilots their first taste of combat against the Luftwaffe. By 4th June 450 aircraft, mostly Hurricanes, had been lost but more critically some 140 trained pilots were missing or wounded in action, many experienced pre-war airmen, and their replacement became a major problem. During the Battle of Britain it was not the lack of aircraft that caused the greatest concern but the supply of trained pilots.

The Battle officially lasted from 10th July until 31st October, the designated period for the award of the Battle of Britain Clasp - a gilt rose emblem worn on the ribbon on the 1939-45 Star, and presented to 2,927 airmen. The Command had a front-line strength of 57 squadrons, with six of these being non-operational, giving Dowding some 1,100 pilots - 'The Few' - to defend the country from a Luftwaffe force then estimated to have in excess of 2,000 'attack' aircraft.

The pilots were clearly instructed: '..it must be constantly borne in mind that our aim is *the destruction of the enemy bombers*, and that action against fighters is only a means to an end.' The bombers were the twin-engined Heinkel 111s, the Junkers 87 'Stuka' dive bombers, the Junkers 88s, strong and manoeuvrable twin-engined bombers, and the Dornier 17s, probably the least effective. Their fighter escorts were the Messerschmitt 109E, one of the classic fighters of the war, with a superior performance to the Hurricane, and the much-vaunted 110C or Zerstörer ('Destroyer'), a twin-engined and heavily armed fighter. Both had been designed by Willy Messerschmitt, and the correct definition of these aircraft should be 'Bf' for Bayerische Flugzeugwerke, their manufacturer, but as the Luftwaffe records showed both 'Bf' and 'Me', the latter will be used here for ease of identification.

During the Battle it was No 11 that carried the heavier burden, with the three other Groups providing the reserve squadrons. The fighter airfields in Cambridgeshire, at Duxford and Wittering with their satellites at Fowlmere and Collyweston, were under No 12 Group's control, whereas Castle Camps later came under No 11 Group. This Group was commanded by Air Vice-Marshal Keith Park, a highly effective and popular leader, and his calm and measured tactics proved decisive during the Battle.

His counterpart at No 12 Group, Air Vice-Marshal Trafford Leigh-Mallory, had commanded the Group since 1937; he was energetic and decisive with an abundance of self-confidence. Leigh-Mallory held strong views on the conduct of aerial combat, favouring the use of fighter wings of three or more squadrons, rather than operating singly or at the most in pairs. There was no love lost between the two

*A typical 'scramble' - pilots racing to their Spitfires.*

commanders and Leigh-Mallory was particularly outspoken in his criticism of Park and his use of resources during the Battle. The 'Big Wing' controversy would greatly damage the reputations of both Dowding and Park, whereas Leigh-Mallory became the head of Fighter Command and later commanded the Second Tactical Air Force.

The Battle can be divided into separate phases. The first German attacks were directed at shipping in the Channel, coastal airfields and radar stations, then the Luftwaffe attempted to destroy Fighter Command in the air. This was followed by an assault on the fighter airfields and radar stations; between 24th August and 7th September there were 33 bombing attacks mostly directed at the airfields in No 11 Group, though Duxford and Fowlmere were targeted. It was during this critical period that No 12 Group's squadrons became involved in the Battle, and their deployment started the bitter argument over fighter tactics. From then the offensive changed to daylight bombing raids on London, which continued well into the autumn.

The Luftwaffe knew the Battle as Adlerangriff ('Eagles Attack') when, according to Goering, they expected to 'wipe the British Air Force from the sky'. It was a prelude to Operation Sealion, the invasion of England. Although planned to commence on 10th August - Adlertag ('Eagles Day') - it was postponed for three days because of unfavourable weather. On the 15th, airfields, aircraft factories and radar stations came under heavy attack; 75 enemy aircraft were destroyed for the loss of 30 fighters and 17 pilots. The next day the newspapers reported that 144 enemy aircraft had been destroyed and loudly proclaimed a great victory. Throughout the Battle, the Air Ministry issued figures of enemy aircraft destroyed which, to say the least, were overstated when compared with the actual Luftwaffe losses. The speed, intensity and confusion of the aerial combats may have caused genuine over-claims by the pilots, but the inflated figures did have a most beneficial effect on the morale of the pilots and the public alike.

Sunday (the 18th) saw the heaviest fighting so far, and has since become known as 'The Hardest Day'. Sixty-nine aircraft were destroyed for the loss of 31 fighters in the air, although newspaper headlines boasted, '115 out of 600 raiders destroyed...the biggest defeat of Nazis so far.' This day's battles occasioned Winston Churchill's famous speech: 'Never in the field of human conflict was so much owed by so many to so few.'

On the last day of August the Command suffered its heaviest loss, 39 aircraft, and the strain of constant combat was beginning to show on the pilots. There was deep concern at the high loss of squadron and flight commanders. Sunday, 15th September has rightly become known as 'Battle of Britain Day' because the almost non-stop aerial combats were critical to the final outcome of the Battle. The Air Ministry claimed 185 aircraft destroyed (the true figure was 56) for the loss of 29 fighters and twelve pilots killed. It was hailed as a great victory, and from that eventful day the German High Command realised that they had failed to destroy Fighter Command. Two days later Operation Sealion was postponed.

It had been a close but costly victory: 507 pilots killed and another 500 seriously injured. Churchill considered it, 'one of the decisive battles of the war'. Nevertheless, by November, the architects of this memorable victory - Dowding and Park - had been relieved of their posts in favour of Air Marshal W. Sholto Douglas and Air Vice-Marshal T. L. Leigh-Mallory. It seemed scant gratitude for their valiant work, but time has righted the balance, and their tarnished reputations have been fully restored.

The Command now had the difficult task of opposing the nightly armadas of German bombers. The Spitfires and, to a lesser extent,

Hurricanes were not suited to night-operations; a few squadrons of Beaufighters were hastily brought into service, and aided by Defiants and Blenheims they provided some spirited opposition. Until the AI (Aircraft Interception) radar was improved the night-fighter force would always operate at a considerable disadvantage. Under its new Chief, the Command moved onto the offensive with a new type of operation, 'Circus', followed by others known as 'Rhubarbs', 'Ramrods', 'Jim Crows', 'Rodeos' and 'Roadsteads'. They were a mixture of combined operations with light or medium bombers and individual or squadron fighter sweeps to attack airfields and transportation targets in France and the Low Countries, as well as anti-shipping strikes.

With Leigh-Mallory in charge of No 11 Group, wings were established at his sector airfields. They became especially effective in 1942 with the improved Spitfire marks, commanded by some of the heroes of the Battle of Britain. In September 1941 the new Luftwaffe fighter, the Focke-Wulf 190, made its appearance with an all-round performance superior to Spitfire Vs. Until the Typhoon became more reliable and numerous and the new Rolls-Royce engines resulted in improved Spitfires, the aircraft caused Fighter Command considerable problems.

By 1942 the Command numbered 100 squadrons, mainly operating by day, and it had become a most cosmopolitan force with a third of them manned by Polish, Czech, Belgian, Norwegian, Canadian, Australian and American pilots. The onset of the 'Baedeker' raids on cathedral cities highlighted the vulnerability of the home defences to these random but heavy bombing raids, and in four months only 67 aircraft were shot down, over one third falling to the new Mosquito night-fighters. In August came the ill-famed Dieppe operation, when the Command mounted almost 3,000 sorties and claimed 91 enemy aircraft destroyed for the loss of a similar number. After the war it was discovered that the actual German losses were less than 50, effectively a serious defeat for the Command!

Twelve months later, the Command was treble its size at the beginning of the war with a massive force of fighters. Its main roles were intruder raids and large fighter sweeps over the Continent, as well as escorting the American daylight bombers. In November 1943 it lost almost two-thirds of its squadrons, along with its name, when the Second Tactical Air Force was formed. The small fighter force that remained was renamed The Air Defence of Great Britain, echoing the early 1930s. In January 1944 this force faced a new German night-bombing offensive mainly directed at London, Operation Steinbock, a retaliation for Bomber Command's heavy raids on Berlin. The night-fighter force was far better equipped, and the Luftwaffe lost almost 300 aircraft to the Mosquito night-fighters.

Faced with such a crippling defeat by conventional weapons the Germans turned to their Vergeltungswaffe or 'revenge weapons' - the V1 and V2 rockets. Again the fighter pilots had found their true metier - single-handed aerial combat against the rockets or 'divers' as they called them. In the V1 rocket campaign they managed to destroy over 1,800, about 46% of the total destroyed with nearly one third falling to Tempest pilots. In August another new fighter was in action against the 'divers' - the Gloster Meteor I, the first RAF jet aircraft. In September the first V2 rocket landed at Chiswick. These missiles travelling at more than 3,000 mph were impossible to intercept, so fighters were engaged in attacking their launching sites.

The name Fighter Command was restored in October with Air Vice-Marshal Sir Roderic Hill continuing as Commander, and it was mainly engaged in escorting the daylight operations mounted by Bomber Command during the last nine months of the war. Fighter Command brought its wartime operations to a close on 9th May 1945, providing air cover for the forces landing on Guernsey. Over 5,000 enemy aircraft had been destroyed for the loss of 3,690 aircrew. Without doubt its greatest hour had been in those summer months in 1940 when its pilots held the fate of the country in their hands. For that Battle alone, they should never be forgotten.

# Bomber Command

On 1st September 1939, the US President appealed to Britain, France and Germany to refrain from bombing any undefended towns or any targets where civilians might be injured. Britain and France readily gave the necessary assurances and 18 days later Hitler followed suit, maintaining that, 'Germany would conduct war in a most chivalrous and humane manner'. Suddenly the goalposts had been moved and Bomber Command found that its immediate and sole available target was the German fleet, which was twelfth of thirteen targets listed in the Western Air Plans that had been formulated in 1938 as the Command's war strategy. At least this moratorium allowed some precious breathing space.

*'Take off: Interior of a Bomber Aircraft' – an oil painting by Dame Laura Knight RA. (Imperial War Museum)*

At this time, Bomber Command had 23 operational squadrons – effectively only about 300 twin-engined serviceable aircraft with trained crews ready to take up the bombing offensive. Considering this meagre strike force it was not surprising that earlier in the year, Sir Edgar Ludlow-Hewitt, the Chief of Bomber Command, had informed the Air Council that, 'his Command would not within any predictable period attain the strength in efficiency to declare it ready for war'.

This was a realistic and disturbing assessment of his bomber force, which proved to be inadequate in several other respects. Although the crews were highly trained in most aspects, they were quite inexperienced in long-range flights, especially at night. Furthermore, their aircraft lacked adequate heating for high altitude operations, the fuel tanks and systems were unprotected from bullets and flak, and their defensive armament - hand held guns of merely rifle calibre - was woefully inadequate against fighters.

The first bombing operation was launched on 4th September. The crews' orders were carefully worded: 'The greatest care is to be taken not to injure the civilian population. The intention is to destroy the German fleet. *There is no alternative target.*' Seven Blenheims and Wellingtons failed to return (24%) and sadly two Danish civilians were killed at Esbjerg as a result of a serious navigational error. At least the Command was granted permission to fly over Germany to drop propaganda leaflets and ten Whitleys delivered over five million on the first night of the war. These operations, which would continue for several years, thus quickly countered Goering's pre-war empty bombast that, 'No enemy aircraft will ever fly over the Reich'!

In December 1939 Bomber Command suffered a resounding set-back; the hallowed tenet that 'the bomber will always get through', which had been central to pre-war planning, was found to be patently flawed. The belief that a tight formation of heavy bombers flying by day would be self-defensive was shown to be illusionary by the raids on 14th and 18th December, when 17 out of 34 Wellingtons were shot down on shipping strikes near Wilhelmshaven. In the New Year it was reluctantly accepted that if German war industries were to be attacked by day, then the bombers would require a fighter escort. However, both Spitfires and Hurricanes lacked the necessary range for this task, and moreover they were urgently needed for the country's air defence. The only alternative was to operate at night and without escort.

It was accepted that bombing accuracy would suffer, but night-navigation was not considered too serious a problem, despite the fact that it had never figured large in pre-war training, and more pertinently, in two years there had been 450 forced landings in Great Britain at night due to crews losing their way! Thus night-bombing was introduced more by expediency rather than by any pre-conceived plan. It was a policy that would be pursued whole-heartedly by Bomber Command for the majority of the war, and ultimate success rested on the determination and courage of its crews, along with the arrival of various navigational and bombing aids.

Any slim hope that the December operations were minor aberrations disappeared in April 1940 when the largest bombing operation so far was launched against shipping at Stavanger and nine aircraft were lost (15%). This proved to be the last straw for Air Marshal Sir Charles Portal, the new Chief, and in future he used his heavy bombers by night.

In the following month the air war took a dramatic turn with Blenheims and Battles engaged in a bitter and bloody contest over the near Continent. On the night of 11/12th May, 37 heavy bombers bombed Mönchengladbach, the first Bomber Command raid on a German town, and three aircraft were lost. Four nights later over 100 bombers attacked industrial targets in the Ruhr and Belgium; this heralded the strategic bombing offensive, which would continue almost unabated for the next five years. Although slow and hesitant at first, it steadily grew in strength and severity until it became an utterly devastating demonstration of air power, bringing death and destruction to many German cities and towns.

In May 1940 the Air Ministry issued a bombing directive to the Command, the first of many over the next few years. Four priority targets were identified - aircraft and ammunition factories, oil plants and transport communications. It was estimated that 75% of Germany's industrial production was centred in the Ruhr valley, so targets there would be attacked throughout the war. The crews soon dubbed it 'The Happy Valley', or more grimly, 'The Land of No Return' because of the number of aircrews lost on Ruhr operations. The Command gained its first minor victory during the month, when the Blenheim crews managed to impose a slight but critical delay on the German forces advancing on Dunkirk.

On 25th August the War Cabinet sanctioned the first raid on Berlin as a direct reply to the Luftwaffe's first bombing of London on the previous night. About 50 aircraft attempted to bomb specific targets but because of heavy cloud they were frustrated. More operations were mounted in the coming weeks but they were equally unsuccessful and were really nothing more than 'morale boosting' raids. Bomber Command was not in a position to launch a major and effective offensive against Berlin until March 1943.

During September 1940 the Command attacked invasion barges in the Channel ports - a lesser known aspect of the Battle of Britain. After one operation to Antwerp on the 15/16th, a young wireless operator was awarded the Victoria Cross - the second to be won by a Command airman. Another 18 would be awarded to airmen in bombing operations over Europe.

As a direct result of the Luftwaffe's heavy night-raids, the War Cabinet authorised the first major 'area' attack of a German city centre. The operation was codenamed Abigail Rachel, and Mannheim was selected as the target. On 16/17th December 1940, 134 aircraft bombed, but without much accuracy or effect.

In the New Year Sir Richard Pierse, who had replaced Portal in October, was directed to make the German oil industry, 'the sole primary aim of your bomber offensive'. Nine major oil plants were named - Leuna, Pölitz, Nordstern, Zeitz, Scholven/Buer, Ruhland, Böhlen, Magdeburg and Lützendorf. All would figure in operations mounted by both Bomber Command and the Eighth Air Force in 1944. This oil directive was quickly overtaken by another new priority - U-boat yards and bases - because of the severe losses suffered by the vital North Atlantic convoys. From March until July 1941, German U-boat yards and the French Atlantic ports were attacked, often at a high cost.

Sir Richard Pierse now had the new four-engined Stirlings, followed shortly by Manchesters and Halifaxes, and his Command was growing in strength and power. From the summer of 1941 attention was directed back to German industrial targets with the squadrons active almost nightly. Several operations exceeded the 'tolerable' 5% loss rate, and daylight raids by light bombers were also proving costly. Over 1,100 aircraft had been lost in the nine months up to September. Clearly, no force could sustain such losses for long and still remain operational.

Perhaps more damaging was the report, compiled by D. M. Butt of the War Cabinet Secretariat for the Air Ministry, which was based on 600 aerial photographs taken in two months of operations. It revealed that only 25% of the aircraft came closer than five miles of the aiming point. Over the Ruhr, where intense flak and ground haze affected the bombing, the figure dropped alarmingly to 10%. The situation was even more serious as the report was based on the performance of experienced crews, as they were the only ones provided with cameras. It was also known, from debriefings, that on average one third of the crews had been unable to bomb the primary targets for a variety of reasons. In the face of such dire and damning evidence, allied to the operational losses, the future of the Command's strategic offensive looked very bleak.

Matters came to a head after 7/8th November 1941 when Berlin was attacked in some strength, and 21 aircraft were lost (12%) with a total of 37 missing on the night's operations - the heaviest loss of the war. Sir Richard Pierse was ordered to carry out only 'limited operations' whilst the whole future of Bomber Command and its night-bombing offensive was considered. Sir Charles Portal, now the Chief of the Air Staff, argued persuasively not only to retain the existing Command but also for an outright offensive on German cities - effectively a policy of 'area bombing'. Portal gained Churchill's approval for the all-out offensive, and on 14th February 1942 a directive was issued that stated, 'the bombing should be focused on the morale of the enemy civil population and in particular that of the industrial workers', with a caveat, 'to use the utmost resources at all times.'

Bomber Command had not only survived but it had been given the green light to expand its operations. Harris later wrote, 'without Portal there would have been no bomber offensive'. Sir Richard Pierse was made the scapegoat for the ills of his Command, although they were not of his making. He had been replaced, in January, by a temporary Commander, Air Vice-Marshal Baldwin, until Portal's personal choice - Air Chief Marshal Arthur Harris - took over on 22nd February 1942.

Harris led Bomber Command for the duration of the war, and his name became synonymous with his Command; Churchill dubbed him 'Bomber', though to his crews he was known as 'Butch'! A born leader, who engendered a fierce and total loyalty from his airmen, Harris was unswerving in his commitment to outright area bombing, and prosecuted it with a grim and ruthless determination. He had the advantage of taking over Bomber Command when the most out-standing heavy bomber of the war - the Lancaster - was coming into service, the first navigational aid, GEE, would shortly be available for operations, and the American Eighth Air Force would soon share the strategic air offensive.

His mettle as a Commander was shown with the attack on Lübeck on 28/29th March 1942. It was a heavy fire-raising raid on area bombing lines, and the first real major success for Bomber Command. This was followed by the three famous '1,000' raids on Cologne, Essen and Bremen, which were heralded as 'The Greatest Air Raids in History' and did so much to lift the morale of the British people. In those grim, dark days Bomber Command seemed to be the only Allied force taking the offensive to the enemy. Harris is attributed with the famous phrase, 'Hitler has sowed the breeze and now the German people will reap the whirlwind', and this certainly summed up his uncompromising attitude to the bombing offensive. However, operations on such a

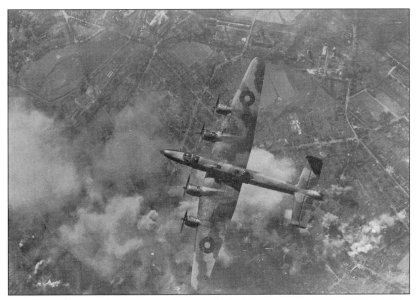

*A Halifax of No 6 Group over Wanne Eickel on 12th October 1944. (Imperial War Museum)*

scale proved costly and losses were on average above 4%. At this casualty rate aircrews had about a 13% chance of completing a tour of 30 operations - a grim and sobering statistic.

Early in 1943 an Allied conference at Casablanca agreed a combined bombing strategy. This directive listed the essential targets in order of priority - U-boat yards, German aircraft industry, road/rail transportation, oil industry and other war industrial targets - with the objective of 'undermining the morale of the German people'. In June the main priority changed at the behest of the Eighth Air Force, with the German aircraft industry heading the list. This new directive was named Pointblank, and except for minor adjustments it would remain in force almost until the end of the war. Harris, somewhat ingenuously, considered that Pointblank had not changed anything as far as his Command was concerned!

By early March, Harris had over 600 heavy bombers at his disposal. The Pathfinder Force (see later) had been operating since the previous August, and he now felt the time was ripe for his ferocious and sustained offensive against targets in the Ruhr. These were followed by the devastating fire-raids on Hamburg and two spectacular and highly publicised operations to the dams and the Peenemunde rocket research

23

establishment, both demonstrating the Command's growing skills in locating and accurately bombing small individual targets. For some time Harris had been pressing the Air Ministry to give him control over the other ancillary forces involved in the bombing offensive, and in December 1943 a new Group was formed - No 100 (Bomber Support). Its squadrons were engaged in various RCM (Radio Countermeasures) operations against the night-fighters and the German radar defences. Bomber Command had come a very long way from those pioneering days of 1940/1.

On 23/24th August 1943 Harris opened his Battle of Berlin campaign, which proved to be a vicious and costly offensive that gained momentum during the winter and continued until the following March. Over 30,000 tons of bombs were dropped in 19 raids, for the loss of over 600 aircraft and 3,347 airmen killed, many of whom are buried in the British War Cemetery at Berlin. Six nights after the last Berlin operation the Command lost its highest single total of aircraft when 95 failed to return from Nuremberg on 30/31st March. This was a major disaster, with more airmen killed on this one night (545) than in the whole of the Battle of Britain.

Two weeks later the overall control of Bomber Command (and USAAF) was passed to General Eisenhower, the Supreme Allied Commander in Europe, and much of the Command's efforts were directed towards support for Overlord - the invasion of mainland Europe. Coastal batteries, Luftwaffe airfields in France and road and rail communications in France and Belgium became the main targets. The latter were part of the Transportation Plan, an air offensive that had been hotly argued mainly because of the high risk to the French civilian population. Harris, along with the Eighth Air Force chiefs, opposed the plan on the grounds that their forces would be better deployed over German industrial targets. Nevertheless, 'The Plan' was approved with the Command being allocated 37 targets, and well over a half were destroyed by D-Day. Before returning in force to Germany the crews were active in support of the Allied armies in Normandy, as well as attacking V1 rocket sites.

The first major daylight raid to a German target since August 1941 was mounted on 27th August 1944 to Homberg and its oil refinery. The bombers were well escorted by a strong fighter force and not a single aircraft was lost. During the coming months the Command's daylight operations would increase in size and severity. What has become known as the Second Battle of the Ruhr was launched in early October, when very familiar Ruhr targets suffered the full fury of Bomber

*The British and Commonwealth War Graves Commission Cemetery, Berlin. (Bryan Jones)*

Command. By January 1945 it was at the zenith of its power, a massive air force with over 1,600 aircraft - a highly technical and totally professional strike force that could attack all types of targets with terrifying and awesome power. In the first four months of the year it conducted 36 major operations over Germany, dropping 180,000 tons of bombs, which was 20% of the total tonnage delivered throughout the war.

On 16th April 1945 it was announced that the objectives of Pointblank had been achieved and only 'necessary' operations should be mounted over Germany. On 25/26th April over 100 Lancasters attacked an oil refinery at Tonsberg in southern Norway. This was the final operation flown by heavy bombers, and a Lancaster came down in Sweden - the last of more than 3,400 to go missing in the war. The final operation was mounted on 2/3rd May 1945 to Kiel by the Mosquitos of No 8 Group - the Pathfinders.

Without doubt the strategic bombing offensive was very costly in human terms; 55,500 airmen were killed, and some 9,800 made prisoners. Air Chief Marshal Harris estimated that about 125,000 aircrew served with Bomber Command during the war, which means over half of them were either killed or made prisoner, with another

8,400 wounded - an enormous price to pay. The Command's fatalities were over three-quarters of the RAF's total for the whole of the war.

The bomber crews waged a special kind of war; a matter of hours separated the quiet and peace of the English countryside and a flight through hell. They had to contend with adverse weather, phalanxes of searchlights, heavy flak batteries and the Luftwaffe night-fighters, to return, if they were lucky, to normality with the certain knowledge that the next night they would face them again ... and again until their tour was over or they did not return, like so many of their friends. And yet these brave airmen did not receive a special Campaign Medal, nor did their Chief gain any post-war honours - a scant regard for their valiant and sterling efforts.

It is virtually impossible to find adequate words to express the immense contribution made by the men of Bomber Command. Even their own Commander found this task difficult: 'There are no words with which I can do justice to the aircrew who fought under my command. There is no parallel in warfare to such courage and determination...it was the courage of the small hours with long drawn out apprehensions of "going over the top". Such devotion must not be forgotten. It is unforgettable by anyone whose contacts gave them knowledge and understanding of what these young men experienced and faced.'

# The Pathfinders: No 8 (PFF) Group

The concept of using an elite force of bomber crews of proven navigational skills to locate targets was not new. The Luftwaffe had established a special pathfinding force - Kampfgruppe 100 - during 1940. Although Bomber Command quickly realised the importance of radio-navigational aids, the idea of a 'Target Finding Force' was not actively canvassed until late 1941. Its main proponent was Group Captain S. O. Bufton DSO, DFC, recently appointed Deputy Director of Bomber Operations at the Air Ministry.

Unlike many of the 'backroom boys', Bufton had current operational experience with No 4 Group, and had pioneered various projects aimed at helping the best crews to locate targets by using flares and guiding other crews by means of coloured Verey lights. His proposal envisaged six squadrons 'based in close proximity to each other', manned with normal crews but including 'at least 40 experienced crews of high navigational abilities'. Faced with the disturbing and damning report by D.M. Butt, Bufton was well able to convince his fellow staff officers of the need for such a force, but to persuade the AOC of Bomber Command and his Group Commanders was another matter!

When Air Chief Marshal Harris arrived at Bomber Command he was approached on the subject, but he was firmly opposed to such a proposal. He considered that the establishment of a 'corps d'elite', which would syphon off the best crews, would be detrimental to squadron morale and could jeopardise the crews' promotion prospects. Harris favoured a system of 'raid leaders', with one selected squadron operating in each Group. He was also aware that the time was close when all crews would have GEE, as well as bombing cameras, and then, he felt, natural competitiveness would bring about improved bombing accuracy. After months of debate and endless correspondence on the subject, Sir Charles Portal, who strongly supported Bufton, overruled Harris and in June 1942 a Target Finding Force was approved.

Despite his initial opposition, Harris managed to engineer some important and dramatic changes to the format of the new force. He instructed the commanders of his four 'heavy' Groups to nominate a squadron to form the force, rather than transferring their best crews. The original name did not really appeal to him, so instead he proposed The Pathfinder Force (PFF), which he thought suggested 'a navigational aid'. To compensate for the possible loss of promotion and for the fact that the crews would be required to complete a tour of 60 operations (including those already completed), he cajoled the Air Ministry (and the Treasury) to concede that PFF crews would be accorded one rank higher than they held. Finally and surprisingly, considering his views on elitism, he gained approval, by Royal Warrant, for the force's own special badge - the famous gilt hovering eagle - to be worn on the flap of the left-hand breast pocket below the medal ribbons, but with the strict embargo not whilst on operations!

The force came into being on 15th August 1942 under the command of Group Captain Donald C. T. Bennett, DSO. He was a young Australian pilot with a distinguished pre-war flying record, both with the RAF and Imperial Airways, and was probably the service's leading navigational expert. Bennett had commanded Halifax squadrons in No 4 Group, and had only recently returned from Sweden after being shot down over Norway. It was an inspirational choice, and much of the Pathfinders' success was due to his strong leadership, vision, drive and

*Air Vice-Marshal D.C.T. Bennett, CBE, DSO. (Imperial War Museum)*

determination. Harris later described him as, 'the most efficient airman I have ever met. His courage, both moral and physical, is outstanding, and as a technician he is unrivalled.'

Bennett set up his headquarters at Wyton, moving later to Castle Hill House in Huntingdon. Although the PFF was nominally under the control of No 3 Group, Bennett reported directly to Command Headquarters. On 17th August the four squadrons were transferred in, with 156 Squadron (Wellingtons) coming from No 1 Group, 7 Squadron (Stirlings) from No 3 Group, 35 Squadron (Halifaxes) from No 4 Group, and 83 Squadron (Lancasters) 'loaned' from No 5 Group. They were based at Warboys, Oakington, Graveley and Wyton respectively.

The PFF squadrons were thrown into the maelstrom with high hopes of success but with few, if any, advantages. The crews held no more especial skills than other airmen, and there was no new equipment or bombs for marking targets. Also, they had entered into their difficult and dangerous role when the enemy's ground defences were on the increase, the night-fighters were becoming more effective, and the Germans had discovered the means to jam GEE. It was difficult to conceive of a more hazardous time to test the mettle of the pioneer Pathfinders.

Their first PFF operation was mounted against Flensburg on 18/19th August 1942, and although 16 of the 31 PFF crews claimed to have marked the target, the bombing was less than impressive. Six nights later the Frankfurt operation was not too successful, and although Kassel was heavily bombed on the 27/28th there was little cloud so the PFF crews were able to visually illuminate the target well. The force already had its critics within the service, and worse was to follow when on 1/2nd September Saarbrücken was the target, but Saarlouis, a town 13 miles to the north-west, was marked and bombed in error. The word quickly went round the Command that the Pathfinders had 'put up a black' - RAF slang for an error of judgement.

Despite these disappointing results Bennett was determined to prove the worth of his force. A hard taskmaster, uncompromising, with very high operational standards, he demanded the same from his crews, and was ruthless in weeding out those who did not measure up. On 2/3rd September the PFF led a most successful operation over Karlsruhe, followed two nights later by a damaging attack on Bremen. In this raid the PFF used techniques which would be improved and refined over the coming months. The PFF crews were allocated separate marking tasks – blind markers and backers-up, visual markers and backers-up, route markers and supporters – each with carefully defined functions within the bombing operation. The intricate and precise marking procedure with different coloured flares, target indicators and

*The Avro Lancaster, the most famous RAF heavy bomber of the war.*

incendiaries was completed despite the phalanx of searchlights and the concentration of heavy flak batteries. The PFF operated mainly in advance of the main force, before the mass of bombers flooded the enemy defences.

During the next six months or so, PFF marking would become somewhat complicated as new techniques and methods were tried and developed. Bennett strenuously pursued the development of a whole range of target indicator pyrotechnics. He was an enthusiastic supporter of Oboe - the blind bombing device - and took an active interest in his solitary Mosquito squadron, No 109, which was trialling the new device right under his nose at Wyton. Bennett devoted his considerable energies to acquiring a totally Lancaster heavy force, all to be provided with H2S, the new radar bombing aid. Indeed, he tried to retain H2S as the sole preserve of his force, arguing that only his highly trained and experienced crews could get the maximum benefit from the device. But even he found it impossible to convince the Air Ministry that all the best crews were serving in his squadrons!

On 8th January 1943 the force was granted Group status - No 8 - with Bennett promoted to Air Commodore, the youngest to hold an Air rank, later being promoted to Air Vice-Marshal. His 'Oboe' Mosquitos had become operational, he now had two precious Flights of H2S aircraft, and during the month the first standard marker or target indicator became available. This was a 250 pound bomb casing packed

*A Mosquito BIX. Mosquitos were an integral part of the Pathfinder Force.*

with pyrotechnic candles, which could be ejected at various heights by a barometric fuse and allowed to fall slowly in a mass of vivid colours - red, green and yellow usually.

From these and later technical improvements, the Pathfinders developed three standard methods of marking targets. The first was visual, used when weather conditions enabled the aiming point to be clearly identified, and was known as Newhaven. The second, called Parramatta, was a system of ground marking used when the aiming point was obscured. And finally skymarking, which employed a variety of coloured flares to hang in the air, was named Waganui. When Oboe-equipped aircraft dropped the target indicators, the prefix 'Musical' was applied to the above names.

It was the Battle of the Ruhr that proved the ultimate worth of the PFF, which played a major and critical role in this series of sustained and devastating raids. The PFF Mosquitos marked accurately with Oboe, with the heavy PFF squadrons which were backing up coming in straight and level through heavy flak to drop their coloured markers. Many operations were potent and striking demonstrations of PFF techniques and methods, and Harris acknowledged that without the PFF, the Battle would have been barely possible, let alone so successful.

The Group had received some welcome reinforcements - 97 Squadron came from No 5 Group and 405 Squadron from the recently formed No 6 (Canadian) Group. His Oboe force was doubled with the addition of 105 Squadron, and another Mosquito squadron, 139, was acquired. Bennett had long been a devoted admirer of the fast little

31

bomber, which he called 'a master aircraft', and he had ambitious plans for their role in his Group. First to operate as a 'diversionary' force and then, more spectacularly, as a 'light night striking force' - his words.

The Hamburg raids in late July 1943 only added glory to the Pathfinders' reputation, as Bennett later wrote: 'Towards the end of July 1943 we achieved what I regard as the greatest victory of the war, land, sea, or air. This victory was in the Battle of Hamburg. The result was staggering!'

If the summer of 1943 had amply demonstrated the excellence of the Pathfinders, the Battle of Berlin during the winter of 1943/4 brought forth fresh criticism. Berlin was outside the range of Oboe so the PFF had to rely largely on H2S, and the images of the amorphous mass of the city as portrayed on the screens defied accurate identification. Even the most experienced PFF crews had difficulty in locating and marking targets accurately. Although there were impressive operations in the campaign, others were less than successful with scattered marking, some caused by adverse weather conditions. Nevertheless the PFF crews fought bravely over Berlin, sustaining heavy casualties and losing many squadron and flight commanders as well as many experienced crews, with 7 and 156 Squadrons suffering particularly harshly.

It is interesting to note that while PFF techniques were being seriously questioned within the service, the Luftwaffe had no doubt about the force's efficacy and expertise. A staff paper in March 1944 reported: 'The operational tactics of the Pathfinders have been under constant development ever since the earliest days, and even now cannot be considered as firmly established or completed. New methods of target location and marking, as well as extensive deceptive and diversionary measures against the German defences are evident in almost every operation...The realisation of these aims was made possible by the conscientious work of the Pathfinder group and by the high training standard (especially regarding navigation) of the crews.' Fine praise indeed from the enemy!

Nevertheless, for some time No 5 Group had been experimenting with a different kind of marking, which it considered an improvement on PFF methods. It was based on the low-level identification of targets and Air Vice-Marshal The Hon R. A. Cochrane, the Group's AOC, was able to convince Harris of the soundness of their techniques. As a result his Group became virtually an independent force, responsible for their own marking. Much to Bennett's opposition and patent displeasure, his Group lost three squadrons - two heavies and one Mosquito - to

Cochrane. From now on, Bennett was determined to obtain as many Mosquitos as possible to build up his Light Night Strike Force - ultimately eight in total. This Force wrought havoc over many German targets, but more especially Berlin, which was bombed night after night, with an amazingly low loss rate (0.2%).

The PFF still continued to lead the way, with its Oboe Mosquito and Lancaster H2S squadrons serving most of Bomber Command for the rest of the war. It was often stretched to its limits marking several operations at once, fully justifying its motto, 'We Guide to Strike'. The gallantry of the Pathfinder crews became legendary, with three of its pilots being awarded posthumous Victoria Crosses. Their contribution was immense, over 50,000 sorties were made for the loss of 675 aircraft, most sustained by the heavy squadrons; 3,727 airmen were killed in action, almost equivalent to 20 complete Lancaster squadrons.

As Bennett expressed in his victory message to his airmen: 'The Pathfinder Force has shouldered a grave responsibility. It has led Bomber Command, the greatest striking force ever known. That we have been successful can be seen in the far-reaching results we have achieved. That is the greatest reward the Pathfinder Force ever hopes to receive, for those results have benefited all law-abiding peoples... I want to thank you, each man and woman of you personally, and to congratulate you on your unrelenting spirit and energy and on the results you have achieved.'

On 12th May Bennett was succeeded by Air Vice-Marshal J. R. Whitley, and Bennett made a brief appearance as a Liberal Member of Parliament before resuming his career in civil aviation. Sadly, he was the only Group Commander not to be knighted.

The Group was quietly disbanded in December as there was no future envisaged for it in post-war Bomber Command, but over 50 years later the exploits of the Pathfinders are still spoken about with awe. They were, and remain, an 'elite' band of airmen.

# USAAF

The United States Army Air Force that served in the United Kingdom during the Second World War comprised two large and separate Air Forces - the Eighth and the Ninth - but only units of the Eighth Air Force occupied airfields in the county. Compared with its RAF

*Three Eighth Air Force generals in early 1944 – (l to r) Carl A. Spaatz, James Doolittle and William Kepner. (USAF)*

counterparts it was a mere babe in arms, having been formed in January 1942 as the 'Fifth', only to be redesignated a few days later. It had been activated to provide the air support for an invasion of North Africa, but when that was postponed Major General Carl A. Spaatz, the Air Force Commander in Europe, persuaded the Pentagon that the Eighth should move to the United Kingdom to form the nucleus of the USAAF in Europe.

Matters then moved rather swiftly, after Brigadier General Ira C. Eaker, along with six fellow officers, arrived at Hendon on 20th February 1942 with the purpose of establishing the new Air Force in the United Kingdom. Their task was truly formidable. The planned build-up was not only most ambitious but quite staggering in its immensity: 60 combat groups - 33 Bombardment, twelve Fighter, eight Transport and seven Observation - with some 3,500 aircraft were to be in place by April 1943, the target date for the invasion of Europe.

If this figure had been realised then the Eighth Air Force would have been larger than the whole of the RAF's operational Commands serving in the United Kingdom. However, the original plan did not come to fruition, being modified and changed by operational dictates and the demands of other war fronts. That does not alter the fact, though, that it became a large and powerful Air Force, fully justifying its sobriquet, 'the Mighty Eighth'.

*A B-17 of the 91st Bomb Group in formation. (USAF)*

The first essential was airfields. No less than 75 would be required and most would need to be sited in eastern England. As their Bomb Groups comprised four squadrons, it was thought that each Group would require two airfields, although this policy changed quite early on, with the result that each Group - Bomb or Fighter - had its own airfield. Ultimately, the Eighth occupied 63. Fortunately the Air Ministry had been aware of the possible need for extra airfields back in 1941 and 36 sites, as well as existing RAF airfields, had been already ear-marked for the USAAF. Nevertheless, the sheer volume of planning and all the logistics involved in accommodating such a vast force was a massive undertaking, and the debt the Eighth owed to Eaker and his coterie of hard-working officers was immense.

The USAAF was dedicated to high-altitude precision bombing with large formations of self-defensive bombers operating solely by day. For this type of aerial warfare the Americans felt they had the best weapons - the B-17 (Flying Fortress) and B-24 (Liberator). Each was equipped with a satisfactory oxygen system and the so-called 'wonder' Norden bomb-sight, which was believed to be deadly accurate even from high altitudes. With this concept in mind, fighters had taken rather a back seat, their main role being as strike aircraft rather than pure bomber escorts. General Eaker was a dedicated advocate of daylight bombing, and he struck up a good working relationship with Air Chief Marshal Harris, who had recently been appointed C-in-C of Bomber Command. This was essential for the Allied air offensive, but the two men also became personal friends.

The Eighth Air Force comprised two separate operational Commands - Bombardment and Fighter. The first would ultimately be composed of three Divisions, almost air forces in their own right. Eaker served as its Commander until early January 1944, taking it through its harsh and costly growing pains, and the Eighth owed much to his vision, courage and leadership. The Fighter Command, under Brigadier General Frank Hunter, was planned to have three Wings; but because of the nature of the bombing offensive, the pressure of the North African campaign, and an acute shortage of suitable aircraft, its build-up was far slower.

The first American units began to arrive in May 1942, with the B-17s appearing in July along with P-38s (Lightnings), then considered the best long-range fighters. The B-17s moved into the East Midlands and other Groups of the First Bomb Wing (later Division) would find homes in the same general area, five of them in the County. The Second and Third Divisions would be based in Norfolk and Suffolk. The Fighter Groups tended to be spread throughout East Anglia, with four operating from Cambridgeshire. When Major General Carl Spaatz arrived, the Eighth Air Force could be said to be in business. Eaker is reported to have said, 'We won't do much talking until we've done more flying. We hope that when we leave, you'll be glad we came.'

The USAAF entered the European air war on 29th June 1942 in a low key affair with light bombers borrowed from the RAF. It was not until 17th August that the first heavies were ready to be tested over enemy territory. On this historic mission, just twelve B-17s of 97th Bomb Group took off from Grafton Underwood. The formation was led by Colonel Frank Armstrong, the Group's Commanding Officer and one of the original six officers that had arrived with Eaker. On this occasion General Eaker sneaked a ride in the appropriately named *Yankee Doodle*, and the target was Rouen, with the small force being well outnumbered by RAF Spitfire escorts. All the aircraft returned safely and Air Chief Marshal Harris sent a congratulatory message to Eaker: 'Yankee Doodle certainly went to town and you can stick another well-earned feather in his cap.' However, it would be another six months or so before the Eighth was able to make a significant contribution to the air offensive over Germany.

Just two Fighter Groups saw some action towards the end of the month, but on 29th September the three RAF 'Eagle' squadrons were handed over to the USAAF to become the 4th Fighter Group. Ten days later the first B-24s entered the action; indeed, on this mission (9th October) the Eighth were able to send out over 100 heavy bombers, quite an achievement in such a short space of time, and which would not be bettered until the following spring. It was a slow build-up and it was 27th January 1943 before the Eighth bombed their first German target - Wilhelmshaven.

In the first six months, over 70 heavy bombers had been lost in action or damaged beyond repair, as well as many destroyed in accidents. The Eighth found that the European winter weather greatly hampered their operations and the theory of the self-defensive bomber formation was not quite working out as planned. It was obvious that until a strong fighter escort was available, the losses would mount and the operational range of their heavies would be restricted. Unfortunately the P-38s had been diverted to North Africa, and in their place came the P-47s (Thunderbolts), which although strong and very effective fighters, were rather limited in their range.

Throughout the spring and the early summer of 1943, the Eighth Air Force, despite sustaining heavy losses, continued to wage a most courageous and determined campaign against targets laid down in the 'Pointblank' directive. The Eighth's commanders held their nerve and doggedly persevered with daylight operations, convinced that such bombing would ultimately prove decisive. Little did they know that quite horrendous losses would soon place even greater strain on their faith in daylight bombing. There was, however, one major change to the original operational plans of the Eighth. The early missions with their medium bombers - B-26 (Marauders) - had proved none too successful. Furthermore, General Eaker did not consider that these aircraft sat happily in his Command, which was devoted to high-altitude bombing, so they were used in a support role until transferred to the Ninth Air Force later in the year. They actually turned out to be a most efficient, effective and economic strike force.

The high losses sustained by the Eighth during the second half of 1943 can be attributed in some part to the lack of long-range escort fighters, but they were also due to an increase in the Luftwaffe's day-fighter force. Earlier in the year the German High Command had not taken the American daylight offensive very seriously. It was convinced that, like the Luftwaffe and the RAF, the Americans would be compelled to turn to night-bombing because of their escalating losses.

But as more and more American bombers appeared, it was decided to vastly increase the Luftwaffe forces based in Germany and units were pulled back from other war fronts. In a few short months the Luftwaffe day-fighters had almost doubled to about 800 - mainly Me 109s and FW 190s. Also their pilots had, by battle experience, evolved tactics to counter the concentrated firepower of the American bomber formations. Thus the scene was set for one of the major battles of the European air war - a war of attrition between the gunners and fighters ('little friends') and the Luftwaffe day-fighters. It proved to be a critical battle, which continued almost unabated up to the last days of the war.

The first major defeat suffered by the Eighth came in August 1943, with Schweinfurt and Regensburg passing into the annals of American Air Force history - 60 heavy bombers out of a total force of 376 were lost. But far worse was to come because, in just seven days in October, 173 aircraft were shot down along with 1,500 airmen; this figure included 60 more aircraft lost over Schweinfurt. The Eighth's conviction in daylight bombing was shaken to its very core by such horrendous casualties, and a change to night-bombing was seriously considered, although the Eighth had little experience of such operations. Mercifully the losses at the end of 1943 were relatively light, at least compared with the horrors of earlier operations, and in December the first North American P-51s began to appear in the USAAF. This legendary long-range fighter, which had such an impact on the European air war, was first placed in the Ninth Air Force (which had arrived in England in October 1943) in a ground attack role, and it would be several months before its true metier was recognised - as a superb long-range escort fighter.

The New Year ushered in several changes. It saw the formation of the United States Strategic Air Forces in Europe (USSTAF) with General Spaatz returning (he had left in December 1942) from North Africa to take over the new organisation. He brought with him Lieutenant General James H. Doolittle, to replace Eaker, who was to take over air affairs in the Mediterranean. Doolittle was an excellent pilot and a fine tactician, but perhaps his main claim to fame was that he had led the first bombing mission to Tokyo. He remained in command for the rest of the war.

Within days of Doolittle's arrival the American heavies suffered once again at the hands of the Luftwaffe when, on 11th January, 42 aircraft were lost attacking aircraft factories. This did not augur well for the Allies' planned major offensive against the German aircraft industry, Operation Argument. In just five days of concentrated action, over

*P-51Ds awaiting delivery in late 1944. (San Diego Aerospace Museum)*

3,000 aircraft were involved in bombing targets throughout Germany for the loss of 177 aircraft. Although expensive in terms of men and machines, such losses could now be sustained due to new aircraft and replacement crews arriving from the States almost daily. The American war machine had gathered a prodigious pace and momentum.

In March 1944 the Eighth turned its attention to Berlin and five operations to the ultimate target were mounted, but like the RAF the American crews found it a most fearsome target. The month of May saw the Eighth take its share of the road and rail installations in central France, as well as many enemy airfields, part of the Transportation Plan. However, on the 12th of the month, the Eighth began its offensive against the German oil industry. Targets that day included Merseburg, Lutzendorf, Zwickau, Brux, Böhlen and Zeitz. These, along with many others, would figure prominently in the minds of its crews over the next six months or so. The Eighth's concentrated offensive against the oil industry was a major contribution to the demise of the Luftwaffe as a fighting force. It was a victory achieved at a very high cost, no single priority target in Germany caused the loss of so many American airmen and aircraft.

*The American Military Cemetery and Memorial at Madingley, near Cambridge.*

By D-Day, the Eighth was at the height of its strength and power - a massive force of heavy bombers, with B-17s in the preponderance, supported by a huge number of fighters, still mainly P-47s. Over 2,500 bomber sorties were mounted with the fighter pilots flying almost continuous escorts and patrols on the momentous day. Before the end of June the Eighth returned to German targets and from then until the end of the war their operations would be mounted at a rapid rate, in great numbers and on a grand scale. An increasing number of these were co-ordinated with Bomber Command with several targets being bombed day and night. Certainly, 'round the clock' bombing became a grim reality for many German cities. This was the bombing philosophy that both Eaker and Harris had envisaged in 1942, but which had all too infrequently been achieved.

During September 1944 the Eighth Air Force was fully engaged in supporting the airborne landings in Holland, but their largest contribution as a tactical strike force came in December in support of their ground forces battling in the Ardennes. On Christmas Eve over 2,000 heavy bombers attacked targets in western Germany, which proved to be the largest air strike mounted by the Eighth. In the autumn many more P-51s became available and they made their presence felt in operation after operation. The Luftwaffe was not only being destroyed in the skies, but also on the ground, as the American fighter pilots became adept at ground-strafing.

The arrival of the rocket-propelled Me 163s and Me 262 turbo-jet fighters did give rise to some concern, and had they appeared in greater numbers they certainly would have posed a considerable threat to the Eighth Air Force. The menace of these jet fighters brought about an increased bombardment of aircraft factories and airfields known to be their bases. One of the last operations mounted by the Eighth during the war, on 10th April 1945, was directed at such airfields, although the final and major battle with the Luftwaffe took place nine days later.

The Eighth's 968th and final operation of the war took place on 25th April. For almost three years it had fought a harsh, harrowing and costly battle; over 6,000 aircraft had been lost with some 43,000 airmen killed or missing in action and another 1,900 seriously injured. The sacrifice of these brave American airmen has not been forgotten; there are many poignant and dignified memorials around East Anglia, and many are remembered on the 'Wall of the Missing' at the awesome and moving American Military Cemetery and Memorial at Madingley near Cambridge. Air Chief Marshal Harris called them, 'the bravest of the brave', and certainly they made an immense contribution to the ultimate defeat of Germany.

# The Airfields

Cambridgeshire had always been in the forefront of service aviation, and more especially of flying training. There were several small landing grounds in use during the First World War, notably at Fowlmere, Wyton, Stamford (Wittering) and Bury (Upwood), with Duxford opening in 1919. Although Wyton can claim to be the oldest service airfield in the county, there was a landing strip at Oakington where, in 1913, a monoplane was built and flown, but the Royal Flying Corps did not make use of this small landing field.

The decade after the First World War, known as 'The Days of the Locust' in the RAF, took a heavy toll of wartime airfields as well as squadrons, but both Duxford and Wittering managed to survive the savage cuts. It was not until the Expansion of the RAF from 1934 onwards that some of the more famous airfields began to appear. In

1933 there were only 27 RAF stations housing operational squadrons, and yet by the outbreak of war this figure had risen to 53, with Wyton, Bassingbourn, Alconbury and Upwood already open and Oakington and Waterbeach planned and in the process of construction.

Each permanent station was built to a similar plan and pattern, and cost on average £750,000, a wise investment as all the above have survived. They were all grass airfields at least 1,100 yards in diameter - the required minimum. Their most prominent features were the massive hangars, which fronted onto a large apron of concrete, where the daily maintenance of aircraft was undertaken. These formidable steel structures were up to 98 feet wide and half as high with huge sliding doors, the interiors were as large as a football pitch and usually one was supplied for each squadron. Surrounding them were a mixture of workshops, stores, flight offices and crew rooms. On most airfields another large hangar was sited further back for major repairs with the various equipment stores nearby. The airmen's quarters and dining rooms in brick barrack blocks two or three storeys high were built on an H-shaped plan and near or off the concrete parade square, with the sergeants' quarters and mess perhaps closer to the main gate. Further away and usually outside the station's perimeter and across the public access road, were the officers' mess, married quarters, squash court, tennis courts and sports field.

The architecture of the pre-war stations bore a striking similarity wherever they were built; this was largely due to the architect commissioned by the Air Ministry Aerodromes Board - Sir Edwin Lutyens. He stamped his very distinctive style on so many RAF stations, which is still evident today. The main buildings were imposing brick structures, well-proportioned with impressive neo-Georgian fronts and high porched entrances. They have been described as, 'a cross between a country house and a large hotel'. Even the main gate-houses were given a distinct look with their formal pillars and curved arches! These buildings had a certain grace, and could almost be described as elegant, outwardly confirming the belief that the pre-war RAF was 'the best flying club in the world'; a monument to Imperial days.

The standard of comfort provided was almost luxurious, at least compared with wartime stations. All barrack blocks were centrally-heated and the officers' messes were splendid buildings containing a grand entrance hall, a large dining room and bar, and sitting rooms or ante-rooms, all with high ceilings. They gave the right ambience and setting for the rather formal ceremonies of the pre-war service. They also provided bedroom accommodation. Most stations were situated away from large towns and became closed communities, virtually self-sufficient. They did have a marked impact on the local villages and the strong links forged with neighbouring communities have been acknowledged in several village signs - Bourn, Bassingbourn and Upwood, for instance. In any case, these airfields had already made their indelible marks on the local landscape; the sheer bulk of the large hangars, the high water towers and the presence of low-flying aircraft ensured that the countryside would never be the same again.

Few pre-war stations were initially built with concrete runways, these were added later. Not until December 1940 would all new bomber airfields be provided with a main runway of 1,400 yards by 50 yards wide and two subsidiaries of 1,100 yards. Two years later these requirements had been extended to 2,000 yards and 1,400 yards respectively, which also applied to extensions to existing runways. This became the specification for a 'Class A Standard Bomber Station' and most of the county's wartime airfields were constructed to this norm. The runways were laid down in the shape of a capital A with the main one aligned to the prevailing wind, depending on any natural or man-made obstruction in the surrounding area. They were linked by a 50 foot wide perimeter road, which could stretch up to three miles or more, and gave access to at least 50 concrete dispersal points (hardstandings) for the aircraft. Some 40,000 square yards of concrete had to be laid, along with almost 50 miles of pipes and conduits.

The outstanding features of these wartime airfields were the black hangars, normally three in number - two of which were T (Transportable) types, with another smaller B type. The T hangars were produced by Tees-Side Bridge and Engineering Works and were 240 feet long and almost 40 feet high with varying spans, although the 90 foot span was most frequently provided. Several wartime hangars have survived and are now used for industrial or agricultural purposes.

Perhaps the most familiar sight on any wartime airfield was the watch-house, or control tower as it was known in the USAAF. By 1942 it had evolved into a standard design; a functional two-storied brick building with concrete rendering, and provided with a railed balcony on the first floor as well as railings on the roof. It was used for flying control and was full of radio, radar and teleprinting equipment as well as housing the meteorological office. The control tower was the nerve-centre of the airfield when operations were mounted, and there are many poignant wartime images of the balcony crowded with senior

*The wartime control tower at Little Staughton has survived to the present day.*

officers waiting in apprehension for the first sound or sight of the returning aircraft.

Compared with the permanent stations, life on these wartime airfields could be rather rugged and somewhat less than comfortable. Most of the buildings were nothing more than pre-fabricated huts, some of timber and plasterboard, whilst others were of pre-cast concrete slabs, with Orlit or Maycrete huts being the most prevalent. There was no shortage of the famous curved corrugated iron-sheeted Nissen huts, some 36 feet long by 16 feet wide, which invariably provided the living and sleeping quarters for the airmen. They were normally grouped in separate units spread around the countryside a mile or so from the operational side of the airfield, which meant that a bicycle became a valuable requisite. These huts provided little in the way of comfort or warmth in the winter; nevertheless they are still fondly remembered by wartime airmen, though perhaps distance of time has lent enchantment to the view!

Wartime operational airfields had many and various buildings - armoury, technical workshops, equipment and parachute stores, motor repair shops, headquarters section, briefing rooms, photographic section, sick quarters, guardroom and the operations block. For the material welfare of the airmen (and airwomen) there was usually a

*Aerial view of Wratting Common in March 1956. (D.o.E).*

dental surgery, NAAFI (or PX), a church and/or chapel, often a cinema, and other communal areas. For obvious safety reasons the bomb and ammunition stores were sited well away from the living and working quarters, and usually two large underground fuel tanks were built, each containing about 100,000 gallons of aviation fuel.

Each airfield cost in the region of £1 million - an enormous investment considering that over 440 were built during the early war years. The Air Ministry Works Directorate, also known as 'Works and Bricks' or 'Wonders and Blunders', were responsible for the construction programme, although most of the large construction companies were engaged on this massive building project - John Laing, McAlpine, W. C. French, Richard Costain et al - as well as hundreds upon hundreds of small sub-contractors.

Each airfield was given a unique two-letter identification code. This was especially necessary when so many were crowded together as they were in East Anglia. These codes really dated from pre-war days when the location of each airfield was prominently displayed in large white letters that could be seen from a height of 2,000 feet. For obvious security reasons this system was changed with the outbreak of war and the two-letter code was introduced, which was displayed prominently near the control tower. Most of the codes had some relation to the name of the airfield - AY for Alconbury, CC for Castle Camps and DX identified Duxford. Other codes bore no relation to the airfield's name - KR for Steeple Morden, for instance, and IM for Bottisham (the reason being that the obvious codes SM and BO had already been allocated to Swanton Morden and Bodney). For night identification purposes a mobile beacon unit known as a 'pundit' was used to flash in red the identity letters in morse code, which is why the letters became more commonly known as the 'pundit code'.

Over one third of these airfields have survived, with many of them still in the hands of the Ministry of Defence, although only Wittering, Wyton and Molesworth remain occupied by the RAF. Most of the others have long since disappeared under the soil, though the odd building has survived the ravages of time. Wartime concrete seems more impervious to aging and wear, and strips of runways, perimeter roads and hardstandings can still be discovered in and around the fields. Their brief days of action and glory have been suitably remembered in the fine memorials that are dotted around the countryside.

It is not the intention of this book to trace all the squadrons and units that served at these airfields, or indeed all the operations mounted from them. If any reader feels that I have not adequately covered a squadron or Group's wartime activities then I apologise in advance and plead a shortage of space. It has been possible only to cover the more important bombing operations undertaken by the RAF and American squadrons and Groups, as well as merely outlining the part played by the fighter airfields in the air defence of the country.

# 2
# ALCONBURY

The original site, to the east of Alconbury Hill, was acquired in 1938 to provide a satellite landing ground for Upwood, and by May of that year a detachment of Fairey Battles from 63 Squadron was using the airfield, with the crews sleeping under canvas. The concept of dispersing aircraft away from the main station was then in its infancy, and Alconbury was treated as a guinea pig to test the practicalities of the idea. The aircraft returned to the permanent station for fuelling, maintenance and repair, as there were no plans to provide such facilities at these basic airfields. These enhancements only came with the exigencies of the war, when most satellite airfields gained full station status.

At the outbreak of the war Alconbury was placed under the control of Wyton, then in No 2 Group of Bomber Command. Blenheim IVs of 139 and 114 Squadrons used the airfield for periods until both were transferred to the Advanced Air Striking Force in France. In their place came more Blenheims on detachment from Wyton, this time the new aircraft of 15 and 40 Squadrons, which had returned from France in December, having suffered heavily with their Battles.

No 15 Squadron was always better known as 'XV', and the Roman numerals appeared on its badge along with its motto 'Aim Sure'. It was one of the oldest operational squadrons, first formed in 1915, and would serve continuously in the war, operating five different bombers. The squadron mainly used Alconbury in April/May 1940, with its first operation leaving there on 10th May when nine aircraft attacked Waalhaven airfield near Rotterdam. All arrived safely back. It was a very different affair two days later when bridges over the Albert Canal at Maastricht were attacked. The whole operation was costly; eleven out of 42 Blenheims were destroyed and the squadron lost six out of twelve despatched. Even the surviving aircraft were heavily damaged.

XV Squadron was left with only two serviceable aircraft. Ultimately, the squadron lost 27 Blenheims in 97 raids.

In November, as a result of Wyton and its satellites being transferred into No 3 Group, both squadrons began to convert to Vickers Wellingtons. This famous bomber had been designed by Barnes Wallis (of 'bouncing bomb' fame) in response to an Air Ministry specification (B9/32) for a twin-engined medium bomber. It first flew in June 1936 but two years would pass before the aircraft entered the service. Its unique geodetic design - metal lattices covered with fabric - proved to be immensely strong and durable, able to sustain considerable damage and still survive. The early variant - Mark IC - was powered with Pegasus XVIII engines, giving it a speed of 235 mph at 15,500 feet and a ceiling height of 19,000 feet with a maximum bomb load of 4,500 pounds. They were the first bombers adapted to take the 4,000 pound bomb.

The Wellington proved to be a most reliable aircraft and popular with its six-man crews, being dubbed the 'Wimpy' after the famous cartoon character, J. Wellington Wimpy! Its fame with the British public was ensured by the early and successful propaganda film *Target for Tonight* in which it had the starring part. Over 11,400 were produced - more than any other RAF bomber. With an operational range of 1,200 miles they formed the backbone of Bomber Command, and carried a large part of the bombing offensive during the early war years.

The first Wellington ICs to arrive at Alconbury belonged to B Flight of 40 Squadron, although in February 1941 the whole squadron moved in. The first casualties came on 12/13th March when Squadron Leader E. Hugh Lynch-Blosse's aircraft was shot down over Berlin; all the crew baled out and were taken prisoner. Years later, Lynch-Blosse recalled that this occurred on the 13th, when he was on his 13th mission in aircraft R1013 - although he stoutly maintained he was not superstitious. Another Wellington failed to return on the same night. It disappeared over the Pas de Calais with a young crew (average age 20 years) and sadly they were on their first operation.

During the summer the crews were in action over Hanover, Cologne, Essen, Berlin, Düsseldorf and Stettin; the latter target involved over nine hours of flying time. Although Wellingtons were equipped with early versions of auto-pilots they did not always work, nor at times did the rather unreliable cabin heating system, so these long flights could be most exhausting and thoroughly uncomfortable without the constant threat of enemy action both from the ground and in the air.

Two operations in October added to the squadron's growing

casualty list. Three crews were lost on the 14/15th when severe weather conditions, thick cloud and heavy icing were encountered on a trip to Nuremberg – and only 15 out of 80 crews claimed to have bombed the primary target! Two nights later whilst on a Duisburg raid, Squadron Leader T. G. Kirby-Green and his crew went missing; it was the only aircraft lost on the operation. Kirby-Green was the only survivor of the crash, and less than three years later he was shot by the Gestapo following the famous mass escape from Stalag Luft III in March 1944.

It had been a difficult time for the squadron, 32 aircraft had been lost in action along with many experienced crews, including five squadron leaders. Towards the end of October, 16 aircraft and crews were moved to Malta, but the remnants of the squadron still operated from Alconbury. A few Wellingtons were lost in early 1942 but, on 14th February, the Flight was absorbed into a reformed squadron - No 156.

This squadron had been first formed in September 1918 but never became operational, as it was disbanded two months later. 156 was destined to have a most distinguished war record, operating for the majority of the time as a PFF squadron from Warboys and Upwood. It was given the code 'GT', which was prominently marked on the fuselages along with the aircraft's individual letter, either side of the RAF roundel; all RAF squadrons carried identification letters. Within days of its formation one crew was sent out to 'Nickel' the Lille area. Nickel was the codename used for the dropping of propaganda leaflets, though the aircrews called it 'confetti throwing'. These operations were considered good night-flying training for inexperienced crews, though this was the only Nickel sortie made by the squadron. By the end of the war it was reckoned that 30 leaflets had been dropped for every single man, woman and child in Western Europe!

On the following night (17/18th February 1942) three Wellingtons left on what were called roving commissions, when a small number of aircraft were directed to many German targets. This time Emden, Hamburg, Kassel and Aachen were selected, but because of poor visibility it was impossible to judge the bombing results. The first of the squadron's 308 bombing raids had passed without incident. Unfortunately, 156 Squadron would suffer heavy losses during its time at Alconbury, and indeed at Warboys, with in total 39 Wellingtons missing in over 650 sorties (6%). Most were Mark IIIs; their Hercules XI engines improved the aircraft's speed by some 25 mph and they were provided with increased fire-power by having eight .303 machine guns instead of the six in the earlier Marks.

*Shoot Luke, a B-24 of the 93rd Bomb Group being bombed up. (USAF)*

The squadron was engaged in the three '1,000' raids as well as many Ruhr operations. On 29/30th April the Gnome and Rhône aero-factory at Gennevilliers in Paris was attacked but without much success, and one crew failed to return. A month later 156 Squadron returned to the same target and its commander, Wing Commander P. G. R. Heath and his crew were shot down over Paris. His replacement, Wing Commander H. L. Price, DFC, was lost over Hamburg on 28/29th July in a particularly fraught operation as bad weather over numerous bomber bases prevented many of the squadrons taking part. The weather worsened and the bombing was very scattered. No 3 Group's squadrons suffered heavily, 25 were lost (15%). Another two of the squadron's crews failed to return. By the middle of August 1942, 156 Squadron had been selected to become part of the new Pathfinder Force, and it moved away to Warboys.

The airfield had already been allocated to the USAAF and its first American residents, part of the 93rd Bomb Group, the oldest B-24 unit in the USAAF, moved in on 6th September. Prior to their transfer to Europe the crews had been engaged on anti-U-boat patrols over the Gulf of Mexico, and had claimed three U-boats destroyed. The Group, commanded by Colonel Edward J. 'Ted' Timberlake Jr, ultimately flew

*A B-17 of the 92nd Bomb Group, 25th August 1943. (Smithsonian Institution)*

the greatest number of B-24 operations, although during its short stay only eight were mounted from Alconbury. Two squadrons, the 330th and 490th, were detached to RAF Coastal Command, with another moving to Bungay in Norfolk to undertake experiments with the RAF's GEE navigational device.

The Consolidated B-24 was one of the two heavy bombers used by the Eighth Air Force. First designed in 1939, it entered service in late 1941 and was produced in greater numbers than any other American wartime aircraft - over 18,000! Unlike its close rival, the B-17, it was not a particularly attractive aircraft with its twin tails and slab-like appearance, but it proved to be particularly durable with the Eighth Air Force operating with 14 B-24 Groups from bases mainly in Norfolk. The aircraft was known as the Liberator in the RAF, and it served in 15 Allied air forces, becoming one of the most versatile and enduring aircraft of the war.

On 13th November 1942 Alconbury received a visit from HM King George VI, the first time an Eighth Air Force base had been honoured by royalty. Almost a month later, 24 B-24s left for North Africa and temporary service with the Twelfth Air Force, but when the crews returned in the New Year it was to a new base at Hardwick in Norfolk. Already their place had been taken by another Heavy Bomb Group, the

92nd, which had moved from Bovingdon in Hertfordshire during the first week of January 1943. Its crews were the first to fly their aircraft, Boeing B-17s, non-stop across the Atlantic from Gandar to Prestwick - no mean feat considering the distance was 2,120 miles and the first commercial transatlantic service had only started in early 1939. The Group received a Special Commendation for this pioneering flight.

B-17s will forever epitomise the Eighth Air Force during their time in England. The aircraft had first flown in July 1935 and as the first all-metal four-engined monoplane it was way ahead of its time. The slender, almost sleek, design made it visually attractive and it bristled with so many guns that the American press dubbed it 'The Flying Fortress' - by which name it became universally known. It was designed to operate at high altitudes and to be self-defensive. Certainly in the late 1930s it looked a most formidable heavy bomber, especially when compared with its contemporaries. The aircraft, in its several models, operated with 26 of the Eighth's Groups, providing a massive phalanx of destruction. The B-17 ranked with the Lancaster as the most famous wartime bombers, and they spearheaded the Allied strategic bombing offensive. The aircraft was fondly admired by its crews, who had a complete faith in their 'ship' to bring them back safely despite, at times, quite crippling damage.

The 92nd was operating as the training and replacement unit for new aircrews entering the Eighth, although it had been in action whilst at Bovingdon and held the unenviable record of losing the first heavy bomber in action on 6th September 1942 - its first mission. For a brief period during the early summer of 1943 another Bomb Group, the 95th, used the airfield for a handful of missions. Sadly, whilst it was in residence at Alconbury a terrible accident occurred when, on 27th May, a bomb detonated while a B-17 was being loaded. In the massive explosion 18 men were killed and another 21 seriously injured, with five B-17s destroyed, which was more than the Group lost in action whilst at Alconbury. By the second week of June the 95th had moved away to another temporary home at Framlingham in Suffolk.

Since April the 92nd had been relieved of its training commitments and had been brought up to a fully operational standard. The crews restarted their bombing operations on 14th May by attacking the U-boat yards at Kiel and one aircraft was lost. During this period the Group was supplied with a new secret version of the bomber - YB-40. This was an experimental B-17, virtually a flying gun platform to be used purely for the defence of bomber formations. It had been modified by the addition of another two power gun turrets, which gave a total of

*A B-17 of the 92nd Bomb Group taking off in wintry conditions. (Smithsonian Institution)*

14 .5 inch machine guns, and extra armour plating was provided for the crew. The aircraft were first used operationally on 29th May, but were not particularly successful and taken off operations in August.

The Group was detailed for an operation against the Continental Gummi Werke, a large synthetic rubber plant at Hanover, on 26th July. On the way over the Group suffered a frontal attack from FW 190s, in which one aircraft, *Ruthie II*, was badly damaged, leaving the pilot mortally wounded and most of the crew unconscious because the oxygen lines had been shattered. The second pilot, Flying Officer John C. Morgan, fought to keep the aircraft within the formation despite the fact that the pilot's body was slumped over the controls and the windscreen had been shattered. Morgan managed to bring the aircraft over the target and then coax it back to England, making a safe emergency landing at RAF Foulsham. For this remarkable feat of flying, Morgan was awarded the Congressional Medal of Honor - equivalent to the Victoria Cross; only 17 were awarded to Eighth Air Force airmen. Morgan was later shot down over Berlin, in March 1944, but he survived as a prisoner of war.

Before the 92nd left for Podington in Bedfordshire, it suffered its heaviest loss on a single mission. This was the disastrous Stuttgart operation on 6th September 1943 when, because of worsening weather conditions, the mission should have been aborted. Heavy clouds not only frustrated the bombing but also caused the bomber formations to fragment, which was exploited to the full by the strong Luftwaffe fighter force. Forty-five out of 338 B-17s were lost in action (13%), with another 20 either ditching in the sea or crash-landing because of fuel shortages. This operation was a severe blow to the Eighth, as it was to the 92nd with seven crews missing and another B-17 written off. The Group left Alconbury during the second week of September. Perhaps as befitted the oldest Bomb Group in the Eighth Air Force, it was later to lead the final bombing mission of the war.

The reason for the Group's enforced move was that on 10th August 1943 a new Group was formed at Alconbury - the 482nd - the only Eighth Bomb Group to be activated in the United Kingdom. Its function was to provide a Pathfinder Force of radar-equipped aircraft to precede the main force and locate and mark targets obscured by poor weather conditions. It was almost a year to the day since the RAF had formed their own Pathfinder Force.

The new Group was commanded by Colonel Baskin R. Lawrence, Jr, and the nucleus of its first aircraft and crews came from the 92nd. It would comprise three squadrons - 812, 813 and 814 - the first two equipped with B-17s and the latter with B-24s. The aircraft were supplied with H2S, the RAF's airborne radar scanner, and some with Oboe Mk I, although difficulties were experienced fitting Oboe into B-17s. The B-17s with H2S were most distinctive, having the appearance, or so it was said, of 'a bath tub slung under the nose' - the scanner had to extend clear beneath the aircraft. The Americans called their H2S sets 'Stinky' and when their own version H2X appeared, it was dubbed 'Mickey' from the Disney character!

After several trials, the first PFF-led mission was mounted on 27th September to Emden. This target was chosen as it was felt that the strong contrast of land and sea would show more clearly on the screens. Three PFF aircraft were despatched, two were effective, and there was some improvement in the bombing accuracy so the operation was considered 'a moderate success'. The Group's objective was to train a sufficient number of crews to provide a PFF nucleus for each Bomb Group.

Until 22nd March 1944, when it was taken off operations, the Group had flown 346 sorties and lost their first aircraft to enemy action on 11th January in the torrid mission to the Focke-Wulf plant at Oschersleben, when formations of the First Division suffered heavily in sustained fighter attacks. The Group, along with the rest of the Division, received a Distinguished Unit Citation. The USAAF reserved this high award for a Group's meritorious achievement or performance in a single or succession of operations. Such citations were very highly prized and they were formally presented to the Group's Commanding Officer with due military ceremony.

When the Group was taken off operations it acted primarily as a training unit for radar operators, as well as testing new PFF techniques and radar equipment. It did also get called upon for special duties. One such operation came on the night of 1st June when two crews in Mosquito PRXVIs set off to photograph the French coast from Cherbourg to Le Havre. Their photographs were so detailed and clear that they were used by the 18 PFF crews from the Group that led the Eighth's bomber formations over Normandy on D-Day.

In November 1943 another two special units were formed in the Eighth Air Force - 36 and 406 Squadrons - to drop supplies and arms to resistance forces in occupied territories, mainly in France. They worked closely with the two RAF squadrons based at Tempsford in Bedfordshire, which had long experience of such clandestine operations. The squadrons' B-24s were painted in non-glare black and had been specially adapted for this work. The front ball turrets had been removed and a cargo hatch installed, known as 'Joe Holes', from the American nickname for agents. The first drop was made on 4th January 1944; in the following month they moved to Watton in Norfolk.

During late 1943 the area to the east of the airfield, close to Little Stukeley, had become the scene of considerable construction work, as a new Strategic Air Depôt was taking shape. This work involved laying down a perimeter track and hardstandings, as well as the erection of a multiplicity of technical buildings, workshops, communal and accommodation sites. The air depôt was completely independent from Alconbury and was known as Station 547 or Abbots Ripton; it became operational on 1st March 1944 when the personnel moved in from Little Staughton.

The last American unit to use the airfield arrived at the end of February 1945. It was the 36th Squadron, the Eighth's Radio Counter-Measures Unit, formed in January 1944 to operate with the RAF's No 100 (Special Duties) Group, and equipped with a mixture of B-24s and B-17s, mainly the former. Until the end of the war it operated closely with the 482nd Group. The squadron left Alconbury in October 1945, and in the following month the airfield was handed back to the RAF.

# 3
# BASSINGBOURN

This large pre-war airfield, which is now occupied by the Army Training Regiment, was built alongside the A14 road or Roman Ermine Street, and its situation owes something to a long-established tenet that 'military airfields should, if possible, be placed next to Roman roads, so they would be recognised easily from the air'. Wittering, in the north of the county, was another example of this policy, which somewhat rebounded on the Air Ministry during 1940/1 when the Luftwaffe appeared to be able to locate and bomb both airfields with apparent ease.

Bassingbourn emanated from the RAF's Expansion schemes of the mid 1930s, and opened in March 1938 as part of No 2 Group of Bomber Command. In May two squadrons of Hawker Hinds, the service's last biplane light bombers, arrived to use the grassed airfield, but within twelve months the squadrons - 104 and 108 - had been re-equipped with Blenheim Is. They were soon engaged in training, Volunteer Reserve pilots being called forward for advanced and conversion training. Just before the outbreak of war the two Group Training squadrons moved to a safer airfield further inland, Bicester in Oxfordshire, as part of the Group's Scatter Plan.

For brief periods during September and October 1938, Blenheim IVs of both 21 and 82 Squadrons used the airfield on detachment from their operational base at Watton. However, it was Wellingtons that were destined to become almost permanent residents for the next two and a half years. In late September 215 Squadron arrived and when it was transferred into No 6 Group on 27th October 1939 the airfield's immediate future seemed sealed; it would be mainly involved in operational training.

The Group had been given the charge of the Command's training and Air Vice-Marshal W. F. MacNeece Foster had been brought out of

*A Wellington with 215 Squadron's codes but operating with 11 OTU in July 1940.*

retirement to establish a properly structured training programme for bomber crews. It had been acknowledged that the rather casual peacetime arrangement whereby crews, after basic training, were posted direct to squadrons to gain experience, was completely unsuitable for wartime conditions. The chiefs of Bomber Command did have a dilemma, as their already slim resources would be further depleted to service an adequate operational training programme. Air Marshal Charles Portal, who had been appointed AOC-in-C of Bomber Command on 28th March 1940, made a bold and perceptive decision to establish nine Operational Training Units, and thus, during the first week of April, 215 Squadron formed the nucleus of No 11 Operational Training Unit.

These units provided an intensive eight week operational course, longer during the winter months in order to get the required flying hours completed. The various individual members went through their own specialised training and for the final two weeks came together as a complete crew. Long distance navigation flights, formation flying, bomb aiming, fighter affiliation exercises and escape drills were all part of the course, and on completion crews were posted to operational squadrons. This ambitious training programme drew heavily on the Command's scarce resources - experienced crews, operational aircraft and airfields - and even more critically in 1941, when another eight such units were set up. The units' aircraft and crews were used in certain operations, notably the '1,000 bomber' raids of 1942, and sadly they suffered proportionally heavier losses than operational squadrons.

Bassingbourn first attracted the Luftwaffe's attention during the autumn of 1940 when several bombs landed on or near the airfield. In April 1941 a training Wellington returning from a night flight was shot down on its approach run and it crashed onto another on the ground. The following month a similar incident occurred, with another Wellington being shot down. Then on 22/23rd July as eleven crews

*B-17 Stric Nine of the 91st Bomb Group at Bassingbourn. (USAF)*

were making night circuits of the airfield, one of the pilots banked sharply and collided with an enemy intruder, a Junkers 88. There was a tremendous explosion, lighting up the night sky, and the wreckage of both aircraft came to ground near the village of Ashwell.

The satellite airfields at Steeple Morden and Tempsford became involved in Bassingbourn's training commitments, especially from December 1941 when W. & C. French Ltd moved in to bring the airfield up to a Class A standard bomber station. When the work was completed in April 1942, most of the Wellingtons returned to Bassingbourn and became engaged in a few bombing missions during the summer, with one crew lost over Düsseldorf on 10/11th September – four of the five airmen were New Zealanders. Another of the unit's Wellingtons, which had left Steeple Morden, crashed in Suffolk. Of the 20 Wellingtons lost in this raid, 16 came from training units. At the end of the month the unit moved out to Westcott in Buckinghamshire, to make way for the arrival of the first American airmen.

If the airfield had been relatively inactive so far, at least on the operational front, that situation was about to change with a vengeance, when one of the most famous Bomb Groups of the Eighth Air Force, the 91st, arrived in the middle of October. For the previous month it had been based at Kimbolton, but as the runways there needed repair and extension, the Group's ebullient commanding officer, Colonel Stanley J.

Wray, quickly moved his men and aircraft into the relative comfort and luxury of Bassingbourn, which they later called 'The Country Club'! The Group already occupying the airfield, the 17th, exchanged places as they were only temporary residents having already been earmarked for the Twelfth Air Force in North Africa.

The 91st comprised four squadrons, 322, 323, 324 and 401, and was placed in the 1st Bomb Wing. It became only the third B-17 Group to serve with the Eighth, one of the so-called Pioneer Groups, later to be known by the nickname 'The Ragged Irregulars'. Within three weeks of its arrival, on 7th November 1942, Colonel Wray led 14 B-17s to Brest, the first of 340 operations. It was to be a long and harsh war for the Group's crews. On this operation all the aircraft returned safely, although eleven were damaged, and the gunners claimed one enemy fighter destroyed. Another 419 would be claimed - constituting a Division record. In the first two weeks of operations, the U-boat pens along the French Atlantic coast figured large in the Group's itinerary - Brest, St Nazaire, La Pallice and Lorient.

It was on 23rd November that the crews realised that their part in the air war was going to be none too easy. Along with the 306th Group they were detailed to attack St Nazaire but heavy cloud and bad weather resulted in the force being recalled. However, the Luftwaffe took full advantage of the scattered bombers and two B-17s were shot down and another two badly damaged, one of which crash-landed killing two of its crew. Of the ten aircraft that left Bassingbourn, only one, *Quitchurbitchin* managed to make it back to the airfield. Two squadron commanders were amongst the 25 airmen lost in action, and yet not a single bomb was dropped on the target.

Until the New Year, the Eighth Air Force mainly concentrated on airfields and rail marshalling yards in France, but on 27th January 1943 it tackled its first German target - Wilhelmshaven. This was a major naval port, which had attracted attacks from Bomber Command since the outbreak of the war. The 91st survived the mission intact, although in the next twelve months the port would be bombed on six occasions, in which the Group lost ten aircraft. Eight days later another German port - Emden - was targeted. This mission was led by Captain R. Morgan, accompanied by Colonel Wray in *Memphis Belle* - without a shadow of a doubt the most famous B-17 in the Eighth Air Force. Two B-17s were shot down, and crews reported that for the first time they had been attacked by twin-engined fighters. They were Me 110Gs, which had been specifically developed for night-fighting, although they later proved no match for the American P-47s.

*Captain Robert K. Morgan and crew of the* Memphis Belle *before leaving for the US on 9th June 1943. (Smithsonian Institution)*

The Eighth attempted to bomb a Ruhr target for the first time on 14th February but the mission was abandoned because of severe weather conditions. It was postponed until 4th March, with the large marshalling yards at Hamm as the primary target. This had been so frequently bombed by Bomber Command that its crews had dubbed it 'Ham and Eggs'! Again heavy clouds hampered the bombing force but Major Paul Fishborne in *Chief Sly II*, who was leading the Group, decided to press on to the target and the crews succeeded in bombing with quite excellent results. On the return flight the crews came under strong fighter attacks for almost an hour, in which three B-17s were downed and a fourth ditched in the North Sea. The Major was awarded the DFC (US) for his leadership, and two years after the war ended the Group was belatedly given a Distinguished Unit Citation for this operation.

During May 1943 the Group mounted nine operations and lost nine aircraft, with almost 100 airmen missing in action, including a British war correspondent killed over Kiel. The *Memphis Belle* was chosen to be sent back to the United States for promotional purposes and to undertake a War Bond-raising tour of the country. The aircraft's name was said to have been taken from the part Joan Blondell played in the film, *Lady for a Night*, wherein she was described as a 'Memphis Belle'! With due military ceremony Captain R. Morgan and his crew left for the States on 9th June. The aircraft's fame was ensured by William Wyler's fine documentary film of the Eighth Air Force operations, entitled *Memphis Belle*. Wyler, a well-known Hollywood producer, had taken much colour footage at Bassingbourn and one of the Group's aircraft, *Bad Penny*, was used for the aerial photography of combat action. The successful remake of the film in 1989 only added to the celebrity of the aircraft, which had been restored to its former glory in the 1980s and is now on display in Memphis.

In the middle of April another B-17 Group, the 94th, had arrived at the airfield, under the command of Colonel John G. 'Dinty' Moore. Five aircraft were lost in six operations mounted from Bassingbourn, but the Group would operate more successfully from Bury St Edmunds in Suffolk. Before it moved away to another temporary base at Earls Colne on 27th May, on several days over 50 B-17s could be seen taking off for targets in France and Germany - an impressive and awesome sight.

The names of Schweinfurt and Regensburg have become etched on the collective memories of all those crews who took part in what is now accepted as 'the most intensive air battle of the Second World War'. August 17th 1943 proved to be a day of destiny for the Eighth Air Force and for those 16 Bomb Groups that took part in the historic mission. It also happened to be the first anniversary of the Eighth's operations in Europe. The vital ball-bearing plants at Schweinfurt, situated about 70 miles east of Frankfurt in southern Germany, were the targets for 230 B-17s of 1st Wing. They would be led by the 91st, with its popular and very able commander, Lieutenant Colonel Clemens L. Wurtzback in charge and several of the top-ranking officers from Wing Headquarters (also based at the airfield) flying with the Group. The other B-17 Wing - the 4th - would attack the Messerschmitt factories at Regensburg, 100 miles or so further south-east, and after bombing would continue south to land at airfields in North Africa.

It was the most ambitious operation yet mounted by the Eighth Air Force. It necessitated the deepest penetration into Germany by their aircraft, and was planned to be a potent demonstration of its daytime bombing policy. Unfortunately, the British weather intervened with the result that the start of the operation was delayed with the Schweinfurt force leaving about three and a half hours after the 4th Wing, rather than the shorter time-lapse originally envisaged. This time delay proved critical and, indeed, fatal for so many crews; it allowed the

*Captain Birdsong placing a replica DFC against B-17* Delta Rebel 2 *of the 91st Bomb Group. (Smithsonian Institution)*

Luftwaffe a valuable breathing space for its fighters to land, refuel, rearm and regroup. In contrast, there was insufficient time for the escorting fighters to return to their home bases to refuel, but in any case the escorting P-47s and RAF Spitfires were limited in range to the German/Dutch border. In retrospect, the operation seemed a blueprint for the disaster it proved to be.

Before the formations had reached Schweinfurt 24 B-17s had been shot down and then on the return flight another twelve came to grief - 36 aircraft (15.5%). Most of the casualties came from the 91st and 381st Groups, losing ten and eleven respectively. With another 24 lost on the Regensburg mission, the air battle was one of the most intense conflicts of the Second World War. It was a severe blow for the Eighth and destroyed forever the belief that B-17s flying in close formation during daylight were self-defensive. Ninety eight airmen missing in action was the 'blood count' at Bassingbourn, with another ten rescued from the sea. As Colonel Wurzbach commented, 'My Group was so seriously crippled after that Schweinfurt mission that it took several months to build up into a first class fighting organization'. Yet despite this the Group was still able to put up eleven aircraft when the Eighth bravely

*The handover of Bassingbourn by the USAAF on 15th July 1945. (Smithsonian Institution)*

returned to Schweinfurt on 14th October. Due to problems on the outward flight, the small band of crews found themselves again in the lead onto the target, but this time only one failed to return to Bassingbourn. A minor blemish on a day which has passed into USAAF folklore as 'Black Thursday', because of the loss of another 60 aircraft (20%).

The Group's one hundredth mission was mounted on 5th January 1944; it was the first to reach this milestone. Six days later the Division was engaged in yet another difficult and costly operation, this time over Oschersleben, when 34 aircraft were shot down, five from Bassingbourn. All the Groups taking part were awarded a coveted Distinguished Unit Citation. During February, in just five days and four operations, the Group lost 13 aircraft. Things were not getting any easier for the crews, nor indeed was their life expectancy improving!

In March the Eighth Air Force tackled the ultimate target, Berlin, just as the RAF's long offensive was coming to its bitter conclusion. It was now the turn of the American airmen to face the frightening array of flak batteries that surrounded the German capital. The first operation was planned for 3rd March but because of heavy cloud formations the bombers were recalled. Sadly, one of the Group's aircraft collided head-on with another B-17.

Three days later (the Eighth's 250th operation) over 700 heavies, escorted by even more fighters, bombed several targets in and around Berlin, but because of the heavy cloud cover the bombing was not particularly effective. Of these aircraft, 69 bombers and eleven fighters failed to return, and again it fell to the 91st to bear the brunt of the Division's losses - six out of 18 lost. Despite the awesome flak, over two-thirds of the bombers fell to the Luftwaffe, the gunners and fighter pilots claiming 178 fighters, though the true figures were closer to 70. Nevertheless, it had been an air battle on a grand and frightening scale. One of the Group's pilots, Lieutenant Rentmeester, thought, 'It was a turning point similar in some respects to Vicksburg and Gettysburg during the Civil War.' Certainly, the Eighth had been heavily mauled, but so had the Luftwaffe and the USAAF was able to replace both aircraft and crews far quicker and easier than the Luftwaffe could make good their lost pilots and machines.

Since the Eighth's first raid against Merseburg and its large synthetic oil complex at Leuna, in April 1944, the flak defences had been greatly strengthened, and it was reckoned that over 1,000 batteries were in place around Leipzig. Many American crews considered it to be the heaviest defended place in Germany, 'one that sent shivers down your spine.' The operation involved a long flight over hostile territory (about 500 miles from the bases) before facing the fearsome corridor of batteries leading up to Leuna. On 2nd November 1944 the Luftwaffe opposed the bomber formations in greater strength than for several months; it was estimated that some 400 enemy fighters were in action. The 1st Division despatched 223 B-17s, of which 26 were destroyed and

150 damaged. The Group lost 13 - a crippling blow even for a battle-hardened outfit that had become somewhat inured to heavy losses. It was perhaps some comfort to the surviving crews that their 'little friends' had claimed over 100 fighters destroyed.

One of the survivors of this mission was Lieutenant Colonel Immanuel J. Klette, who had joined the 91st in July 1944. Klette became a living legend in the Eighth. He had flown his first operation in March 1943, survived 25 operations and then volunteered for a second tour. A bad crash in September 1943 almost finished his flying career, but he finally convinced the Command's chiefs that he was fit for operations again. His old squadron Commander, Colonel Henry W. Terry, was now the Group's CO, and he welcomed with open arms such an experienced pilot. Klette was given command of the 324th 'Wild Hare' Squadron, which had been awarded more Distinguished Service Crosses than any other squadron in the Eighth Air Force. Klette flew one of the Group's Pathfinder B-17s and led its final mission on 25th April to Pilsen in Czechoslovakia. It was his 91st - a record unsurpassed by any pilot in the Eighth.

The two aircraft lost over Halberstadt on 8th April 1945 were the last to fall to enemy action. One, *Wee Willie*, had survived 120 missions, but a direct hit by flak cleanly removed a wing. Some of the crew escaped, including the pilot, First Lieutenant Robert Fuller. Another B-17, *Nine O Nine*, completed 120 missions without having a single aborted operation. The most unenviable record held by the Group was the largest number of aircraft lost – 197.

It had been a long and bitter war and to do justice to the immense contribution made by the airmen of the 91st would require a far larger volume. Just inside the main gates of the airfield today there is a propellor and stone memorial, which simply states, 'Never Forgotten, Forever Honored' - a fitting epitaph for the Group. The last B-17, appropriately piloted by Lieutenant Colonel Klette, left Bassingbourn in June 1945, and the airfield was handed back to the RAF on 15th July; few of those present at the formal ceremony would have thought that American airmen would return to Bassingbourn some five years later!

# 4
# BOTTISHAM

Perhaps no Cambridgeshire village has so faithfully honoured its wartime associations with the USAAF than Bottisham, where a road has been named Thomas Christian Way in memory of the first commanding officer of the 361st Fighter Group, which served there during 1943/4. Colonel Thomas J. J. Christian Jr was killed in action on 12th August 1944. A fine memorial lych gate to commemorate him was unveiled by his daughter in October 1988. There is also a memorial plaque in Holy Trinity church, as well as a montage of wartime photographs in the Village College.

Before the Americans arrived, the airfield had been in existence for almost three years. During the early summer of 1940, a stretch of open farmland close to the A45 road from Cambridge to Newmarket was requisitioned and prepared as an auxiliary landing ground for a new bomber station then being constructed at Waterbeach. As the main airfield did not open until January 1941, there was little flying activity at Bottisham save for the occasional de Havilland Tiger Moth from Cambridge using the grass airfield for training.

In July 1941 the airfield was handed over to the Army Co-operation Command, which had been formed in December, and one of its squadrons, No 241, arrived with Westland Lysander IIs. These aircraft had entered the service in 1938, and had been specially designed for army support duties, mainly flying observation and reconnaissance patrols. As they were already becoming rather obsolete, even for these mundane duties, it was decided to re-equip many of the Command's squadrons with Curtiss Tomahawks.

This aircraft was introduced into the US Army Air Corps in late 1939, and was known as a P-40 or Warhawk; at the time of Pearl Harbor it

*A Curtiss Wright Tomahawk.*

was the main American fighter. The RAF ordered 140, as well as taking those produced for the now non-existent French Air Force. They were intended to operate as escort fighters. However, the aircraft's overall performance proved rather disappointing, especially its rate of climb and manoeuvrability, and was considered unsuitable for escort duties. They were primarily used for training until transferred to an army support role, and ultimately twelve Army Co-operation squadrons were equipped with Mark Is. They later served admirably in North Africa, where their ability to absorb considerable punishment became almost legendary.

During late 1941 the provision of two runways of Sommerfeld tracking improved the landing facilities of the airfield. This was 13 gauge, 3" mesh wire netting secured by metal pickets and strengthened with flat steel bars. Originating in the First World War, it was developed during 1940 by an Austrian engineer, Kurt Sommerfeld, for runway construction at grass landing grounds, mainly because it was cheap, easy and quick to lay. The tracking was used with particular success in the North African desert, where it gained its nickname 'tin lino'! Many British airfields were provided with Sommerfeld track. It gave a reasonably secure and dry landing surface, especially during the winter months, but was not really robust enough to contend with the heavy American fighters that appeared in England during the winter of 1943/4.

Before 241 Squadron moved off to Ayr in May 1942, it received another new American aircraft, the Mustang I. This fighter, which was destined to have such a dramatic affect and influence on the European air war, owed its existence to the British Air Purchasing Commission in America. In April 1940 the Commission had ordered more P-40s than Curtiss could deliver on time and it was suggested that North American Aviation might set up a supplementary production line for a 'substitute' P-40/Tomahawk. The company responded to the challenge with alacrity, and its chief designer, Edgar Schmued, a German-born Austrian, produced a prototype of a new fighter in no less than 102 days. After certain modifications, it first flew in September 1940. It was designated the P-51.

The Air Ministry was most impressed with its design and specifications and certainly it possessed some striking similarities to the Tomahawk, not least in its dimensions, area, and engine; indeed, one American aviation engineer called it 'the first cousin to a P-40'. From the outset the P-51 looked a winner. It had clean fine lines, an ideal cockpit layout, good performance and, unusually, squared wings. The Army Air Corps showed little interest in the aircraft, preferring their P-40s and P-38s (Lightnings), a decision that it would later rue. The Air Ministry immediately placed an order for 320 aircraft.

The first aircraft arrived in Britain during October 1941, and was named the Mustang, although the company had originally considered calling the fighter the 'Apache'. During its initial trials the RAF soon discovered that although it had an impressive speed at low altitudes (almost 400 mph), its performance fell off considerably at higher altitudes. This was due, it was thought, to an under-powered and 'asthmatic' engine, the Allison V1710, which was very similar to the Tomahawk's engine. Sadly, like the Tomahawk, it did not quite fit the bill as an escort fighter and it was also relegated to army support duties, becoming operational with the Command in July 1942.

The next squadron to use the airfield was No 168, which had been formed at Snailwell equipped with Tomahawks. It was commanded by Squadron Leader F. G. Watson-Smythe, who had made a couple of trips to Bottisham to inspect the airfield and its accommodation, such were the rumours of its poor and rather basic facilities! Nevertheless, the squadron moved in on 3rd July 1942, another Army Co-operation unit with its pilots engaged in army support exercises and training flights.

Early in November the Mustangs made a welcome return when eight flew in from Scotland to join the squadron, but by the middle of the month there was an unusual amount of activity at the airfield when some Armstrong Whitworth Whitleys towing Horsa gliders arrived. They proved to be merely the 'removal men' to uplift the squadron to its new base at Odiham in Hampshire.

It would have been difficult to find a greater contrast in the aircraft that replaced the sleek and powerful Tomahawks and Mustangs at Bottisham. In their place came Tiger Moths and Taylorcraft Austers of No 652 AOP (Air Observation Post). The Moths were small biplanes dating back to the early 1930s, which were being phased out of army duties and replaced by Austers. The small aircraft remained at the airfield until early January 1943 before returning to their original home base of Westley on the outskirts of Bury St Edmunds.

In the following month one of the RAF's oldest squadrons came for a brief stay - No 2. Its origins dated back to May 1912 and, in 1915, one of its pilots, Lieutenant W. B. Rhodes Moorhouse, was awarded the first air Victoria Cross. From its inception the squadron had been engaged on army support duties and nothing had changed, in fact the squadron was in action in France as early as October 1939. Since those days it had spent much of its time at Sawbridgeworth and was now commanded by Wing Commander P. W. Stansfield. The pilots had been operational with Mustangs since November, and were mainly engaged in shipping patrols along the Dutch coast, often from nearby Fowlmere. When the squadron returned to Sawbridgeworth in April, Bottisham became virtually devoid of aircraft.

Fresh construction work was now put in hand. The runways were extended and more accommodation sites built, with most of the temporary living quarters being sited in and around the village. The airfield had been allocated to the Eighth Air Force and its 361st Fighter Group, which would make Bottisham its home for about nine months, had sailed from New York on 23rd November 1943. They came to their journey's end on the last day of the month. Within days of their arrival yet another American fighter made its appearance, the Republic P-47D or Thunderbolt.

This aircraft was probably the most famous American fighter of the Second World War, being built in larger numbers than any other. It was variously described as the 'Jug' (Juggernaut), the 'Flying Milk Bottle', or 'The Repulsive Scatterbolt' because it was so unlike the conventional idea of a sleek and streamlined fighter. The first prototype had flown in May 1941 and it was in service with the USAAF by September 1942. The P-47 was noticeably different from its contemporaries. It was heavy, almost twice the weight of a Spitfire, very rugged and capable of sustaining heavy damage. Despite its bulk the P-47 was fast, especially at high altitudes, with a quite frightening rate of dive, and was probably the heaviest armed fighter of its time with a devastating fire power provided by eight .5 machine guns. The aircraft did have a few bad habits but engendered terrific loyalty from its pilots. The two top fighter aces of the Eighth flew P-47s throughout the war, a sufficient testimony to the aircraft's ability and success as a combat fighter.

The 361st Group was the last P-47 unit to join the Eighth Fighter Command, which meant that its fighter force now totalled some 550 aircraft, still short of its planned complement. It was placed in the 66th Fighter Wing, and ultimately the 65th, which had its headquarters at the Saffron Walden Grammar School, and would control five Groups. Each Group comprised three squadrons, normally commanded by a Major (equivalent to Squadron Leader). The squadrons, Nos 374 to 376, were each given an identity code - B7, E2 and E9 respectively - which was painted on the aircraft's fuselage to the left of the American white star, and all were further identified by yellow nose markings.

The heavy P-47s played havoc with the Sommerfeld runway, making take-offs and landings rather hazardous affairs. In January a team of American engineers was called in to improve the runways, and within three days they had laid a 1,470 yard runway made up of PSP (Pierced Steel Plank), which came in panels ten feet long with stiffening ribs and punched holes to reduce weight and assist drainage. The speed of this remedial work was a record, and it certainly resolved most of the problems.

On 21st January 1944, Colonel Christian led the Group on its first operational mission - part of a large fighter escort to V1 targets in the Pas de Calais. All the aircraft arrived back safely. Eight days later, whilst operating over Frankfurt, the first pilot was lost in action. On the next day, four enemy aircraft were destroyed for the loss of a P-47. In their first eight weeks of operations the newcomers made an impressive start, with 20 victories for the loss of three pilots and another three aircraft written off in crash landings. The missions during this period included such formidable targets as Berlin, Regensburg, Schweinfurt and Brunswick, so it had not been an easy baptism for them. Their best performance so far came in early April when escorting bombers to Brunswick - nine victories claimed for the loss of a P-47. It was particularly impressive as the Luftwaffe units defending this target had gained quite a reputation in the Eighth for their proven determination, expertise and successes.

*P-51s of the 374th Fighter Squadron, 361st Fighter Group, at Bottisham 15th May 1944. (Smithsonian Institution)*

During the second week of May, Mustangs returned to Bottisham in the guise of P-51Bs and Cs. Early in 1944 it had been decided that all P-47 Groups would be converted to P-51s, as and when supplies of this scarce aircraft became available. Only the 56th Group at Boxted in Essex would retain P-47s throughout the war. The P-51 was now a far different beast to the earlier Mustang; because of the aircraft's poor performance at altitude the RAE at Farnborough had, during the autumn of 1942, experimented with exchanging the existing Allison engine for a Rolls-Royce Merlin V power unit. There was a dramatic improvement in its performance, especially at high altitudes, and the manufacturer was persuaded that its engines should be changed. By mutual agreement the American car company, Packard, produced Merlin engines in the United States under licence.

The P-51 had now come of age. With a maximum speed of 440 mph at 30,000 feet, it was able to cruise swiftly at low-power settings, and with the addition of two drop tanks its operational range had extended to about 750 miles. In air combat it proved to be some 50 mph faster than FW 190s and Me 109Gs at 28,000 feet, with the margin increasing at higher altitudes. Although it was the lightest armed Allied fighter with six .5 inch machine guns, the aircraft established a marked

*P-51s from the same squadron in formation. (USAF)*

ascendancy over the Luftwaffe day-fighters, and it became one of the outstanding pursuit fighters of the Second World War. According to Air Vice-Marshal J.E. 'Johnnie' Johnson, CB, CBE, DSO, DFC, it was 'the best offensive fighter of the war'.

On 21st May 1944 the Group was engaged on a major ground-strafing operation - a concerted attack by the Eighth Fighter Command on the German railway system which had been rather appropriately codenamed 'Chattanooga Choo-Choo'! Each P-51 Group was given a different area in southern Germany to attack, whilst the other Groups were allocated areas in northern Germany. In this massive operation over 550 fighters were active and 91 locomotives were destroyed, of which the 361st were credited with 23. Two pilots were lost. Two days later, along with the 359th Group (based at East Wretham in Norfolk), it was detailed to destroy a railway bridge at Hasselt in Belgium. Each P-51 was loaded with a pair of 1,000 pound bombs, the first occasion that they were used as fighter/bombers, and some 17 tons of explosives were dropped for the loss of one aircraft.

The month of June was a hectic time. So many missions were launched that many of the Group's pilots completed their operational tours in a very speedy time, despite the fact that in May the tour for fighter pilots had been increased from 200 to 300 combat hours. In the same month, the Eighth Fighter Command let it be known that enemy aircraft destroyed on the ground counted equally with those shot down.

Although it was generally accepted that ground-strafing could be very dangerous, many pilots felt that victories gained in air combat were harder to achieve and thus deserved greater merit. On 29th June the Group's pilots scored heavily on both counts. Led by Lieutenant

*The memorial lych gate to Colonel Thomas J. Christian Jr, the Commanding Officer of 361st Fighter Group.*

Colonel Webb, they were escorting B-17s to Leipzig when they became engaged in a fierce air combat with Me 109s, and managed to account for four without loss. Shortly afterwards, Webb led a flight attack on an airfield near Oschersleben, where at least 16 aircraft were destroyed and many more damaged. Because this particular airfield was relatively lightly defended, the pilots made eight separate attacking passes without a single loss.

The inherent dangers of strafing were highlighted on 12th August 1944 when Colonel Christian led his pilots in an attack on rail targets in northern France. They encountered fierce and accurate ground fire with Colonel Christian's aircraft, *Lou IV*, receiving a direct hit and seen to crash in flames. Another three pilots were lost on the same mission. For the next five weeks the Group had two commanding officers until Lieutenant Colonel Joseph 'Joe' J. Kruzel, the Group Executive Officer, took charge on 20th September. Kruzel had fought in 'the Pacific theater' and had three Japanese aircraft to his credit when he was shot down, but he evaded capture and made his escape from Java. By the time he left the Group in November four German victories had been added to his tally.

The Group's time at Bottisham was coming to a close. The airfield at Little Walden in Essex had been earmarked for them as soon as the

Ninth Air Force Bomb Group had moved on to France. It was suggested that the proposed move was because the facilities there were far superior to those at Bottisham, which certainly could not be denied. But perhaps the real reason was that, on 15th September 1944, the Eighth Fighter Command had been reorganised with the various Groups being allocated to the three Bomb Divisions for their direct control. As the 361st had been seconded to the Second Division, its move into Essex would at least bring it closer to the Division, which operated mainly from airfields in Norfolk. The American airmen left on 26th September, which effectively brought about the demise of Bottisham as an operational airfield.

Until it was formally closed in April 1946, the airfield was used for training by Belgian airmen from their flying school at Snailwell. The dual carriageway of the A45 has now cut across the site, but the village of Bottisham has not forgotten those days of 1944 when the countryside echoed to the sound of P-51s thundering overhead.

# 5
# BOURN

In 1942 Bourn was described as 'a straggling wasteland of mud and Nissen huts'; not a particularly flattering or comforting picture but no doubt completely honest for all that. Such a description could have applied equally to countless wartime airfields throughout Eastern England, where thick mud was a constant problem, followed a close second by the bitterly cold and damp conditions experienced in the omnipresent Nissen huts.

The airfield was constructed during 1940/1 on a corner site, bordered in the north by the A45 Cambridge to St Neots road, and in the west by a minor road to the village of Bourn. It was planned as a satellite for Oakington and, in late July 1941, some Wellingtons of 101 Squadron from the parent station carried out trial landings and circuits. It was not until the autumn that the airfield came into more general use when Wellingtons and Stirlings (of 7 Squadron) were dispersed there during congested periods at Oakington. The increased activity had not gone unnoticed by the Luftwaffe and on 3/4th October a Stirling was returning from Brest when it was attacked six times by a Junkers 88C whilst on the landing circuit above Bourn. Two of the crew baled out at 700 feet and survived, the other five, including the pilot - Squadron Leader D. I. MacLeod – were killed. One of the survivors, Sergeant I. H. Hunter, RNZAF, was tragically killed six weeks later when his Wellington crashed shortly after take-off from Oakington.

Towards the end of the year three large hangars were erected to the east of the airfield, for the use of Short Brothers to repair damaged Stirlings of No 3 Group. The unit was known as SEBRO (Short Bros. Repair Organisation), which had its main factory and offices in Madingley Road, some two miles out of Cambridge. If the aircraft were airworthy they were flown into Bourn for damage appraisal; category A were repaired at Bourn, with the others being dismantled for either

*An artist's early impression of the new Wellington bomber – 101 Squadron operated Mark IIIs from Bourn.*

repair or cannibalisation at the main factory.

101 Squadron moved over from Oakington on 11th February 1942. It was in the process of exchanging its Wellington ICs for Mark IIIs, and frequently the crews ferried their new aircraft from the Vickers

*A Short Stirling being bombed up.*

factories at Blackpool and Chester. The conversion programme was not completed until July, by which time the first 'III' had been lost in action. It crashed in Luxembourg on 16th April after a Dortmund operation; all the crew were killed. Two nights later two crews went missing on a Hamburg operation, one of the airmen, Flight Sergeant G. M. Mason, DFM, being an experienced observer with 50 operations to his credit.

On the first '1,000' raid to Cologne on 30/31st May, 17 Wellingtons left Bourn, five from 23 OTU based at Pershore, which had arrived a few days earlier. Three failed to return, two from the squadron. The training Wellingtons remained for the next '1,000' raid to Essen on 1/2nd June, when two were lost. During July seven crews were lost in action, including two missing from laying mines off Heligoland. Five days before the squadron moved to Stradishall in Suffolk, on 11th August 1942, a Wellington III was destroyed on the ground when an aircraft lost control on take-off.

As the Wimpys disappeared they were replaced the following day by Stirlings of XV Squadron, which had been pushed out of Wyton by the arrival of a PFF squadron. The four-engined Stirling was the only wartime bomber to be so designed; both the Lancaster and Halifax were originally planned to have just two engines. It was one of the series of heavy bombers designed to Air Ministry specification B12/36, which really dictated the format of Bomber Command's wartime strike force.

The first prototype had flown in May 1939 but unfortunately it crashed on landing, which delayed the test flight programme. Nevertheless, the first production aircraft appeared twelve months later. Of the three main wartime bombers, the Stirling was the tallest (22 feet from ground to cockpit), the longest at 87 feet, and had the shortest wing-span at 99 feet (limited to be housed in the existing hangars!). With a cruising speed of 200 mph and a ceiling height of 17,000 feet, it suffered proportionally heavier losses than either the Lancaster or Halifax - 3.3% against 2.2%.

The aircraft looked most ungainly and, at first sight, could be daunting to new crews. In flight it proved to be very manoeuvrable, gaining the name of the 'fighter bomber', and not solely because of its eight .303 machine guns in three turrets; it was said that it could turn inside a Spitfire. The Stirling was a very sturdy aircraft, able to sustain considerable damage - 'built like a battleship but flew like a bird'. The aircraft had a maximum bomb load of 14,000 pounds with a range capable of delivering what Winston Churchill called, 'the shattering strikes of retributive justice'. The *Official History* considered its performance 'disappointing' and Air Chief Marshal Harris held little love for the aircraft, but it served his Command well, and later operated as a transport, glider tower and troop carrier, with over 2,700 being produced in various marks.

XV Squadron, under the command of Wing Commander D. J. H. Lay, DFC, was quickly into action, with seven crews despatched to Düsseldorf on 15/16th August 1942 and all survived. Two nights later, whilst returning from Osnabrück, a badly damaged aircraft crashed in Norfolk, though all the crew escaped injuries. Kassel and Nuremberg in the last week of the month saw the loss of three aircraft, and in October the crews were involved in an intensive training programme before they returned to operations, with Italian targets to the fore.

On 20/21st November the Fiat works at Turin received its heaviest raid so far, and one of the squadron's aircraft, piloted by Squadron Leader M. Wyatt, DFC, had engine trouble over the Alps. The crew continued to the target, bombed and then set course for Spain, where the Stirling was force-landed. After a short period of internment the

*An Avro Lancaster III of 97 Squadron. (RAF Museum)*

crew were safely back in the United Kingdom by the end of January 1943. Wyatt later commanded 75 (NZ) and 514 Squadrons.

In the New Year the squadron was re-equipped with Mark III Stirlings. These were powered by Hercules XVI engines, which had marginally improved the aircraft's speed and ceiling height. It was now commanded by Wing Commander Stewart Menual, one of its famous 'old boys'. During February 1943, Wilhelmshaven was attacked on four nights, and in the third raid, on 19/20th, five Stirlings out of 56 failed to return. Three belonged to XV Squadron, including its first Mark III to go missing. Twenty-four airmen were killed. It is now believed that all three aircraft were shot down by the same Luftwaffe pilot.

Berlin was the target on 1/2nd March for a 300-strong force led by the Pathfinders. The operation caused more damage than any previous raid, mainly because of the number of aircraft taking part and their increased bomb load. Seventeen aircraft were lost, of which two came from XV, both victims of night-fighters. During the raid a captured H2S set, which was being reassembled in the Telefunken works, was completely destroyed in the bombing. Later that night a Halifax, with an almost intact set, crashed in Holland, enabling the Germans to carry on their research into H2S without interruption!

Once again the squadron found itself being moved to accommodate a PFF unit. Bourn had been transferred to No 8 Group and a Lancaster squadron drafted in to strengthen the PFF would arrive on 18th April. XV Squadron mounted its last operation from Bourn on 10/11th of that month to Frankfurt, losing a Stirling on the night. Three days later it left for Mildenhall, which proved to be its last wartime station.

The new PFF squadron, No 97 (Straits Settlements), was never a particularly lucky squadron, suffering heavy losses throughout the war, especially during its time at Bourn. Under its commanding officer, Wing Commander G. D. Jones, DFC, the crews began training on PFF techniques. After mounting its first mission from Bourn on 26/27th April 1943, when all eight aircraft returned safely from Duisburg, the squadron was mainly engaged on targets in the Ruhr through most of the summer.

In June, four crews were sent on a special mission - to illuminate the Zeppelin works at Friedrichshafen on the shores of Lake Constance for No 5 Group Lancasters. The factory made Wurzburg radar sets for the German fighter interception system. The 60-strong force was controlled by just one pilot, which later came to be known as the Master Bomber system. All the aircraft survived and flew south to land at Maison Blanche in North Africa. Two days later (the 23rd) they returned to England after bombing the Italian port of La Spetzia en route. This was the first shuttle mission flown by Bomber Command.

The squadron now comprised three Flights, giving it an operational strength of 24 aircraft with another six in reserve. In August seven crews were lost in four separate operations to Berlin and Nuremberg. Wing Commander K. H. Burns, DFC and his experienced and decorated crew (two DFCs and four DFMs) were shot down over Berlin on 31st August/1st September. Two were killed and the rest made prisoner. Burns, who lost a hand in the explosion, was subsequently repatriated and, after having a false hand fitted, returned to flying. For about two weeks urgent repair work was carried out on the runways and the three Flights were temporarily out-housed at Gransden Lodge, Graveley and Oakington.

The most traumatic mission ever mounted from Bourn came on 16/17th December 1943 with Berlin as the target. At the briefing the Met Officer was convinced that the operation would be cancelled because of the strong probability of fog over the home bases later in the night. Nevertheless, the operation went ahead with the squadrons being despatched far earlier than usual in the hope that they would arrive back before the weather closed in. Thus it was that 21 Lancasters left Bourn in the late afternoon.

Enemy action accounted for 25 Lancasters in all - one from 97

Squadron; but it was on their return that the problems started. Most of the bases in No 1 and 8 Groups were closed in by low cloud. Eight crews did manage to land safely at Bourn, three made Graveley, and another Wyton. One damaged Lancaster made an emergency landing at Downham Market in Norfolk. Five of the squadron's Lancasters crashed in Cambridgeshire (two at the airfield), and two were abandoned on orders with the crews baling out. The squadron had lost eight aircraft with 36 airmen (including two Squadron Leaders) killed and another seven injured. This was the heaviest wartime loss for the squadron and a deep sense of numbness pervaded Bourn for several weeks. It was a tragic start for the new CO, Wing Commander C. M. Dunnicliffe, who had only taken over from Group Captain N. H. Fresson, DFC, on the previous day.

Fourteen Lancasters were despatched to Berlin on 24/25th March 1944; 97 Squadron was now down to two flights as C Flight had moved to Downham Market to form the nucleus of 635 Squadron. Two aircraft were lost, one of which ditched in the English Channel with six of the crew being picked up by a German rescue launch. In the Berlin Offensive, 97 Squadron had sent out 342 Lancasters in 19 raids and lost 25 aircraft, with 150 airmen killed or missing in action. By the middle of April the squadron had been loaned back to No 5 Group, leaving for Coningsby on the 18th. In twelve months its crews had flown 1,465 sorties for the loss of 58 Lancasters (4%) - a valuable, if costly, contribution to the PFF.

The first Mosquitos arrived at Bourn on 23rd March 1944. They came from Marham and belonged to 105 Squadron, one of only two Oboe PFF units. The squadron had already achieved a fine wartime record - first flying Blenheims in No 2 Group with Wing Commander H. I. Edwards DFC, and being awarded a Victoria Cross in July 1941, before pioneering the Mosquito into Bomber Command and blazing the trail with some daring low-level daylight raids. It had been transferred to the PFF in the previous June, and was now commanded by Wing Commander J. H. Cundall, AFC.

The arrival of the matt-black Mosquitos was rather appropriate, because earlier in the month one of the top Mosquito pilots, Group Captain H. E. Bufton, DSO, DFC, AFC, had been appointed Station Commander. He had pioneered the use of Oboe in Mosquitos with 109 Squadron. Oboe was really a variation of the system of wireless beams that had been used successfully by the Luftwaffe during their night raids of 1940/1, and had been first devised in early 1941. In simple terms, it was a blind bombing system based on pulses transmitted from two ground stations, about 100 miles apart. The aircraft followed a continuous signal from one station (the 'Cat') and the markers or bombs were released at the exact point of intersection on a signal from the second station (the 'Mouse').

There were limitations to the system: its range was about 260/280 miles and the stations could only cope with six Oboe aircraft in an hour, although a second pair of stations were established, doubling the operational capacity. Instead of being given to the main force, only PFF aircraft were equipped with Oboe, mainly Mosquitos. In this way the aircraft's high speed greatly nullified the enemy's attempts to target Oboe aircraft, and their operational ceiling extended the range of the system. Later, further ground stations were established on the Continent bringing other targets into range, although it was not until April 1945 that Berlin was attacked using Oboe. It was an effective and reliable blind-bombing and marking aid, and although the enemy managed to jam the earlier version, Mark II, 'Album Leaf' was brought into service with an accuracy of 0.01 of a mile - at least in theory.

The Mosquito was the most successful aircraft of the Second World War with well over 5,500 being produced during the war in Great Britain, Canada and Australia. It could operate with equal facility as a low-level or high altitude bomber, a day or night fighter, an anti-shipping strike aircraft, and was ideal for photo-reconnaissance; but its greatest success was found with the Pathfinders. It had been planned in 1938 and, like the Blenheim, was developed by private enterprise. The idea of a twin-engined, high speed unarmed wooden bomber was treated with scorn by the Air Ministry, but despite a sad lack of official commitment Geoffrey de Havilland, the designer and manufacturer, had sufficient faith in his aircraft to carry on with the project, and the DH98 prototype flew in November 1940. The aircraft did have one dedicated service supporter, Air Marshal Sir William Freeman, who as the Air Member of the Air Council for Development and Production, ordered the RAF's first 50 Mosquitos against strong opposition. In fact, in the early days of the project the aircraft was dubbed 'Freeman's Folly'!

The Mosquito I was powered by two Rolls-Royce Merlin 21 engines and proved to be faster than the current Spitfire. It entered the service in July 1941 and made its first photo-reconnaissance sortie on 18th September. The bomber version, BIV, arrived about two months later and 105 Squadron made its first Mosquito bombing operation at the end of May 1942. It was originally designed to carry a bomb load of 2,000 pounds. By March 1944 the squadron had been equipped with the sophisticated BIXs and BXVIs; the former had been specially developed as a high altitude bomber and was powered by two-stage Merlin 72 engines. It was capable of over 400 mph at 26,000 feet, equal to the P-51. The BXVIs were enhanced versions provided with pressurised cabins, and both were adapted to take a 4,000 pound bomb or 'Cookie', thus giving them a greater bomb load over Berlin than B-17s.

On their first night at Bourn six crews left to lay flares over the marshalling yards at Laon. Three nights later (26/27th March 1944) they were active over Essen, successfully marking the targets for a large force of Lancasters and Halifaxes, in what proved to be a most effective operation with minimal losses. At the end of the month the crews marked the railway yards at Vaires near Paris. This operation was conducted in bright moonlight and the subsequent bombing was very accurate with two ammunition trains being blown up. The success of this mission brought forth a congratulatory message from the C-in-C of Bomber Command.

Another commendation was received from Air Chief Marshal Harris as a result of the squadron's participation in Operation Flashlight - the destruction of the coastal batteries defending the Normandy coast. For three nights in the first week of June 1944, the crews sky-marked the batteries in the Pas de Calais, part of the invasion deception plan; then, on 5/6th June, they marked ten heavy batteries along the Normandy coast. The operation commenced just before midnight with two crews marking the batteries at Crisbecq and it ended five and a half hours later with an attack on Ouistreham. Over 1,000 heavy bombers took part and some 5,000 tons of bombs were dropped - the heaviest tonnage in a single night so far. The message from Harris read: 'You did famously last night in the face of no mean difficulties. Fire from coastal batteries, which were your targets, was virtually negligible... Calls upon you may be heavy and weather conditions may not be easy; but I know you will do your damnedest to meet all with that efficiency and determination, which has so characterised your share of Operation Overlord to date.'

After D-Day ammunition dumps, road/rail junctions and marshalling yards were marked and V1 rocket sites came in for special attention during the second half of the month. Indeed, by the end of June 105 Squadron had launched some 380 sorties. As planning allowed, oil refineries and plants in the Ruhr were marked and attacked as well as targets further afield in Germany. The squadron's losses had been light, to say the least, despite two accidents in April

*LR503-F of C Flight, 105 Squadron flew 203 sorties. (Canadian Aviation Museum)*

and May which had killed both crews. On 5/6th July one Mosquito was lost when the Buer synthetic oil plant at Scholen was attacked.

The following day, when enemy strongpoints to the north of Caen were bombed, A Flight commander, Squadron Leader W. W. Blessing, DSO, DFC, one of the legendary Mosquito pilots, was killed when his aircraft broke up after being attacked by enemy fighters at 32,000 feet. His navigator, Pilot Officer Burke, managed to escape. This operation brought more praise from Air Chief Marshal Harris: 'The efforts by your chaps over Caen tonight made us all very proud to belong to the Royal Air Force.'

On 18th December 1944 another Mosquito squadron was formed at Bourn - No 162. Some of the Mosquitos were equipped with H2S and in order to gain experience with their sets the crews were sent out on Siren Tours. Four or five towns throughout Germany were selected and a single 500 pound bomb was dropped. Once the Mosquitos appeared over the towns, the sirens were sounded, factories stopped production, the workers lost their sleep and the night defences were kept on the alert. The new squadron went out on the night of 21/22nd December to attack the Nippes marshalling yards at Cologne, which served the German forces in the Ardennes; all six crews returned. 162 Squadron became a welcome addition to Bennett's Light Night Strike Force and during February and March 1945 was involved in the long series of night attacks on Berlin.

Both squadrons were engaged in the Command's last operation over

Berlin on 20th April. 162 Squadron completed its brief but effective war on 2/3rd May when 16 aircraft in three waves attacked Kiel. Only one Mosquito had been lost to enemy action in 89 raids - the lowest loss rate in Bomber Command.

The crews of 105 Squadron were also in action for the last time on the same night, attacking airfields at Eggebeck and Husum, whilst others marked and bombed Kiel. 105 had carried out more PFF raids and flown more sorties, almost 5,000, than any other Mosquito squadron and lost only ten aircraft whilst with the PFF. During the war it carried out the most bombing raids in the whole of the Command - 713 for the loss of 58 aircraft (0.9%), an amazing record. One of its aircraft, LR503, completed over 200 operations, and came to grief whilst on a victory tour of Canada in May 1945!

By early July all the Mosquitos had left Bourn, the last to go being the remnants of 162 Squadron which flew off to Blackbushe on the 9th. In October 1945 the airfield was handed over to No 3 Group. It finally closed down three years later although the land was not sold until 1961. Civilian aircraft began to use what was left of the airfield in 1967, and today there is still some club flying from Bourn with part of the old runway being used.

# 6
# CAMBRIDGE

Cambridge Airport is perhaps the only privately owned international airfield in the country that can lay claim to almost 60 years of continuous flying. Even more impressive is the fact that for all that time it has remained in the hands of one company - Marshall of Cambridge - a name that is synonymous with aviation. The Marshall link with flying can be traced back to September 1912 when the airship *Beta II* was repaired by them. But the most direct connection comes from the original Cambridge aerodrome established at Whitehill in 1929 by Arthur Marshall, in partnership with his father, David Gregory Marshall, and the formation of Marshall's Flying School.

The site of the old airfield has long since disappeared under a housing estate. The present airport, to the east of Cambridge off the A45 road, opened in October 1937, although the official ceremony was delayed for twelve months. It was at this formal opening, on 8th October 1938, that the Spitfire made its first public appearance; pilots of 19 Squadron led by Squadron Leader H. I. Cozens brought their precious and unique fighters from nearby Duxford.

Countless pilots had already received their flying training at Marshall's Flying School when, in January 1938, the Company was selected to operate No 22 Elementary and Reserve Flying Training School at Cambridge as well as No 26 at Kidlington near Oxford. These schools were intended to provide basic flying instruction to RAF volunteer reservists and also to members of the Cambridge and Oxford University Air Squadrons, both of which ultimately supplied so many RAF pilots; RAFVR pilots and crewmen became the backbone of the service during the early war years. By the outbreak of the war the E & RFT Schools had already trained over 600 pilots.

Many RAF pilots gained their first flying experience at Cambridge. On their arrival at No 1 Initial Training Wing their flying kit would be

*Cambridge airport in 1937. (Marshall of Cambridge Aerospace Ltd)*

issued - a leather helmet, earphones, Sidcot suit, inner garment of padded silk and wool, gauntlets, silk undergloves and flying boots lined with lamb's wool. At least now they would look like airmen! Soon they would be inculcated with the theories of navigation, armaments, and signals, as well as more mundane subjects such as mathematics, service organisation and law. The initial course could take up to eight weeks. Already they were being assessed as to their initiative, leadership qualities and willingness to accept responsibilities, with a recommendation being recorded as to whether they were 'officer material'.

For the actual flying training the u/t (under training) pilots were grouped into four under one flying instructor - Marshall's had a total of 35 instructors at Cambridge and Oxford. The RAF Flying Training Manual soon became their 'bible', laying down proper flying procedures that had been established by the RAF's Central Flying School. They were introduced to their parachutes and how to operate and take care of them, with great emphasis placed on their cost (then about £70)! The Link trainer, which was a miniature aircraft with hooded fuselage and complete with tail and wings, simulated flying whilst on *terra firma*. Its automatic recorder, known as 'the crab',

*A student pilot climbs into the rear cockpit of a Tiger Moth – the great moment has arrived!*

faithfully traced all their errors. Then, the first tremulous step into the rear cockpit of a de Havilland Tiger Moth to begin the real flying training!

The Tiger Moth or 'Tiggy' was a biplane and the military version of the very successful civil Moth Trainer. It had first flown in October 1931 and a month later was delivered to No 3 Flying Training School. De Havilland developed an improved version with a 130 hp Gipsy Moth engine, a plywood rear fuselage in place of the fabric coating and a fitted hood which could be pulled over the rear seat for instrument flying training. The aircraft was designated DH 82A, but in the service it was known as a Tiger Moth II. It had a maximum speed of 109 mph at 1,000 feet but cruised at around 90 mph with a ceiling height of 13,000 feet and a range of 300 miles.

Despite its fragile appearance the Moth was sturdy and well able to survive the rough handling it received at the hands of trainee pilots, moreover the engine was most reliable. Almost 70 EFT Schools throughout the United Kingdom and the Empire were equipped with Tiger Moths and they were, and still are, fondly remembered by all pilots. Certainly the skies around Cambridge literally buzzed with

Moths, although other nearby airfields were also used for training circuits and landings.

22 EFTS was the largest school then in operation and it achieved several records for the speed of its flying courses (normally five to six weeks depending on the weather) and the number of hours flown over a period; at least 29 hours dual with 26 hours solo. In August 1941 the company opened another school (No 29) at Clyffe Pypard in Wiltshire, and two months later an Air Observers Navigation School at Bobbington. The several Marshall schools trained in excess of 20,000 pilots, observers and flying instructors during the war.

Perhaps the most famous old boy was J. E. 'Johnnie' Johnson. He arrived at 22 EFTS in December 1939, although not as an *ab initio* student, having already completed some pre-war weekend flying training at Stapleford Tawney in Essex. Johnson left Cambridge in the spring of 1940 with 84 flying hours in his log and he, like thousands of others, moved off to one of a number of the service's flying schools, where he graduated to monoplanes, usually Miles Masters. Even at the end of August, Johnson was not considered ready to join a front-line fighter squadron, No 19 at Fowlmere. This shows the length of time needed to train pilots and highlights Air Chief Marshal Dowding's greatest concern during the Battle of Britain - the shortage of trained pilots. Johnson finished the war as the highest scoring RAF pilot with 38 victories, and retired from the RAF in 1966 as a much decorated Air Vice Marshal.

At the height of the invasion threat in the summer of 1940 the school became part of the Air Ministry's 'Banquet Light' plan, an attempt to use all available resources to counter any German invasion. Two flights (ten aircraft) of the school's Tiger Moths, each armed with eight 50 pound bombs would be used, if the occasion arose, in support of the home forces. They would be required to dive or level bomb enemy troops attempting a landing. The aircraft - unarmed and carrying no protective armour - would be flown by instructors with orders to bomb from about 50 feet. Their only defence was the aircraft's manoeuvrability. The Flights were affiliated to the Lysanders of 268 Squadron, then at Westley. It certainly seemed a most hazardous operation, which thankfully did not materialise, although 'bombing practice would be undertaken at the home training school'!

In the summer of 1940 the Tiger Moths were joined by the rather battle-scarred Lysander IIs of 16 Squadron, which had recently returned from service in France. The Westland Lysander had been specially designed as an Army Co-operation aircraft to an Air Ministry

*A Westland Lysander II – 16 Squadron operated 'Lizzies' from Cambridge.*

specification (A39/34). It was a high wing-braced monoplane provided with a glass cabin that gave the pilot an excellent field of vision. It had first flown in June 1936 and was delivered to the RAF exactly two years later, with 16 Squadron being supplied with the first 14. The squadron dated back to 1916 and had always been used for army support duties. Lysander IIs were powered by Bristol Perseus XII engines, which gave them a maximum speed of about 230 mph. The 'Lizzies', as they were familiarly known, were particularly suited to small or improvised landing grounds, as they could take off and land on a very short run (about 245 yards).

At the outbreak of the war there were seven Lysander squadrons but over France and the Low Countries their inadequacies were cruelly exposed; 118 were lost up to May 1940 - about 20% of the total force sent to France. The Lysanders soon became relegated to air-sea rescue work and target towing duties, but their wartime fame quite rightly resides with the two (Special Duties) squadrons - 138 and 161 - who used them constantly on their Special Operations Executive missions. About 1,650 Lysanders were built during the war, and it is interesting to note that its Luftwaffe counterpart - the Henschel 126 - bore a striking resemblance in design, and the two aircraft were frequently misidentified.

From July a pair of Lysanders could be seen leaving Cambridge airfield just before dusk and returning early the following morning, after completing their nightly patrol of the East Coast searching for any

*Armstrong Whitworth Albemarles were frequent visitors to Cambridge, especially in 1944.*

signs of an enemy invasion. The entire coastline from Land's End to Duncansby Head had been divided into separate 'beats', which were continually patrolled by Lysanders throughout the hours of darkness.

The Lysanders were dispersed along the Newmarket road at the eastern boundary of the airfield, and this road was closed for security reasons until July 1941. They attracted the Luftwaffe's attention, and in the late evening of 28th August a Junkers 88 dropped some high explosives and incendiaries close to their dispersal area but no damage was sustained. Later, in December, a Dornier 215 bombed the airfield, causing damage to a few Tiger Moths and some other aircraft, but apart from these two isolated incidents the airfield survived the war relatively unscathed.

Another important wartime task entrusted to Marshall was to repair, rebuild and convert a wide variety of aircraft. The company was part of the nationwide Civilian Repair Organisation, which had been formed by Lord Nuffield. At first Whitleys, Oxfords and Gladiators arrived at Cambridge, followed later by Dakotas, Typhoons and Albemarles. This latter aircraft had been designed by the Bristol Aeroplane Company as a twin-engined bomber, but its production was undertaken by Armstrong Whitworth. When the Albemarles entered the service in late 1941 their role had changed to transport duties as well as acting as glider towers. Many of these aircraft in their invasion strip - black and white stripes - could be seen around the airfield during the summer of

1944. The Company also undertook on-site repairs to Spitfires, Hurricanes, Blenheims and Wellingtons, completing the repair and rebuilding of over 5,000 aircraft.

Perhaps its most famous wartime work was the conversion of de Havilland Mosquitos. The first Mark IIs arrived at the airfield in early January 1943, to be converted to night-fighters and redesignated Mark XIIs. The work involved installing AI VIII radar in a new nose radome, or so-called 'thimble nose'. The first completed XIIs were delivered to 85 Squadron; only 97 were produced during the war and all originated at Marshall. The other Mosquito conversion to be undertaken by the company was the NFXVII, differing from the XIIs by the inclusion of the American radar - AISCR 720. In total, 133 Mosquitos were converted at Cambridge.

After the war the airfield established a record when on 1st January 1946, the day that the ban on civil flying was lifted, the Mayor of Cambridge, Lady Bragg, became the first post-war civilian passenger. Rather appropriately, she flew in the rear seat of a Tiger Moth. The Elementary Flying Training School survived until April 1947 when it was redesignated 22 Reserve Flying School and continued the proud tradition of service flying training until April 1954. By then the first concrete runway had been laid down, and since those days the Company and its airport have gone from strength to strength. Many famous post-war aircraft, service and civil, both large and small, have used the 6,400 feet runway and the superb modern facilities now provided – certainly a far cry from those bygone days of wartime flying.

# 7
# CASTLE CAMPS

During the hot summer of 1940, when the sun shone most days, this airfield was described by Squadron Leader Peter W. Townsend, DFC, as, 'a meadow where the sweet-smelling grass mingled with the rank and thrilling odour of aircraft.' An evocative description of a small grass airfield, just one of many, that became operational in those stirring days. It nestled almost hidden in the folds of the East Anglian Heights on the boundary with Essex, and became largely forgotten after the war; at least until September 1994 when a small brick memorial was dedicated to the 13 RAF squadrons that served there.

In late September 1939 this rather bleak and isolated site was selected for the dispersal of aircraft from nearby Debden. The facilities provided were a little primitive; a grass landing ground with the pilots living and sleeping in tents, their mess a large marquee. A vast difference from the relative comfort and luxury of Debden, a pre-war permanent station, but most airmen who served at Castle Camps enjoyed the informal and relaxed atmosphere. By the middle of June 1940 the airfield was considered ready to receive its first aircraft - a detachment of Hurricanes from Debden - and in the early months it was only these doughty fighters that flew from Castle Camps.

The aircraft had been designed by Sidney Camm, the chief designer of the Hawker Company, and the first prototype flew on 6th November 1935. The Air Ministry deliberated more than six months before placing an order for 600 'Fury Interceptor Monoplanes', as the aircraft was known until Camm suggested the name 'Hurricane'. In 1938, the Air Ministry increased their order to 1,000, and eventually over 14,000 were produced in various marks of this remarkable fighter.

The early Hurricanes were powered by Rolls-Royce Merlin II engines, armed with eight .303 machine guns, and capable of a top speed of 330 mph. When they entered the service in December 1937 they ushered in a new and glorious era for Fighter Command as its first

*Squadron Leader Peter Townsend, DFC, with pilots of 85 Squadron. (Imperial War Museum)*

monoplane fighter. Although the Hurricane was slower than both the Spitfire and the Me 109, it was sturdy and reliable, highly manoeuvrable and able to withstand considerable damage. It became the mainstay of Fighter Command during the Battle of Britain, destroying more enemy aircraft than all the other defences combined. The 'Hurry' was admired and trusted by all who flew it, inspiring immense loyalty, and there was always a keen debate as to which was the best fighter - it or the Spitfire.

It fell to 85 Squadron to open the airfield. This was a famous fighter squadron which, during the First World War, had been commanded by two VC aces - Majors Bishop and Mannock. According to Debden's commander, Wing Commander Larry Fullergood, '[85] will always be the first Fighter Squadron of the RAF.' It had just returned from a torrid time in France and was now commanded by Squadron Leader Peter W. Townsend, who was destined to become a celebrated fighter pilot, rising to the rank of Group Captain. He remained with the squadron until well into 1941. Except for a mere handful of veterans, it was now manned by young and green pilots, most with barely ten hours of Hurricane experience. They were constantly engaged in exhausting and rather monotonous convoy patrols along the coast, but as Townsend later maintained, 'this was an excellent training ground to learn flying discipline, loyalty and vigilance.'

During July 1940 some of the experienced pilots began to fly night patrols as well as day sorties. It was the Flight commanded by Flight Lieutenant Richard Lee, DSO, DFC, that used the airfield more regularly, although Townsend retained a soft spot for Castle Camps and he tried to operate from there as much as possible. During the month the squadron began to make their presence felt, especially some of the old hands like Flight Sergeant Geoffrey 'Sammy' Allard, DFM, Pilot Officer Albert Lewis, DFC, and Flying Officer P. P. Woods-Scawen, DFC. The latter would be killed in action on 1st September, the day before his younger brother Chris was killed with 43 Squadron.

Unfortunately, not all losses were as a result of enemy action. On 22nd July a pilot was killed when his Hurricane crashed on approach to Castle Camps; this was the first fatal casualty at the airfield, which had already gained a certain notoriety because of rather tricky cross-winds. The day before the squadron moved to Croydon (19th August), Flight Lieutenant Lee was lost, last seen chasing three enemy aircraft over the sea. He had been a brilliant young pilot and leader with nine victories to his name.

The replacement squadron, No 111, which had introduced the Hurricane into the service, had been moved from Croydon for 'a rest', which proved anything but as the Luftwaffe turned its attention towards the fighter airfields at North Weald, Debden and Duxford. Indeed, the squadron carried out a successful interception on 31st August, turning back a raid which was bound for Duxford. Two days later the squadron became heavily engaged in a fierce aerial combat over the Thames Estuary. Two Hurricanes were damaged for just one enemy aircraft destroyed and one pilot killed. Sadly he was Sergeant W. Dymond, DFM, a most experienced pilot with eleven victories to his credit.

During their brief stay 111 Squadron only operated with nine aircraft rather than a full complement of twelve. On 3rd September it returned to Croydon to relieve 85 Squadron, which had suffered quite heavy losses whilst accounting for 44 enemy aircraft during August. After only two days, 85 moved north to Church Fenton for a well-earned rest, but without its CO, as Townsend had been shot down and injured on 26th August 1940.

It was quickly followed into the airfield by another famous squadron, No 73, which had served with distinction in France. Since the middle of June the pilots had been training for night-flying in Yorkshire but they now found themselves fully engaged on daytime operations as the Battle of Britain reached its critical stage. Their first patrols proved costly with five Hurricanes lost and two pilots killed, but in the next week or so they managed to right the balance, claiming six victories for two losses. During the autumn as the night blitz on London intensified, the squadron operated nightly but with scant success and several Hurricanes were lost to 'friendly' anti-aircraft fire. Towards the end of October 1940, the squadron was taken off operations pending a move to warmer climes - Malta. Within two weeks most of the aircraft and personnel had departed, leaving the airfield strangely quiet and tranquil.

The peace did not last very long as building contractors moved in. The airfield was to be improved with the addition of tarmac runways, hardstandings, and proper, if temporary, living accommodation. Three runways, 1,950, 1,600 and 1,070 yards long, were constructed and quarters for some 1,300 officers, men and women were erected. Before the end of 1941 the station headquarters was ready and other than a lack of hangars (they appeared later) it could be said that the airfield was ready to become operational again.

For some unaccountable reason this rather remote airfield was chosen to house one of only two Mosquito night-fighter squadrons. Perhaps its very isolation made the airfield a perfect site as the Mosquito was then a rare bird. The first fighter version - Mark II - had made its appearance in May 1941, and fitted with a AI Mark V set, was quickly brought into service to fill a night-fighting role. The first to be equipped with Mosquito IIs was 157 Squadron. It had recently been reformed at Debden, with its personnel moving into Castle Camps at the end of the year to await their new aircraft.

On 26th January 1942, the squadron's commander, Wing Commander Gordon Slade, landed the first Mosquito at the airfield. He was one of the few RAF pilots with any experience of the new 'wonder' aircraft, although Squadron Leader Rupert F. H. Clerke, a Flight Commander, was probably the most experienced Mosquito pilot in the service, having served with No 1 Photographic Reconnaissance Unit and flown its first Mosquito sortie on 17th September 1941. Due to production problems at the de Havilland factory at Hatfield, this black Mosquito trainer was the only one to arrive at the airfield for several weeks, although by March fourteen had been supplied and the crews were fully engaged in flight trials as well as resolving problems with their AI sets.

The squadron was in friendly rivalry with the other Mosquito night-fighter squadron, 151 at Wittering, as to which would first become operational. It was on 26/27th April 1942 that 157 was ready - a few days before 151. By coincidence this was the same night that Norwich

*Mosquito IIs of 605 Squadron.*

was heavily bombed, and three Mosquitos were in action for the first time but without any success. On 30th May, Squadron Leader G. Ashfield almost certainly destroyed a Do 217, with another 'probable' in July. However, it was left to the CO to make the first positive kill on 22/23rd August - a Do 217 - followed about a month later by the destruction of a Ju 88 on a daylight operation, with two more downed in October.

With relatively little enemy action over England during the winter of 1942/3, the 'Mossie' crews were eager to take their aircraft on night intruder raids but the Command was loath to sanction the use of Mosquitos on this type of operation, as the aircraft was still considered a 'secret weapon'! In January 1943 Gordon Slade left the squadron, his place being taken by Wing Commander V.J. Wheeler, MC, DFC, and, finally in March the crews began intruder training, but in the middle of the month they moved down to Bradwell Bay on the Essex coast.

Other than for a brief period during the spring of 1944, the airfield would house several Mosquito squadrons operating various marks; for such a small and little known airfield Castle Camps gained quite a reputation as a 'Mossie' station. Apparently the Luftwaffe was fully aware of its growing importance because, during the summer of 1943, several attempts were made to bomb the airfield. On the night of 15th June at least three FW 190s were active over East Anglian airfields. A couple dropped some bombs directed at Castle Camps, one fell harmlessly into a field and the others close to Helions Bumpstead, a delightful Essex village about a mile or so south of the airfield. In September, a solitary Me 410 attacked the airfield just as two Mosquitos were coming in to land, and damage was sustained to a parked aircraft.

At this time 605 (County of Warwick) Squadron was in residence, which had been equipped with Mosquito FB IVs in July and was commanded by Wing Commander George L. Denholm, DFC. He and his pilots were almost fully engaged on night intruder raids over the Low Countries. One such operation occurred just after midnight on 15th April 1943 when a small force of Ju 88s and Do 217s was picked up by radar heading for Chelmsford and intelligence sources revealed their home bases. The squadron was ordered to patrol three airfields in Holland to await the return of the bombers. Although, on this particular night, there was no positive success for the crews, at least Squadron Leader C. D. Tomalin, AFC (who would later command the squadron) claimed to have damaged a Do 217 as it landed at Soesterberg airfield. After some six months at Castle Camps, 605 Squadron also departed for Bradwell Bay in October.

For a brief period the airfield was rather inactive save for the aircraft of 527 Radar Calibration Squadron, with its motley assortment of Blenheim IVs, Hurricane IIs and Hornet Moths occupying one corner of the airfield. It had been formed at the airfield in June 1943 as an amalgamation of the various calibration wings in East Anglia. There had been a growing need to check the accuracy of the defence radar systems by air calibration. The squadron's duties also included checking other radio and radar systems such as blind-landing and homing devices. It moved to Snailwell in February 1944.

Another experienced Mosquito night-fighter squadron, No 410, had moved in from Hunsdon at the end of 1943. This Canadian squadron had been formed in June 1941 and had operated Defiants, Beaufighters and Mosquito IIs, and was re-equipping with Mark XIIs fitted with American radar equipment. Commanded by Wing Commander G. H. Elms, the crews were very active during the so-called 'Little Blitz' in the early months of 1944. They achieved successes in both February and March, with at least six Ju 88s destroyed as well as a couple of probables, including a Me 410. Their last victory from Castle Camps came on 18/19th April when a He 177 was shot down near Saffron Walden, but towards the end of the month the squadron had moved back to Hunsdon.

During March 1944 a new fighter appeared at the airfield, the Hawker Tempest V. They had arrived to re-equip a Typhoon squadron, 486 (RNZAF), that country's second fighter squadron and the first to convert to this superb fighter. The aircraft was essentially a Typhoon with several aerodynamic improvements, and had been designed by Sidney Camm. It had a thinner elliptical wing, an up-rated Sabre IIA

*A Tempest V of 486 Squadron at Castle Camps, 1944. (Imperial War Museum)*

engine, an improved cockpit and longer fuselage. The Tempest had a higher maximum speed, both at low and medium altitudes, than any other Allied or Luftwaffe fighter, and armed with four 20mm cannons, it proved to be a sturdy, powerful and deadly fighter.

A Luftwaffe test pilot, on evaluating a captured Tempest, was forced to admit, 'this exceptional aircraft is an improvement on the Typhoon, which in performance and aerodynamics was quite stunning...but there is no doubt about this one; the Tempest is an impressive highly powered aeroplane by any standards.' It proved to be a devastating ground-strike aircraft that was said to be, 'a superb combat machine...a pleasure to fly'. It really made its name against the V1 rockets - over one third of those shot down by the RAF fell to Tempest pilots.

The squadron had only a brief spell at Castle Camps before moving on to Newchurch in Kent. There it operated as part of No 150 Wing under Wing Commander R. P. Beaumont, DSO Bar, DFC Bar, DFC (USA), whose name was synonymous with Tempests.

Until June 1944 the airfield was rather a quiet backwater, before yet another night-fighter squadron, No 68, arrived with its newly acquired Mosquito XVIIs and XIXs. Since its reformation in January 1941, the squadron had gained a fine reputation for night-fighting, especially under the ebullient Wing Commander Hon. Max Aitken, DFC. It was now commanded by Wing Commander D. Hayley-Bell, DFC, with many Czech airmen, the most famous being Jo Capka. He had started his RAF service in September 1940 with 311 (Czech) Squadron, flying Wellingtons. After completing 55 bombing sorties, he became an instructor, but soon tired of the routine and applied to fly fighters. After much effort he was finally posted to 68 Squadron at Coltishall in December 1942.

On 27th June, Capka was returning from a patrol over the English Channel when he sighted a B-24 limping home on two engines. He thought that the aircraft was a bit of a 'sitting duck', so he moved closer with the intention of escorting it back to its base. The B-24 gunners misidentified the Mosquito and immediately opened fire, badly damaging the aircraft and seriously wounding Capka, who lost the sight in his left eye. He ordered his navigator to bale out, but could not do so himself as the aircraft was most unstable, so he struggled, almost blinded, to bring the Mosquito home. On its landing approach the aircraft crashed into trees and burst into flames, with Capka being badly burned. After prolonged hospital treatment and a period at Queen Victoria Hospital, East Grinstead under Archibald McIndoe, Capka was able to return to flying, joining the Czech Air Force after the war. Capka was just one shining example of how much the RAF owed to so many brave airmen from the occupied countries.

Until the airfield closed in the summer of 1946 it was a Mosquito station pure and simple, with two squadrons - Nos 25 and 307 - ending their war at Castle Camps. Both were operating NF30s or XXXs, a truly excellent night-fighter with a much improved high altitude performance produced by its modified Merlin 76 engine. In June it was rather fitting that NF30s of 85 Squadron came to take up residence at Castle Camps for about four months - shades of Peter Townsend, Dickie Lee, Sammy Allard et al.

The airfield soon passed over to agriculture, but the brick memorial located on the side of a minor road, shows the extent of the airfield and where the runways were sited, providing a very useful and necessary guide.

# 8
# DUXFORD

Duxford is probably the most famous wartime airfield in the country, due to the establishment of a department of the Imperial War Museum there in 1976. Service flying dates back to 1919 and Duxford was ensured of a special place in aviation history when, on 4th August 1938, the first Spitfire arrived to join 19 Squadron. Although the squadron dated back to June 1916, it had been reformed at Duxford as a Flight attached to No 2 Flying Training School, and was brought up to full squadron strength in June 1924, serving almost continuously at Duxford until early 1941.

The Spitfire originated from an Air Ministry Specification F7/30 (later F37/34) to which R. J. Mitchell, the chief designer of Supermarine Aviation, responded with his first design of a revolutionary mono-plane, the F400. His company had gained a fine reputation with seaplanes and the Spitfire was a derivative of the splendid S6B, which won the Schneider Trophy in 1931. But it was the successful marriage of Mitchell's airframe with a Rolls-Royce PV12 engine, later named Merlin, that ensured the aircraft's astounding success. The first prototype flew on 6th March 1936, and was already known as a 'Spitfire', though Mitchell was not impressed with the name. He is reported to have said, 'Sort of bloody silly name they *would* choose'! Mitchell did not live to see its remarkable success, he died in June 1937.

The Spitfire I had a top speed of 360+ mph at 18,500 feet with a fine rate of climb, and was thought to be the fastest fighter in the world. Armed with eight .303 Browning machine guns, it became a formidable fighting machine. Over 20,000 Spitfires were produced in a bewildering

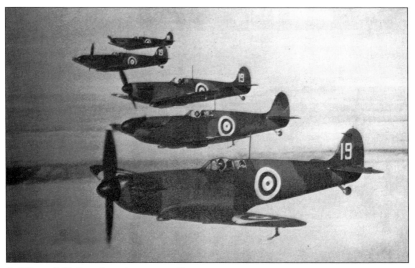

*Spitfires of 19 Squadron in pre-war livery.*

array of marks and its last operational sortie was flown in June 1954. Most of the famous wartime fighter pilots flew Spitfires. 'Sailor' Malan was most impressed, '[She] had style and was an obvious killer...moreover she was a perfect lady. She had no vices. She was beautifully positive.' Douglas Bader considered it, 'the aeroplane of one's dreams.'

At the outbreak of war Duxford was a Sector station in No 12 Group of Fighter Command. It was a large grassed landing field (1,600 yards by 2,000 yards) to the east of the Newmarket to Royston (A505) road, with three Spitfire squadrons in residence - Nos 19, 66 and 611. 66 had reformed at Duxford in July 1936 from C Flight of 19 Squadron, but by comparison, the Auxiliary pilots of 611 were newcomers, having arrived in August for their annual summer camp only to be mobilised into active service. They moved out in October to make way for Blenheim Ifs of 222 Squadron under the command of Squadron Leader H. W. 'Tubby' Mermagen, AFC, which became operational in December flying North Sea patrols.

In the spring of 1940, 222 converted to Spitfires, serving with distinction in the Battle of Britain. As in all RAF squadrons, the aircraft were quickly marked on their fuselages with their new identification codes, the pre-war codes having been comprehensively revised. Bold block letters were normally placed to the front of the RAF rondels, thus QV, LZ and FY would distinguish the three Spitfire squadrons respectively throughout the war; 222 was allocated ZD, which it

*Czech pilots of 310 Squadron.*

retained until the mid-1950s, when most squadrons had changed to coloured markings.

There was little action until May 1940, although 66 claimed its first victory - a Heinkel 111 - in January. Both squadrons spent time operating from Horsham St Faith in Norfolk and were engaged on North Sea patrols. On 11th May, Flight Lieutenant W. G. Clouston claimed 19's first victory, a Junkers 88. In February the squadron had received a new pilot, the legendary Douglas Bader. He had been allowed to rejoin the service at his previous rank of Flying Officer, and had convinced the authorities of his ability to fly fighters despite his age (he was 30) and severe physical disabilities. In May he was promoted to Flight Commander with 222 Squadron, and left Duxford when the squadron moved to Kirton Lindsey.

On 25th May, 19 Squadron moved to Hornchurch to take part in the air cover over the Dunkirk beaches, and in ten days it met the Luftwaffe on five occasions, claiming 30 victories but not without cost. Three pilots were missing, including the CO, Squadron Leader G. D. Stephenson, who was taken prisoner. When the remaining pilots returned to Duxford in June they were commanded by Squadron Leader P. C. Pickham, and soon would be flying night as well as regular day patrols, mainly from nearby Fowlmere.

A new squadron, No 310, was formed in July, equipped with Hurricanes. It became the first Czech unit in Fighter Command, but with a British CO, Squadron Leader G. D. M. Blackwood. On 26th August the Czech pilots, who were said to be 'very keen and eager to have a crack', made their first contact with the Luftwaffe by intercepting a raid bound for Debden. By the end of the year sixteen aircraft had been lost with three pilots killed and another two injured.

Bader returned to Duxford on the 30th when he brought down his Hurricane squadron - No 242 - from Coltishall. He had been promoted to take over this somewhat demoralised squadron mainly manned by Canadian airmen, which had suffered heavy losses whilst serving in France. From 1st September 1940 it would operate under the Duxford Sector Controller and Station Commander, Wing Commander A. B. 'Woody' Woodhall, AFC.

The squadron put up 13 Hurricanes on the 30th and claimed twelve victories. Afterwards, Bader maintained that had there been more fighters with them, 'we could have hacked the Huns down in scores.' As the leading proponent of the 'Big Wing' concept, Bader was utterly convinced that the most effective fighter tactic was to use at least three squadrons as one combined strike force. Air Vice-Marshal Leigh-Mallory strongly supported him, although Keith Park at No 11 Group was less enthusiastic and the 'Big Wing' controversy caused a serious rift between the two commanders.

The Duxford Wing under Bader's leadership made its entrance on 7th September, comprising three squadrons - 19, 242 and 310. By the end of the day, 20 aircraft were claimed destroyed. Two days later the Wing was again in action and another 21 enemy aircraft shot down. It is now known that these claims were overstated, but at the time they were used to prove the effectiveness of the 'Wing' theory. On Battle of Britain Day the Duxford Wing was indeed big - five squadrons of Hurricanes and Spitfires operating in the late morning and early afternoon. 302 (Polish) Squadron had moved into Duxford and 611 had come down from Digby to join the Wing.

At the end of the day 52 victories were claimed - extravagant to say the least, considering that the Luftwaffe's total losses on the day were 56! In fact, the accuracy of the statistics mattered little, such victories were good for the morale of the pilots and public alike. Also the operation of the 'Big Wing' had a quite devastating effect on the Luftwaffe pilots; to face such a large force of fighters, when they had been told that the RAF was 'a spent force and down to its last Spitfires', was more than a little demoralising and a sign that they had lost this particular battle.

The winter of 1940/1 proved to be a quiet time, at least compared with the hectic action of only two months earlier. After some six weeks at Duxford, Bader's squadron moved back to Coltishall in December, and 19 Squadron returned from Fowlmere, although by February it would have left Duxford for good.

From December, the Air Fighting Development Unit moved in from Northolt. This unit was engaged in the testing and trialling of new versions of fighters as well as evaluating captured Luftwaffe aircraft, and comparing their performances with Allied aircraft. The unit also had a Flight - 1426 (Enemy Aircraft) - which took its motley collection of enemy aircraft around on tours of RAF and USAAF stations. There was the occasional accident; on 13th November 1943 a Heinkel 111H, which had been captured in February 1940, crashed at Polebrook killing seven of the eleven on board.

In June 1941 an old and proud squadron dating from the days of the Royal Flying Corps, No 56, arrived under the command of Squadron Leader Prosser Hanks, DFC. The squadron had been fully engaged in the Battle of Britain, mainly from North Weald. It had now been selected to trial a new fighter operationally, the Hawker Typhoon. Like the Hurricane, this aircraft had been designed by Sidney Camm and had first flown in February 1940. Its development had been indecently hastened to counter the Luftwaffe's new threat, the FW 190.

The Typhoon was a large and brutish aircraft, powered by a Napier Sabre engine, heavily armed with twelve .303 machine guns, and with a top speed of over 400 mph. It first appeared in September 1941 but soon some serious problems became apparent. There were instances of structural failure around the tail plane, undercarriages had a tendency to collapse, and the cockpit leaked carbon monoxide; one of the squadron's pilots died of carbon monoxide poisoning. The engine proved somewhat temperamental, on occasions cutting out at high speeds, and the aircraft was very heavy and not easy to control causing a high proportion of training accidents. Ultimately, the problems were resolved but they did delay the operational readiness of the squadron.

During August 601 Squadron flew into Duxford with their rather strange Bell Airacobras, the only RAF unit to be equipped with this rare American fighter. It had really been designed around a large T-9 cannon, which was located in the hub necessitating its Allison engine to be unusually sited midships behind the pilot. The engine caused incessant problems, and although the fighter was fast and heavily armed it was not an easy aircraft to fly. The first two flights ended in forced landings as did several more during the training programme. Although the pilots persevered with their troublesome aircraft, the squadron was re-equipped with Spitfires after leaving Duxford in the New Year.

Towards the end of January 1942 another squadron arrived to re-equip with Typhoons - No 266 (Rhodesian) - but as the production of Typhoons had been delayed because of the various teething problems, it retained its Spitfire Vbs *pro tem*. In March they were joined by another Typhoon squadron - No 609 (West Riding) - with the object of establishing a Typhoon Wing at Duxford. By April it had become a reality and was then commanded by Wing Commander Denys Gillam, DSO, DFC Bar, but it only flew for the first time on 9th June, merely a special demonstration for the Duke of Kent, followed the next day by one for the chiefs of Fighter Command and No 12 Group. The Wing's first test came in August with the ill-fated Dieppe operation, with the squadrons operating from advanced landing grounds.

The Typhoon's performance fell off above 18,000 feet, as did its manoeuvrability, and as a pure day-fighter its use seemed rather limited. During the summer Fighter Command deliberated on its future role and it seemed highly likely that it would be relegated to army support duties. The three Squadron Commanders submitted their opinions. They accepted that the Wing had proved a failure, but proposed that the speed and firepower of the aircraft could be better employed by operating Typhoon squadrons independently at airfields closer to the coast to counter the Luftwaffe's low-level 'tip and run' raids. In the autumn the Wing disbanded, and the three squadrons moved away. Nevertheless, the great potential of the aircraft had been recognised and, on 1st September, a new Typhoon squadron - No 181 - was formed at Duxford, commanded by Squadron Leader D. 'Crow' Crowley-Milling, DFC. Just two years earlier he had been a Pilot Officer in Bader's squadron. Several months were spent working up to readiness but in November the squadron left for Snailwell.

Duxford had now been allocated to the USAAF and during October 1942 the first American personnel arrived, part of 350th Fighter Group, which had been formed in the United Kingdom at the beginning of the month. The Group comprised three squadrons, although only the 345th would serve at Duxford. It was intended to act as a tactical fighter unit for the US forces in North Africa and in January 1943 the pilots left for warmer climes.

More than two months elapsed before Duxford's permanent USAAF residents arrived - 78th Fighter Group. The first P-47s flew in, on 3rd April, from Goxhill where the pilots had been training on P-38s (Lightnings) since December. The commanding officer, Colonel Arman

Peterson, considered the P-47 to be a very poor substitute. He likened it to, 'a change from thoroughbreds to plough horses.'

Despite the change of fighters, just ten days later 40 P-47s, led by Colonel Peterson, went out on a sweep of St Omer in northern France. On their return one suffered engine failure over the English Channel and Lieutenant Colonel Dickman, the Group Executive Officer, was fortunate to be picked up by a RAF air-sea rescue launch some miles off Calais. The pilots had to wait another month (till 14th May) before they met the Luftwaffe in combat for the first time, and then honours were even - three shot down for three P-47s lost. Major James J. Stone, CO of 83rd Squadron, and Captain Charles P. London scored their first victories. In the first two months of operations the 78th had proved to be the most successful of the three Fighter Groups.

The month of July turned out to be most eventful for the Group. On the first day its popular CO was killed in action, and his replacement, Lieutenant Colonel Melvin F. McNickle, was shot down on the 30th whilst on his third operation, but he survived as a prisoner of war. On this mission the Group was providing escorts for bombers returning from Kassel. One pilot, Lieutenant Quince L. Brown Jr, suffered engine problems and lost altitude, and whilst he was hedge-hopping home he shot up a locomotive and a gun battery to the west of Rotterdam.

This was the first recorded ground-strafing by an Eighth fighter pilot. 'Strafing' was a German term adopted by the Allies to describe the destruction of ground targets by fighters; it originated in the First World War - 'Gott strafe England' literally meant 'God punish ...'. Brown was from Oklahoma and had named his P-47 *Okie*; he later became the Group's most successful pilot with a total of 13 victories, four of which he claimed on a single mission. Sadly, Brown, then a Major, was on his second tour and 136th sortie when he was shot down on 6th September 1944.

The July operation set several records. The pilots had claimed 16 victories, then the highest total recorded in a single mission. Major Eugene Roberts in his *Spokane Queen* shot down three aircraft, the highest individual score on a single operation. Captain London added two to his total, making five in all and thus became the first fighter ace of the Eighth Air Force, with Major Roberts becoming the second ace in October. 'Ace' was another term dating back to the First World War, and had been introduced by the French before being taken up by the British and German Air Forces. During the Second World War both the Luftwaffe and the USAAF reintroduced the term. The Americans required five positive victories in air combat to claim ace status,

*A P-47 of the 78th Fighter Group at Duxford, 26th August 1944. (Smithsonian Institution)*

whereas the German pilots needed double that number.

The USAAF was particularly quick to recognise the propaganda value of its ace fighter pilots. On the other hand, the British Air Ministry refused to officially acknowledge 'aces' as such, because it was considered 'bad for squadron morale'. DFCs were normally awarded for five victories, and maybe a Bar to the DFC for a number of subsequent victories. Certainly, the Air Ministry was quite happy to publicise the exploits of their most successful fighter pilots without actually calling them 'aces', although it is thought that over 1,000 RAF pilots could claim the title. The Eighth Air Force had a total of 261 fighter aces by the end of the war, of whom 13 flew with the 78th.

During January 1944 the Group's pilots began ground-strafing of railway targets in earnest, and also to use their P-47s in a fighter/ bomber role. Each aircraft carried two 500 pound bombs on wing shackles with some of their colleagues acting as escorts on these bombing missions. Dive bombing by P-47s was often described by the pilots as more 'by guess and God', although the technique did improve over the coming months. In March the Group's P-47s acquired their distinctive black and white chequerboard markings on their nose bands with red, white and black rudders to distinguish Nos 82 to 84

Squadrons respectively.

Whilst engaged in attacking targets near Brussels on 29th August 1944, Major Joe Myers, CO of 82nd Squadron, sighted an unusual aircraft flying far below his Flight. At first he thought it was a B-26 but then he realised that a B-26 could not travel so quickly! Myers identified it as a 'twin-jet' and as the P-47s closed for the attack, the jet took evasive action and finally crash-landed in flames. Major Myers and his wingman, Lieutenant Manford Croy, were credited with the first destruction by the Eighth of a Me 262. This was the first turbo-jet aircraft to become operational in the war, and with a maximum speed well in excess of 500 mph it easily had the legs of all Allied fighters. But for Hitler's insistence that it should be developed as a fast bomber like the Mosquito, it would have made a far greater impact than it did. As it was, the fighter did pose a considerable threat to the Allies' air superiority during the final stages of the war.

In mid-September the Group was given one of their most daunting and dangerous tasks of the war - to destroy the flak batteries in the path of the Allied airborne landings in Holland. Three other P-47 Groups were also involved, and the pilots were ordered to attack from about 2,500 feet and drop their fragmentation bombs only when the batteries opened fire. It was emphasised that bombing accuracy was the order of the day, and they survived this ordeal of fire with the loss of just one aircraft. The next day (the 18th), along with the other 'veteran' 56th Group, they had to attack from a lower height due to poor visibility, and five pilots were lost. Five days later the Group was sent in 'to neutralise the dropping zones' before RAF transports resupplied the beleaguered airborne forces. For their actions on these missions the Group was awarded its first Distinguished Unit Citation.

In the last quarter of 1944 the Group seemed to lose some headway in the number of victories scored, at least compared with many Groups. Its pilots rarely found themselves in an advantageous position when tackling the Luftwaffe, and could only muster a 'mere' 34 enemy aircraft for the loss of 14 pilots. They were still operating P-47s and did not convert to P-51s until December. At first the change was not welcomed by the pilots, most considered that their Thunderbolts were superior in many respects to P-51s. Bad weather during the month also created problems with the retraining programme, with Duxford fully justifying its nickname 'Duckpool'! Matters became so serious that a 4,100 foot PSP runway was put down. On the last day of the year, Captain Julius Maxwell shot down a FW 190, the final enemy aircraft to fall to their P-47s, and the Group's victories now exceeded 400.

*Lt Col John D. Landers in his P-51* Big Beautiful Doll *at Duxford, 24th March 1945. (Smithsonian Institution)*

On 22nd February 1945, one of the most brilliant and charismatic fighter leaders of the Eighth Air Force arrived to take charge of the Group. He was Colonel John D. Landers, late of the 55th and 357th Groups, who had previously served in the Pacific and quickly demonstrated that he was an excellent fighter pilot as well as a natural leader. Under the tall Texan's guidance the Group's pilots became very successful at ground strafing. In March they claimed 13 jet aircraft downed out of a grand total of 43 - the so-called 'Great Jet Massacre'. Then, on 10th April, they destroyed 52 aircraft on the ground with Landers claiming eight. Six days later, whilst over Pilsen in Czechoslovakia, another 135 were claimed - a record for the Eighth that was not surpassed and which earned the Group their second DUC.

The Group flew its last mission on 25th April 1945. In 450 operations its total victories amounted to three short of 700, with 167 aircraft lost in action; a heavy contribution to the Eighth Fighter Command and not solely because of its length of service. On 1st August 1945, the airfield was opened to the public with the Group's sleek P-51s on display. The Americans remained at Duxford until October, although most of their aircraft had left in the previous month.

The airfield was formally handed back to the RAF on 1st December and almost sixteen years later, on 1st August 1961, the last operational aircraft, a Gloster Meteor, took off from its now concrete runway. Duxford has since gone from strength to strength and is now acknowledged as the most popular aviation museum in Europe. The new American Air Museum was opened by The Queen in August 1997.

# 9
# FOWLMERE

When, as a new Pilot Officer, J. E. 'Johnnie' Johnson arrived at Fowlmere at the end of August 1940 to join 19 Squadron, he found the airfield to be, 'little more than a large grass meadow with the odd hut dotted around the perimeter, and one or two Spitfires dispersed round the field.' Within days he was posted away to 616 Squadron at Coltishall, but his first impressions show that in 1940 Fowlmere was even more primitive than the old First World War training airfield which had been sited close-by. At least in those days it did possess six large hangars and permanent accommodation.

The airfield was resuscitated in the early summer of 1940, around Manor Farm, to act as a satellite for Duxford, about three miles away almost due east. Spitfires from 19 Squadron began using Fowlmere on 25th June, but eight days later the pilots returned to the comfort of Duxford to make way for the Defiants of 264 Squadron, which flew 'just across the road' from the parent station.

The Boulton Paul Defiant was designed and built in Norwich, the only East Anglian 'local' aircraft. The prototype flew in August 1937, and it was the first fighter to have a heavy power-driven turret, with four .303 machine guns, rather than the conventional forward firing armament, which of course demanded a two-man crew. Powered by a Rolls-Royce Merlin III engine, the aircraft was capable of just over 300 mph at 17,000 feet, and entered the service in December 1939 with 264 Squadron. Defiant crews fought valiantly over the Dunkirk beaches with some success, although on 13th May 1940 four out of six aircraft were lost whilst claiming five enemy aircraft. In August the squadron would suffer grievous losses when it entered the Battle of Britain, and within days was withdrawn from the fray. Whilst the squadron

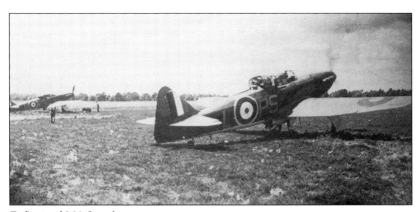

*Defiants of 264 Squadron.*

operated from Duxford and Fowlmere it was mainly engaged in night patrols. The Defiant ultimately became a useful stop-gap night-fighter.

19 Squadron returned to Fowlmere on 24th July, and stayed until the end of the Battle of Britain. The pilots found that in their short absence the airfield had improved somewhat – there were now six Nissen huts instead of only two, but still no hangars! Two days later there was torrential rain and the airfield became a sea of mud. Fowlmere could never be considered a comfortable billet and it is perhaps not surprising that when the Americans occupied the airfield in 1944 they quickly dubbed it 'the hen's puddle'!

It was almost inevitable that, as the RAF's most experienced Spitfire squadron, 19 would be called upon to trial operationally the new Mark IB, which was equipped with two 20mm Hispano cannons. The cannon was of French design and had been selected for its high rate of fire and relatively light weight; it also proved to be an excellent weapon against armour. The Browning guns gave the pilot sufficient ammunition for 18 seconds of firing, whereas the cannons provided only about six seconds. Endless problems were encountered with the cannons and their drum feeds and, by the end of August, 26 cannon stoppages had been experienced in five aerial engagements.

On 31st August 1940, the pilots were engaged in combat with a strong Luftwaffe force over Debden. Two pilots were shot down, one was seriously injured, and another was killed when his aircraft crashed on return to Fowlmere, just for two Me 109s destroyed. It was after this engagement that Air Chief Marshal Dowding agreed with Squadron Leader Philip C. Pinkham that their IBs should be exchanged for 'normal' Spitfires. The squadron was taken off operations whilst the aircraft were changed for Spitfires from an Operational Training Unit.

On 5th September Squadron Leader Pickham was killed in action over Hornchurch and one of the Flight Commanders, Flight Lieutenant B. J. E. 'Sandy' Lane, DFC, was promoted in his place, becoming the squadron's fourth commanding officer in just nine months. He remained in charge until July 1941, but sadly was killed in action in December 1942. His book *Spitfire* was published under the pseudonym B. J. Ellan earlier in the year. The squadron operated as part of the Duxford Wing and on Battle of Britain Day its pilots claimed three Me 109s with another two probables, as well as three Dornier 17Zs shared by a number of other pilots. Two Spitfires were lost, one of them crash-landed with the pilot safe and the other ditched in the Channel with the pilot taken prisoner - a fairly rare occurrence in the Battle.

From the middle of September, 19 Squadron was joined at Fowlmere by the Spitfires of 611 Squadron, then based at Kirton Lindsey. This squadron had suffered harshly during August and was now classified a C unit, which meant it had a nominal five pilots under training. Dowding had been compelled to classify his fighter squadrons in order to ensure a sufficient number of replacement pilots for the front-line squadrons. These latter were classed as A squadrons, and were maintained to the full complement of 26 pilots, whereas B squadrons were kept in reserve and brought up to full strength to rotate with those operating in No 11 Group, which was in the direct firing line. 611 Squadron came down daily to operate from Fowlmere as part of the Duxford Wing, and sometimes the pilots would stay overnight.

On 22nd September 1940 the airfield was bombed when a solitary Dornier 17 dropped a stick of bombs across the landing area, damaging one Spitfire. Four days later the first Mark IIAs arrived for 19 Squadron to trial operationally. These had the higher powered Merlin XII engines, which slightly improved the performance, especially the rate of climb, and were provided with extra armour plating protection for the pilot and fuel tanks.

Although the pilots patrolled almost daily, much of the action had tailed off. The squadron's top-scoring pilot, Flight Sergeant George Unwin, DFM Bar, with 14 victories, left for an instructor's job, because at the age of 28 years he was considered too old for fighter operations! He finally retired from the RAF in 1961 as a Wing Commander and in May 1996 returned to Duxford to take part in the Spitfire Diamond Jubilee Airshow.

After wintering at Duxford, the squadron returned to Fowlmere in February 1941 along with the Czech pilots of 310, and they were largely engaged on coastal patrols, fighter sweeps over the near Continent and later as escorts on daylight bombing missions. When 19 Squadron moved away some four months later, 18 years of almost continuous service at Duxford and Fowlmere came to an end.

On 17th November a new squadron was formed at the airfield - No 154 - and it was also equipped with Spitfires. Under the command of Squadron Leader A. G. Garvin (who had served with 264 Squadron) it took rather a long time to work up to operational readiness, mainly because it frequently lost pilots to other more established squadrons. Its first operation was launched on 24th February 1942 - an abortive East Coast convoy patrol - and soon the pilots were operating from Coltishall as a more convenient base. Early in May the pilots saw their first combat action and lost one pilot, three days later (on the 7th) the squadron moved away to Church Stanton in the West Country.

The first Hurricanes, Mark IIBs, appeared at Fowlmere during July 1942. They had Merlin XX engines, and were supplied with the interchangeable wings with no fewer than twelve .303 machine guns and the carriage of two 250 or 500 pound bombs. They operated in a fighter/bomber role and became known as 'Hurribombers'. The squadron, No 174, had only been formed at Manston in the previous March. After a brief stay the pilots moved back to Manston, from where they operated in the ill-fated Dieppe operation.

Another famous Hurricane squadron, No 111, made Fowlmere a temporary home during the autumn. A First World War squadron that had reformed at Duxford in 1923, it was now a Spitfire squadron and en route to Gibraltar, where it arrived early in November. In the late 1950s it formed the RAF's famed 'Black Arrows' aerobatic flight.

The airfield was rather quiet during the winter of 1942/3, although during February and March several squadrons arrived, mostly on a temporary basis. The first was an Army Co-operation squadron, No 655 (AOP), operating Austers. These aircraft were of an American design and produced by Taylorcraft Aeroplanes (England) Ltd under licence. They were actually a military version of a successful and popular pre-war civilian sports aircraft, and were designed to take off and land from small landing grounds. Although of very light construction and appearing rather fragile, they were in fact quite rugged and proved indispensable for army support duties.

The last RAF aircraft to use Fowlmere were Mustang Is of 2 Squadron, highly appropriate considering that almost twelve months later their American counterparts, P-51s, would operate from the airfield for the rest of the war. The Mustangs, on detachment from

*Pilots of 339th Fighter Group pose beside P-51* Fabasca *in October 1944 – (l to r) Captain Burnsey, Major Gravette, Major Reynolds and Captain Peters. (Smithsonian Institution)*

Bottisham, were mainly engaged on 'lagoons', which involved flying reconnaissance missions, normally in pairs, over the Dutch coast seeking out enemy shipping targets.

For almost the next twelve months the airfield was non-operational. It had been allocated to the USAAF as a fighter base, but in April 1943 it was thought suitable for further development into a Class A bomber station. However, two months later, the USAAF reviewed their ambitious plans for upgrading existing grass airfields, and Fowlmere became re-allocated or 'down graded' to a fighter base again.

During the winter of 1943/4, W & C French Ltd moved in to prepare the airfield for occupation by the USAAF. The road from Fowlmere to Royston was closed and one of the two runways was laid across its path. They were fabricated from Sommerfeld track and a concrete perimeter track was constructed along with 80 pads for the dispersal of aircraft. One T2 hangar appeared along with another seven small blister hangars, and the various living sites were erected close to the village of Fowlmere. During the winter of 1944 when the airfield suffered serious drainage problems, extra Pierced Steel Planking tracking was laid down in an attempt to alleviate the problem.

The American airmen of the 339th Fighter Group arrived on 5th April 1944 under the command of Colonel John B. Henry Jr. It was the penultimate Fighter Group to enter the Eighth Air Force. Most of the pilots had trained on P-39s (Airacobras) in the States, and were complete strangers to the P-51s allocated to the Group. There was a delay of about a week before the first P-51s arrived at Fowlmere, so Colonel Henry had to quickly set up some intense familiarisation exercises and training programmes. Nevertheless, 51 pilots left Fowlmere on the 30th for their first operational mission, a fighter sweep in the Orleans area of France ahead of another Group engaged in a fighter/bomber attack of Bricy airfield. In their first week of operations the pilots flew as escorts for several V1 rocket-site attacks and to Berlin without meeting the Luftwaffe in action, although one aircraft was lost when it crash-landed near Fowlmere, the pilot escaping unharmed.

The pilots had to wait until 9th May before they made their first claim - two enemy aircraft without loss. By the end of May, in only 20 missions, they had accounted for 45 enemy aircraft for the loss of 14 P-51s. As 'greenhorns to the game', as their Colonel described them, his pilots were really making their mark, and would eventually score the highest number of both air and ground victories in twelve months.

During June, the Group was selected to trial the new Berger 'G' suits in operations. These suits were designed to prevent pilots losing consciousness during aerial combat, steep dives and spins. They incorporated inflatable panels, which equalised the pilot's blood pressure. Another Group had already tested the British Frank suits, which operated on water pressure. Both suits were found to be equally effective but the Frank suit was heavier and hotter to wear, so the Eighth Fighter Command opted for the Berger suit; by November they were available in sufficient quantities to supply all fighter pilots in the Eighth.

Another technical innovation that was introduced about the same time was a new gyroscopic gunsight. It was British designed, originally for use in heavy bombers, but cleverly adapted for use in a P-51. The new sight was quickly dubbed 'No miss um' by American pilots and ground crews. It allowed successful firing at nearly twice the previous maximum range, as well as offering deflection shooting. The Americans built their own version of the sight, K-14, which was later installed in all P-51Ds.

*A montage of four Commanding Officers of 339th Fighter Group and P-51* Mary, Queen of Scotts. *(Smithsonian Institution)*

The Group's tally of victories steadily mounted and by the end of August 1944 they had passed the 130 mark, although in the process over 50 aircraft had been lost. These figures do underline just how effective the P-51 had become as a pursuit fighter, but they also demonstrate that it was less able to sustain and survive battle damage compared with the sturdy P-47. On two spectacular days in September, the 10th and 11th, whilst the Group was engaged on escort missions, no less than 58 enemy aircraft were destroyed, many of them on the ground.

It was on the second day that the 339th, led by Major Edgar Gravette, came to the rescue of the 100th Bomb Group, which was being fiercely attacked by a large formation of enemy fighters. Although the 100th (known as 'The Bloody Hundredth' because of the heavy losses it suffered) had eleven B-17s shot down, the Group's pilots managed to save it from utter annihilation, and in the process accounted for 14 fighters for the loss of two pilots. For their actions on these two operations, the 339th was awarded its only Distinguished Unit Citation.

Some of the fiercest fighting of the air war between the Eighth Air Force and the Luftwaffe occurred on several operations during November. For instance, on the 2nd when it was estimated that over 400 enemy fighters were in action, more than a quarter were claimed to have been destroyed, of which the Group's share was 'only' two. Yet on the 26th, when 114 fighters were downed, the 339th claimed the lion's share - 29. It was in this furious and ferocious air battle that Lieutenant Jack Daniell accounted for five FW 190s in his first air combat, thus becoming 'an ace in a day'. He was the thirteenth and last Eighth fighter pilot to achieve such a feat.

From then until the end of the year the pilots' happy knack of scoring heavily seemed to have deserted them. For over a month they did not account for a single enemy aircraft. On the last day of 1944 six victories were claimed, but for the loss of two pilots. This barren period continued into the New Year and the pilots had to wait another five weeks before adding to their total. It was not until early April 1945 that they returned with a vengeance and set two wartime records for the Eighth Fighter Command. On the 4th, 105 enemy aircraft were destroyed in ground-strafing, and leading the Group was Lieutenant Colonel Joe Thury, who added four to his total. This was the first time a Group had exceeded a century on a single mission. Twelve days later they repeated the feat with 118 destroyed on the ground, of which Captain Robert Ammon led with eleven victories - an individual record.

The following day (the 17th) it was decided that Colonel Thury would again lead 505th Squadron in a second attack on the same airfield. The Group's new commanding officer, Lieutenant Colonel William C. Clarke, had ordered the second strike, a rather calculated risk. There was a more than average chance the airfield defences might be prepared and ready for a second attack and, in any case, ground-strafing was a most unpredictable operation at the best of times - the majority of the Eighth's top pilots had been lost whilst strafing rather than in air combat. Seventeen P-51s left Fowlmere in the late morning and about six hours later they all returned, with another 56 aircraft claimed to have been destroyed. This successful mission brought Lieutenant Colonel Thury's grand total to $25\frac{1}{2}$, which made him the second highest scoring ground-strafing pilot in the Eighth Air Force.

Four days later the Group completed their 264th and final mission from Fowlmere, all in a matter of twelve months. In this short time 680 aircraft had been destroyed, a total that was only slightly less than their colleagues at Duxford, who had been operational twelve months

*Memorial to 339th Fighter Group at Fowlmere.*

longer. The Group's total of $440\frac{1}{2}$ ground victories was the third highest in the Eighth. There is no doubt that it was a quite remarkable record, which had been achieved at the cost of 97 aircraft lost in action.

By October 1945 the Americans had left for home, but over the years the 339th Group has maintained close links with the village of Fowlmere; indeed, on their memorial stone, which was dedicated in 1986, it is recorded that, 'Here was our haven in that war'. The airfield was soon turned back to farming, but since then the wartime T2 hangar has been re-clad, a wind-sock still flies and the occasional private aircraft can be seen taking off from the small grass strip.

# 10
# GLATTON

The site of this wartime airfield was one of ten in East Anglia earmarked for development by American engineers, and the only airfield in the county to be constructed by American personnel. The 809th Engineer Aviation Battalion moved in during 1943, with a planned completion date of January 1944.

The airfield lies to the east of the A1, between the villages of Holme and Conington, and within the parish boundaries of the latter, but because there was already a RAF operational station at Coningsby in Lincolnshire, the airfield became known as Glatton (from the village across the other side of the Great North Road) to avoid any confusion in the two names. In one other respect the airfield was quite unusual, as it was built around a working farm, which continued operating throughout the war despite being surrounded by the intense activity of a fully operational bomber station.

The 457th Bomb Group was the last B-17 Group to join the 1st Division and it was placed in the 94th Combat Bomb Wing, which had its headquarters at Polebrook in Northamptonshire. The first B-17s began to arrive at the airfield during the last ten days of January 1944, but sadly two had already been lost when they crashed at Nutts Corner airfield in Northern Ireland. The aircraft were most distinctive, unpainted and resplendent in the original silver finish. However, they soon gained the Group's identification code - a black letter U set inside a white triangle, applied to the vertical tail; also, from August, a blue diagonal band was added and the triangle was changed to black with a white letter. Unlike other Bomb Groups the four squadrons did not have any special markings other than that the propellor hubs were painted red, blue, white and yellow to denote the 748th to 751st respectively.

The Group's aircraft were the latest model of this famous bomber - G

- which also proved to be the final variant. It had been first developed and produced in July 1943, mainly in direct response to operational demands for improved nose armament in an attempt to counter the Luftwaffe's very effective head-on attacks. The new model was equipped with a power-operated Bendix turret of two .5 inch machine guns, giving it 13 guns in the chin, nose, dorsal, centre fuselage, waist and tail positions - a remarkable amount of fire-power! The B-17Gs began to replace the existing F models in the Eighth Air Force in September 1943, with over 8,600 being produced at three different locations by Boeing, Douglas and Lockheed-Vega.

Colonel James R. Luper, the Group's Commanding Officer, was placed under considerable pressure to get his crews to operational standard as soon as possible because the Eighth Air Force was building up to a major offensive against the German aircraft industry. In November 1943 the Allied air chiefs - the Eighth and Ninth in England, the Fifteenth in Italy and RAF Bomber Command - had agreed to mount a concerted and co-ordinated onslaught against German airfields, air-parks, aircraft factories, assembly and components plants, which was codenamed Operation Argument. All that was required to mount these operations was a spell of clear and settled weather and this did not materialise until 19th February 1944 when a favourable forecast suggested a period of clement weather. The RAF opened Operation Argument on the night of 19/20th February with a heavy raid on Leipzig, which resulted in Bomber Command's heaviest loss of the war so far; the following day the Eighth Air Force started their part of the offensive by bombing the same target.

The 457th was brought into action on the second day (the 21st) of what became known in the USAAF as 'The Big Week'. The Group had been left out of the first operation because the target was considered far too distant and daunting a task for completely novice crews. As it was, they saw action first over airfields in western Germany and lost just one aircraft. The next day, the unpredictable weather interfered once again, and the Group's targets were obscured by heavy cloud cover which prevented a satisfactory and effective mission.

Faced with a poor forecast for the following day (the 23rd), the Eighth called for a complete stand down, which was merely a brief respite for the crews before the next big task for the 1st Division - Schweinfurt. The Eighth had not returned to this target since the disaster on Black Thursday in the previous October. The new crews at Glatton would be well aware of the previous two catastrophic operations, so it must have been with no little fear and trepidation that they set off for this infamous target. Of the 266 B-17s that bombed Schweinfurt, eleven were lost, one of which came from Glatton, and probably Colonel Luper breathed a huge sigh of relief to get off so lightly.

The massive air offensive reached a climax on 25th February 1944, with the Eighth mounting its fifth major operation in just six days. The Me 410 assembly plant at Augsburg was laid to the 1st Division, and the Group lost two aircraft. Without doubt, the tyros had experienced a very torrid introduction into battle. As one crewman remarked, 'We went into it like boys and four days later we were men.' During the 'Big Week' the Eighth lost 156 aircraft, compared with the RAF's loss of 141 in four night raids. Three targets - Leipzig, Augsburg and Schweinfurt - had been bombed both by day and night, the first real example of 'round the clock bombing', the Allies' objective ever since the Eighth had joined the European air war. The damage inflicted on the German fighter production was not quite as serious as the Air Chiefs had hoped, because the Luftwaffe was still able to oppose the Eighth in considerable strength by day and Bomber Command at night, if perhaps only on specially selected occasions.

None of the Bomb Groups were given much time to lick their wounds and the 457th was no exception, because ten days later the crews were engaged in the Eighth's first major attack on Berlin. Considering the heavy losses sustained on this mission, the 457th acquitted itself well as only two aircraft were lost and these fell in rather unfortunate circumstances. One of its aircraft collided with a Me 410 and on its way down hit another B-17 in the same formation, and both crashed to the ground.

Four further missions passed without incident and it was only when the crews returned to Augsburg on 16th March that one of its B-17s ditched in the North Sea, with just a few of the crew being rescued. The Group was to lose another three B-17s in the sea during the rest of war, with most of the crew members being rescued; they were rather fortunate, because of the 450 aircraft that ditched in the sea, only just over one third of the crews were saved.

The month of March 1944 saw the appearance at the airfield of a very rare aircraft indeed, at least for European skies - the B-29 Superfortress. This had made its first landfall at St Mawgan in Cornwall on the 7th of the month and five days later it landed at Glatton, creating intense interest amongst all the personnel. The aircraft later visited other Eighth Air Force bases. This massive bomber, with a wing span of 141 feet and almost 100 feet long, had originated in February 1940, and was

*Lieutenant James and the crew of* Home James *of 457th Bomb Group after completion of their 25th mission, 31st May 1944. (Smithsonian Institution)*

first flown in September 1942. It entered the USAAF as a training aircraft in July 1943. Its loaded weight was twice that of a B-17. If brought into operations in Europe, the wear and tear on the runways would require considerable work on the existing airfield facilities, even though some airfields, for instance Marham in Norfolk, had been selected for development into VHB (Very Heavy Bomber) stations. However, the B-29s only flew operationally in the 'Pacific theater'; their first operation was mounted on 5th June 1944. Of course, it was a B-29 - *Enola Gay* - that dropped the first atomic bomb, on 6th August 1945. Just six years later the B-29s would return in numbers to Cambridge-shire; they would also serve with the RAF, where they were known as 'Washingtons'.

On two successive days, 27th and 28th May, the 457th lost three aircraft on each mission, their heaviest losses so far. Such was the tempo of operations during this period leading up to the invasion of Europe that the Group had already passed the half-century mark in barely three months, and it would top a hundred by the middle of August. Crews were also completing their combat tours (30 missions) in record time - one fortunate crew returned to the United States in just 62 days! However, towards the end of the month it was announced that with the increased number of operations and the 'comparatively safer technical missions', the tour would be extended to 35 missions. Perhaps not surprisingly, the Eighth's chiefs noticed 'a definite drop in morale' after issuing this directive, though the USAAF HQ in the Pentagon at Washington went further and directed that 'no relief for combat duty should be determined by the number of missions flown'. In practice, 35 missions became the bench-mark for the completion of a tour and with it a posting back 'State-side'.

On the 7th October oil targets at Pölitz were the Group's primary objective. Pölitz was situated to the north-east of Berlin near Stettin, and because the place was known to be strongly fortified (with over 270 heavy flak batteries) the route planned for this operation allowed an eight minute bomb run. It proved to be a particularly harsh operation with 17 bombers shot down (11.4%), 30 receiving heavy flak damage and only 17 escaping unscathed. The German ground radar had successfully tracked the emissions from the leading H2X aircraft, and accounted for four of the lead 'ships' as well as five deputies. Five crews failed to return to Glatton, including Colonel Luper, but he and his crew managed to bale out, ending up as prisoners of war.

There were heavier losses to come, on 2nd November over the Leuna oil plants at Merseburg. On this operation the Group, like the 91st at

*The lead plane of 457th Bomb Group after the Group had completed 200 missions. (Smithsonian Institution)*

Bassingbourn, suffered grievously at the hands of the Luftwaffe in a brief period when the escorting P-51s were absent, with nine crews failing to return. Six days later the crews were back over Merseburg and another B-17 went missing, and another crew was lost on 12th December when the Eighth attacked this important oil target for the 18th and last time. In just eight operations to various German oil targets, the 457th had lost 28 aircraft. Their losses over oil targets would continue in the New Year with crews missing over Sterkade and Holten.

The last major mission to Berlin was mounted on 18th March 1945, when the German capital, or what was now left of it, suffered once again under the might of the Eighth. This was the 18th major operation mounted by the Eighth to Berlin, in which they lost 391 aircraft and over 3,700 airmen missing in action. This can be compared with the RAF's 19 major night raids during the winter of 1943/4 when 625 aircraft were lost and 4,340 men were either killed or missing in action. Of course, Berlin would be attacked by the RAF on many more

*Memorial to 457th Bomb Group at All Saints' church, Conington.*

occasions, but now exclusively by the PFF Mosquitos.

In this March operation, over 1,100 heavy bombers attacked railway stations and tank plants in and around the city. It did not prove a conspicuous success as poor visibility not only detracted from the accuracy of the bombing, but also caused problems with the escorting fighters, who frequently lost contact with the bomber formations. Some of the Groups were attacked by Me 262s, and their 30mm cannons could be most destructive weapons. One of the Group's aircraft, *Lady Be Good*, survived several attacks from the jets and managed to limp home despite quite heavy damage. Of the 13 bombers lost on the mission, at least eight fell to flak batteries, and one of these belonged to the 457th. Despite the terrific pounding at the hands of Bomber Command and the Eighth Air Force, the Berlin flak was still a potent threat, taking its toll of many brave bomber crews.

From then on until the end of the war just five crews were lost in action, the final casualty falling on 18th April over Rosenheim in southern Germany. Two days later the crews left on their final operation of the war to the marshalling yards at Brandenburg; in just 14 months, 237 operations had been made from Glatton for the loss of 83 aircraft. However, their duties were not completely finished as later in May, after the war in Europe had come to a close, the crews were engaged on the so-called 'Revival' flights, although the official codename was Operation Exodus. With a five man crew, the B-17s were landed on old Luftwaffe airfields to pick up and bring back over 40 prisoners of war on each trip, and even managed to meet friends whom they thought they would never see again. All the crews found these to be the most pleasant and rewarding missions they had flown.

Towards the end of the month the B-17s were moved to depôts in the United Kingdom, and by 21st June the last American personnel had left for the United States. They went home in style on the *Queen Elizabeth*. For a brief period the airfield was used by the RAF, but by the summer of 1946 it had closed down.

Today the main runway has survived and is used by small civil aircraft of Klingair Ltd, and Glatton is now known as Peterborough Business Airfield. There is an attractive memorial to the Group in the churchyard of All Saints' church at Conington, which unlike the nearby airfield has become 'redundant'. It features a bust of an airman on a stone pillar and bears an inscription, 'Fait Accompli', which can be freely translated as, 'Things done and no longer worth arguing about', or more simply, 'The task completed'.

# 11
# GRANSDEN
# LODGE

There is an imposing stained glass window in Great Gransden church commemorating 405 (Vancouver) Squadron, and beneath is a plaque bearing the message: 'The people of these villages cared for the Airmen, who flew from RAF Gransden Lodge. They watched for them and prayed for them.' Sentiments that sum up the close relationships that were established between the wartime stations and the local communities. The villages, Great and Little Gransden, are situated about two miles to the west of Ermine Street (A1198 road) and the airmen remembered were mainly Canadians; the 405th was the only RCAF squadron to serve with the Pathfinders.

The airfield, sited a little to the east of the villages, was built during 1941/2 by John Laing & Son Ltd as a satellite for Tempsford, just over the boundary in Bedfordshire. The first aircraft to appear, in April 1942, were Wellington IIIs of 1418 Flight, which had been formed a couple of months earlier to trial GEE. This was a radio system developed by the Telecommunications Research Establishment (TRE) as an aid to navigation. The device enabled the navigator to fix a position by consulting an instrument or GEE box, which received two sets of pulse signals from three separated ground stations (one 'master' and two 'slaves'). It computed the time difference between the receipt of these signals and gaving an instant 'fix'.

Although relatively simple and reliable to operate, it did have a range limitation - about 350 miles - but this covered targets in the Ruhr. Ultimately the Germans found the means to jam the system, but nevertheless GEE proved invaluable in getting aircraft to the target area and also back home, especially in bad weather. It was first used in a major operation to Essen on 8/9th March 1942, and although GEE was never accurate enough to act as a blind-bombing aid, it marked a considerable step forward.

In the first week of July 1942, Wellington ICs of 1474 Flight arrived. This unit had been formed out of B Flight of 109 Squadron, a special duties unit engaged in the development of radio-counter measures and radar aids. The airfield was now deeply involved in the development of various bombing aids, equipment and techniques, especially with the formation of No 1 Bombing Development Unit, which ultimately was equipped with the four main heavy bombers.

Early in 1943 a new Special Duties squadron was formed at the airfield, No 192, to specialise in gathering information by electronic means; the work was known as 'Elint' from ELectronic INTelligence. Using a variety of Wellingtons, its crews probed the enemy's electronic defences in order that suitable counter-measures could be devised. The squadron was later transferred into No 100 (Bomber Support) Group, formed to co-ordinate all the squadrons engaged in this battle of wits.

The nature of the station changed dramatically in April 1943 when the airfield was transferred into No 8 (PFF) Group, and became a satellite of Oakington, though it became a full station two months later. The Development Unit and 192 Squadron moved away to another Group 3 airfield at Feltwell in Norfolk, and a new unit was set up, dedicated to the final navigation training of aircrews posted to the various PFF squadrons. It was commanded by Wing Commander R.P. Elliott, DSO, DFC, and was programmed to train six crews every three days.

No 405 (Vancouver) Squadron arrived from Leeming in Yorkshire on 19th April. It had been the first RCAF squadron to enter Bomber Command when formed two years earlier, and was adopted by the city of Vancouver in February 1943. Ultimately the RCAF had its own Group (No 6) comprising 14 heavy squadrons, making an immense contribution to the air offensive. Over 9,900 Canadian airmen lost their lives whilst serving with Bomber Command, almost 18% of the total casualties, far more than any other Commonwealth country.

The squadron's transfer into No 8 (PFF) Group brought the return of its most experienced pilot, Group Captain J. E. 'Johnnie' Fauquier, DSO 2 Bars, DFC, as its Commander. He had previously been in charge during 1942. Fauquier was an outstanding leader and earned the nickname 'The King of the Pathfinders'. He remained at the helm until June 1944 when he left to command the famous 617 (Dambusters) Squadron.

*A Halifax II of 405 (Vancouver) Squadron being bombed up, 1943.*

Both the Navigation Training Unit and the squadron were equipped with Handley Page Halifax IIs. This aircraft owed its existence to a specification (13/36) which had called for a twin-engined bomber to be powered by the new Vulture engines. The aircraft was later redesigned to take four Rolls-Royce Merlin X engines. The first prototype flew in October 1939 and entered the service 13 months later, commencing operations in March 1941. It was the first four-engined bomber to make a night attack against a German target. The early Halifaxes cruised at about 260 mph with a total bomb load of 13,000 pounds and had a ceiling height of around 18,000 feet. The aircraft proved to be most durable and inspired a strong loyalty among its crews, who fondly dubbed it the 'Halibag'. The Mark IIs were powered by Merlin 22 or 24 engines, improving performance by about 10%; they were also supplied with a twin-gun Boulton and Paul dorsal turret.

Not everybody was enamoured with the aircraft. Air Chief Marshal Harris considered its performance greatly inferior to his beloved Lancasters, and freely admitted that he would have gladly traded them in for more Lancasters. Certainly the aircraft suffered more heavily than the Lancasters, and at one period during March to August 1942 the losses were sufficiently serious to rest the Halifax squadrons for about a month. Nevertheless, the aircraft served with distinction in three Commands, undertaking a variety of roles, and it was the only aircraft capable of towing the large Hamilcar glider. The much improved Mark IIIs fully restored the bomber's reputation and over 6,100 Halifaxes were finally produced.

At the time of writing, a Halifax is being restored in Canada, but the only completely reconstructed Halifax is in the Yorkshire Air Museum at Elvington; it is resplendent in the markings of *Friday the 13th*, a Halifax II of 158 Squadron, which completed 128 operational sorties before being scrapped. A Halifax - W1048 *'S for Sugar'* - of 35 Squadron, which crashed into a frozen lake in Norway during April 1942, was recovered 30 years later in a remarkable state of preservation, and is now on display at the RAF Museum at Hendon.

The Canadian crews of 405 Squadron had only recently returned from a spell of operations with Coastal Command, and their first PFF mission was mounted on 26/27th April 1943 to Duisburg. The Pathfinders returned utterly convinced that they had marked the target very successfully. However, the following day photographic evidence suggested that much of the attack had fallen outside the target area, mainly on the approach run. The losses on the night were slight, although the squadron lost one aircraft, with the nine-man crew all Canadian bar one.

The number of Halifaxes using the airfield put a considerable strain on the relatively limited facilities. It was decided in June that the PFF Navigation Unit would move to the more commodious surroundings of Upwood, leaving 405 Squadron in splendid isolation at 'The Lodge'.

In the ensuing months 405 became fully engaged in the Battle of the Ruhr, losing crews over Essen, Dortmund, Düsseldorf, Wuppertal, Cologne and Krefeld. On the night of 13/14th July they were engaged over Aachen, only the second time this ancient city had been bombed. A strong tail wind brought the first waves of bombers in early and much of the severe damage occurred in the first ten minutes or so. The German authorities referred to the night as the Terrorangriffe or 'Terror raid'. Over 3,000 buildings were destroyed with perhaps 60% of the city flattened; two months later much of the population had still not returned to the city. The squadron lost only one Halifax, to a night-fighter over Holland, but unfortunately it was manned by a most experienced crew holding three DFCs and two DFMs between them.

The three major Hamburg raids during July passed without incident for the squadron, but on the fourth (2/3rd August) the large and heavy thunderstorm encountered over Holland resulted in the operation

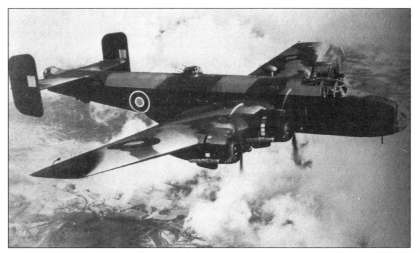

*Both 405 (Vancouver) Squadron and the PFF Navigation Unit operated the Halifax II.*

being an utter failure, and caused the downfall of many crews. Three aircraft failed to return to Gransden Lodge, one of which was abandoned over Sweden - a rare occurrence - with the crew being interned for about six months.

During the month the crews began to exchange their Halifaxes for Lancasters, and the first of the new aircraft was lost in very unusual circumstances. Having landed safely after a successful mission to Nuremberg on 10/11th August, it was being taxied to its dispersal point when it ran into a ditch and was so severely damaged that it was written-off. The unfortunate pilot was none other than the CO, otherwise he might have had some pithy comments to make!

Rather appropriately, the squadron was supplied with the first Lancasters to be built in Canada by the Victory Aircraft Company. They were designated X's and powered by Packard-built Merlin engines. The first of these, KB700, named *Ruhr Express*, completed just two operations with the squadron before being transferred to another Canadian squadron - No 419 (Moose) - in December. During 1944 the squadron also operated a couple of VIs, rather special Lancasters that had been converted by Rolls-Royce. They had an increased wing span of 120 feet and their nose and dorsal turrets removed; they were fitted with improved H2S and early electronic counter-measures equipment. They were never put into full-scale production.

On two successive nights in August 1943 - 16/17th and 17/18th - the crews were involved in two particularly long and arduous operations.

The first was to the Fiat motor works in Turin, which proved to be the last time the Command attacked an Italian target. The Luftwaffe night-fighters were quite active over France both on the outward and return flights and, although only four aircraft were lost, one belonged to 405. The next night the rocket research establishment at Peenemunde was attacked and one of the squadron's crews strayed south of the planned route. The Halifax was shot down over Flensburg, the first to fall to enemy action on that night.

In the first of 19 Berlin raids mounted between August 1943 and March 1944, Fauquier was selected to act as Master Bomber, though the term 'Master of Ceremonies' was still being used. His first Berlin mission had been in November 1941 as a Flight Commander with the squadron, such was his vast operational experience. The operation on 23/24th August would be the first time that a Master Bomber was used over a major German city. It was thought that Fauquier, 'had the ability to impose his will. He was a bright, hard fellow who certainly would have made the Master Bomber method work, if anybody could.' The operation was not a great success, most of the bombs falling outside the city. Of the 56 aircraft lost, two came from Fauquier's squadron. One crashed in southern Sweden after being badly damaged by a night-fighter. It was unusual, if not unique, for one squadron to have two crews interned in Sweden within a month of each other.

By a strange coincidence, on the final Berlin operation (24/25th March 1944) the squadron again supplied the Master Bomber - Wing Commander R. J. Lane, DSO, DFC Bar, who would replace Fauquier as Squadron Commander in June. This raid has become known as the 'Night of the Big Winds' because of the fierce north winds (over 100 mph), which had not been forecast and caused such havoc with the target marking and bomber formations. It was said that Lane's strong Canadian accent could be clearly heard exhorting the crews, 'Those bastards wanted a war, now show them what war is like.'

Seventy-two aircraft were lost on the night (9%), most on the return leg across central Germany and Holland, but remarkably the squadron escaped unscathed. Indeed, for the duration of the Battle of Berlin 405 Squadron sustained the lowest losses in the whole of No 8 Group, although 69 men had been killed with another 24 missing. One of its pilots, Squadron Leader H. W. Trilsbach later considered that this Battle was the worst of his operational flying career: 'worst weather, the most flak, most searchlights and by far the greatest fighter opposition.'

Towards the end of April 1944 the squadron lost another experienced

*142 Squadron became part of the Mosquito LNSF from October 1944.*

and brave Canadian pilot and crew when their Lancaster was the only aircraft not to return from a raid on important railway yards at Montzen, near Aachen. Squadron Leader E. M. Blenkinsopp was acting as Deputy Master Bomber when he was shot down. He managed to evade capture and worked with a Belgian Resistance group until captured by the Germans in December. He was taken to Hamburg to work as a forced labourer, but he later died in Belsen concentration camp. Further crews were lost over French railway targets in June, at Versailles, Tours and Lens. Another Lancaster went missing from a daylight raid on 8th September when enemy positions near Le Havre were attacked.

In eight days, from 20th to 28th September Bomber Command launched over 3,200 sorties dropping some 8,000 tons of bombs on the enemy's defensive positions at Calais and Cap Gris Nez. The five daylight raids were conducted in heavy cloud though the bombing was said to be 'effective', and 13 aircraft were lost (0.4%). One Lancaster that failed to return on the 26th was flown by the squadron's commander, Wing Commander C. W. Palmer, DFC, who had only been in charge of 405 since 23rd August.

The first Mosquitos arrived at the airfield on 27th October 1944, and rather appropriately they were Canadian-built BXXVs, from de Havilland's factory in Toronto. These were identical to the Canadian Mark XXs except that they were powered by Packard Merlin 225 engines. The XXVs were not particularly numerous as only 400 were ever produced. Neither of the Canadian Mosquitos was able to carry the 4,000 pound Cookie bombs. The new Mosquito squadron, No 142, had reformed two days earlier. It had previously served in France with the Advanced Air Striking Force flying Battles, and when it returned to England it converted to Wellingtons, moving to North Africa at the end of 1942. The squadron was disbanded in Italy in October and now became the latest addition to the Pathfinders' Light Night Striking Force.

This amazing force was entirely the concept of Air Commodore Bennett, such was his boundless faith in this spectacular aircraft. The LNSF, sometimes called the Fast Night Strike Force, caused damage and mayhem to German towns and cities and wrought endless havoc to German industry out of all proportion to its size, and to the losses it sustained in action. The figures almost beggar belief: over 12,000 sorties flown for the loss of 46 aircraft (0.37%)! The force raided Berlin on no less than 170 occasions, and from 20/21st February to 27/28th March 1945 on 36 consecutive nights - the so-called Berlin Express or Milk Run. Bomber Command acknowledged this role in 1945: 'The value of the Mosquito attacks as a supplement to the attacks by heavy aircraft is unquestioned and their contribution to the success of the combined bomber offensive was both significant and praiseworthy.' It was arguably the most successful operational force of the war.

Just two crews of the new squadron went out on 29th October, joining a force of 57 Mosquitos attacking Cologne, followed the next day by another two making the journey to Berlin along with another 60 Mosquitos. This was the first of countless operations the squadron made to the 'Big B'. In a little over six months, 142 Squadron mounted almost 1,100 sorties in 116 raids, and all for two aircraft lost in action. The squadron's targets ranged over Hanover, Herford, Stuttgart, Kassel and many oil targets in the Ruhr.

But it was Berlin that occupied the crews for much of their time, especially in 1945. On several occasions some of the aircraft would make two sorties in one night. The first time was on 4/5th January, when the first wave of Mosquitos left in the early evening and on return the crews were changed before the aircraft set off again. One of the largest Berlin attacks occurred on 21/22nd March, when 142 attacked the city for the loss of a single Mosquito. The Mosquitos were almost inviolate, travelling at 400+ mph at a height of 30,000+ feet. Only the Luftwaffe's Me 262 and 163 could catch them, but as these jet fighters were in short supply and engaged elsewhere, the force's losses were minimal and economical in the extreme. In this Berlin raid, one of the pilots' log books read: 'Big raid, over 100 aircraft. Did Dly

Telegraph X-word on way back'!

February 1945 was the squadron's busiest month so far, over 220 sorties flown with 156 tons of bombs being dropped. The crews were engaged in a variety of tasks. For instance, on 13/14th two 'windowed' Bohlen and then went on to bomb Dresden, two made a 'spoof' attack on Bonn, whilst another eight attacked Magdeburg. Ten nights later Berlin, Frankfurt and Darmstadt were attacked; the latter was a mock marking raid. The squadron flew its last mission on 2/3 May 1945 when 16 aircraft attacked Kiel in two waves. Kiel had suffered two heavy raids in the previous week when over 160 Mosquitos attacked this important port, which had featured in Bomber Command's operations since the early days of the war.

The Canadian squadron sent nine Lancasters to Berchtesgaden and Hitler's 'Eagle's Nest', with another four joining the force attacking coastal batteries on the island of Wangerooge - another target that dated back to 1939. Whilst 405 Squadron had served in the PFF it completed 317 raids, losing 62 aircraft, and its wartime record stood at 450 raids with the loss of 167 aircraft and over 750 airmen killed in action. The squadron flew back to Canada in June for further training as it had been selected to be part of the RAF Tiger Force, as its strategic bomber force for the Pacific was named. The sudden end of hostilities resulted in the squadron being disbanded in September.

In the same month, the Mosquito squadron was also disbanded at Gransden Lodge. Although some Liberators arrived at the end of the year, they only stayed for about two months. From then on the airfield remained silent, although the runways survived until the 1950s. Now there is little left of this once busy wartime airfield.

# 12
# GRAVELEY

Graveley has all but disappeared under the plough although the concrete perimeter road has been saved, as has the old control tower, now successfully disguised as a modern farmhouse. A discreet memorial stands beside the entrance to Cotton Farm recording the existence of this little known but active wartime airfield, from where famous bomber pilots flew - Alec Cranswick, Basil Robinson, Pat Daniels, Danny Everett, Julian Sale and Guy Lockhart, to name but a few.

The airfield opened on 1st March 1942 as a satellite for Tempsford, and was first used by 161 (Special Duty) Squadron. This unit had been formed at Newmarket on 14th February under the command of Wing Commander E. H. Fielden, MVO, AFC, who had been Captain of the King's Flight. It would spend the rest of the war transporting agents to and from enemy occupied territories as well as dropping supplies to support the activities of the Resistance forces and the SOE (Special Operations Executive). The squadron was equipped with a mixture of Lysanders, Whitleys and Wellingtons, and one of its pilots, Pilot Officer W. Guy Lockhart, would later return to command a Mosquito squadron. Just three successful clandestine operations were mounted from Graveley, two of them in a Lysander flown by Lockhart, although Tangmere in Surrey was used as the final departure point. During early April the squadron moved away to its permanent base at Tempsford.

The ground staff at Graveley gained their first experience of the tension involved in a large night operation, when Wellington ICs of 26 OTU at Cheddington in Buckinghamshire left Graveley before midnight on 30th May to take part in the '1,000 bomber' raid on Cologne. The vast air armada totalled 1,047 aircraft, well over half of them Wellingtons, clearly demonstrating the growing strength of Bomber Command. Forty-one aircraft were lost, its highest total so far, and it was an unhappy night for the unit as four failed to return. Three were shot down by night-fighters and the other crashed whilst attempting an emergency landing at Soham to the north-east of Cambridge.

The formation of the Pathfinder Force in August 1942 settled Graveley's future as a Pathfinder station. It was transferred to the control of Wyton and on the 15th received one of the first PFF squadrons - No 35 (Madras Presidency). The squadron was equipped with Halifax IIs, and had been specially reformed to introduce the new bomber into service. It mounted the first Halifax operation on 10/11th March 1941, and would continue to operate Halifaxes until March 1944.

On the night of 18/19th August, 31 PFF aircraft left to mark Flensburg for the main force - the first PFF-led raid. Unfortunately, the winds encountered were far stronger than expected and the bombers drifted to the north of the target. Sixteen PFF crews claimed to have marked the target area but it was later disclosed that two Danish towns had been mistakenly bombed. It was not a very auspicious start for the Pathfinders. One of the Halifaxes suffered two attacks from night-fighters and was shot down. A month later (on the 19/20th September), over Saarbrücken, the squadron lost Wing Commander J. H. Marks, DSO, DFC, and another senior pilot, Squadron Leader J. G. Kerry, DFC, went missing over Aachen on 5/6th October.

In November the squadron would have lost another very experienced pilot but for a rather remarkable escape. On the night of the 18/19th when Turin and its Fiat motor works was the target for 77 aircraft, a Halifax piloted by Squadron Leader Basil V. Robinson, DSO, DFC, AFC, was on its return flight when one of the flares in the bomb bay ignited and the fire quickly spread to the port wing. Robinson ordered his crew to bale out but just as he was preparing to make his escape, he realised that the fire had gone out. He remained at the controls and managed to coax the aircraft back home - over 700 miles and some four hours' flying time - completely single-handed.

He finally landed at Colerne in Wiltshire, and for this brilliant solo flight he was awarded a Bar to his DSO; his crew survived as prisoners of war. In December 1941 Robinson had another lucky escape when his Halifax ditched in the sea about 50 miles off the English coast. The aircraft floated for about 20 minutes, enabling the crew to escape safely and all were finally rescued. When Graveley became a full station, in May 1943, Robinson was promoted to Group Captain to become its first Commander.

The first H2S sets to be issued to Bomber Command at the end of 1942 were allocated to the Pathfinders, due in no small measure to Bennett's enthusiasm and support for the new device. H2S was an

*A Lancaster taking off from Graveley with 'FIDO' in operation. (via T. Murphy)*

airborne radar system that could transmit a shadowy image of the ground passing below onto a cathode ray set (or Plan Position Indicator), which was carried on the aircraft. An experienced operator, using predictions and overlays, could analyse and interpret the often confused images that appeared on the screen. Being airborne there were no restrictions on operational range, but the Germans did develop systems to track H2S quite accurately and also managed to produce a homing device - NAXOS - which was used by their night-fighters. The device's unusual codename is the chemical formula for the noxious gas, hydrogen sulphide, and it is said to have originated from 'It stinks!' - Professor Lindemann's retort to the boffins' excuse for the tardy development of the project, although he was told it was short for 'Home Sweet Home'!

At first only certain aircraft in 7 and 35 Squadrons were supplied with H2S, but during 1943 all PFF squadrons received the new equipment. On 30/31st January 1943, seven Stirlings and six Halifaxes led the first H2S operation of the war to Hamburg. Although on this occasion its use was not particularly successful, ultimately H2S, despite its limitations, proved to be quite effective but not, alas, the complete answer to blind-bombing.

Graveley was, on 18th February 1943, the scene of the first flying test of FIDO, or Fog Investigation Dispersal Operation, and the pilot was none other than Air Commodore Bennett. He was a most ardent supporter of the project, and had offered Graveley as the first operational station to be supplied with FIDO. It was a system by which pipelines were laid along each side of the runway into which petrol was injected under pressure, which was then fired by burners set at certain intervals along the pipeline. The intense heat so generated caused an updraught that dispersed the fog in the vicinity of the runway.

The first operational use of FIDO came on 19th November when four Halifaxes successfully landed with visibility down to 100 yards. Ultimately 15 airfields were supplied with FIDO, not only saving the lives of many crews but also enabling Bomber Command to maintain its operational schedule when weather conditions would have dictated otherwise.

During 1943 the squadron was fully engaged in all the Command's major operations, and it proved to be a costly year with 63 aircraft lost in action. Over one third of the Command's total casualties in the war occurred in 1943, with many senior and experienced crews being lost. 35 Squadron lost five Squadron Leaders, including its Navigation Officer, G. D. Waterer. Furthermore there were some close calls, with Squadron Leader D. F. E. 'Dixie' Dean and his crew escaping unharmed from a crash-landing. At the end of the year Squadron Leader Julian Sale, DSO Bar, DFC, brought his blazing Halifax III back to Graveley to make a crash-landing. He and his air-gunner escaped just before the aircraft exploded; the rest of the crew had baled out. This brilliant young Canadian pilot had successfully evaded capture on 12/13th May after being shot down over Holland en route to Dusiburg.

The saddest loss of the year was the death in action of Group Captain Basil Robinson, DSO Bar, DFC, AFC. He had personally briefed the crews before the Berlin operation on 23/24th August, and then took off with a scratch crew. Air Chief Marshal Harris severely restricted station commanders flying operationally - maybe to one or two per month - and Robinson always selected the hardest and most difficult missions. His Halifax was one of the four that failed to return from Berlin.

The Battle of the Ruhr took a heavy toll, especially on the night of 21/22nd June when Krefeld, to the west of the Rhine, was the target. The moon was bright and the PFF produced almost perfect marking. It was reckoned that 75% of the bombing was within three miles of the centre of Krefeld, with devastating results. However, the Luftwaffe were out in strength and six of the 19 Halifaxes failed to return to Graveley - 35 Squadron's heaviest loss of the war. On 11/12th

*A Mosquito being loaded with a 4,000 pound 'Cookie' bomb. (via T. Murphy)*

November the crews were in action over Cannes in the south of France, where the marshalling yards and railway sheds were the target. Four of the 124 Halifaxes were destroyed and three came from No 35.

The squadron was now beginning to receive its first Halifax IIIs, powered by Bristol Hercules VI engines and with increased wing spans, which improved the aircraft's performance and operational ceiling. There was also a new Commanding Officer, Wing Commander 'Pat' Daniels, DSO, DFC, who had previously served with 83 Squadron, and was now on his second PFF tour. Pat Daniels would remain with the squadron until well past D-Day and he acted as Master Bomber on the operation over Caen on 7th July 1944.

On the first day of the New Year a new squadron was formed at the airfield - No 692 (Fellowship of the Bellows). It derived its strange name from a patriotic organisation of Anglo-Argentinian businessmen and families in Buenos Aires, who raised funds to purchase RAF aircraft. It was equipped with Mosquito BIVs, and brought back to Graveley another brave and talented pilot - Wing Commander W. Guy Lockhart, DSO, DFC Bar, Croix de Guerre - as its first Commanding Officer. Lockhart had been a fighter pilot, flown numerous secret missions, successfully evaded capture in France, completed a spell with air intelligence in the Air Ministry, and now would lead a Mosquito squadron with verve and daring. On one remarkable occasion Lockhart 'lost' an engine on the way to Berlin but he carried on regardless, bombed and returned home safely.

The squadron's first sorties were mounted on 1/2nd February 1944 over Berlin and during the month several of its BIVs were modified to accommodate the 4,000 pound High Capacity bomb or 'Cookie'. The conversion of the aircraft was relatively simple but the extra weight altered the aircraft's centre of gravity and induced a certain instability. On 23/24th February three Mosquitos led by Squadron Leader S. D. Watts, who later commanded the squadron, dropped the first Mosquito 'Cookie' on Düsseldorf from about 25,000 feet. More Cookie operations were mounted during March, mainly on Ruhr targets; then, on 13/14th April, the first 4,000 pound bombs were dropped on Berlin by Mosquitos. Because of the increased weight the aircraft required two drop fuel tanks for their Berlin missions, nevertheless they made the journey in two hours, half the time taken by Lancasters. The Mosquito force would land over 1,400 Cookies on the German capital.

For a brief period during the month another Mosquito squadron, No 571, moved into Graveley to work alongside the crews of 692. This squadron, comprising only one Flight, had been formed earlier in the month at Downham Market. After mounting a few sorties from Graveley the crews moved away to Oakington.

In May, 692 Squadron achieved another notable first with their Mosquitos when they were used for mine-laying. Thirteen aircraft, each carrying a single mine, left for the entrance of the Kiel Canal and eleven of the crews successfully dropped their mines from about 50-200 feet. Sadly, one crew was lost on this operation but the canal was closed to shipping for about one week. There seemed to be no operational task that this splendid little aircraft could not accomplish.

Meanwhile, 35 Squadron ploughed on with its bombing offensive and PFF duties. Berlin figured large in January 1944, as did Stettin and Magdeburg, but it was on a raid to Leipzig on 19/20th February that the squadron lost one of its most experienced officers and Flight leaders - Squadron Leader Julian Sale, DSO Bar, DFC. This was a harsh operation for Bomber Command with 78 aircraft shot down and the Halifax squadrons suffering almost a 15% loss. The bomber stream came under almost constant fighter attack from the Dutch coast right to the target. Sale's aircraft was shot down by a Ju 88 night-fighter; all of the crew managed to bale out but Sale later died in captivity from his injuries. Sale's navigator, fellow Canadian Flying Officer G. H. Carter, DFC, made his second successful evasion. On the last major Berlin operation in March another Flight Commander was lost - Squadron Leader R.T. Fitzgerald. Earlier in the month the squadron had begun to exchange its Halifaxes for Lancaster IIIs.

Perhaps the deepest loss experienced by the squadron occurred on 4/5th July over the rail marshalling yards at Villeneuve St Georges to the south of Paris. Sixteen Lancasters left Graveley and because of deep and heavy cloud cover the aircraft were forced to bomb from 4/5,000 feet. The heavy and accurate flak accounted for 14 aircraft, two of which belonged to 35 Squadron. Lancaster TL-J, piloted by Wing Commander Alec P. Cranswick, DSO, DFC, received a direct hit and burst into flames; before the crew could bale out the aircraft broke up. Only the wireless operator survived, he was hurled out by the power of the explosion.

Alec Cranswick was a living legend in Bomber Command. He had started his operational service in June 1940 with 214 Squadron on Wellingtons and by October 1943, whilst serving in 35 Squadron, he had completed no less than three operational tours. After a spell at PFF headquarters, he returned to the squadron in April 1944 to begin his fourth tour. When he was killed he was 24 years old and had been married only eleven weeks. It was thought that Cranswick had completed *at least* 107 missions, although Don Bennett's book *Pathfinder* claims the correct figure was 143! Such was Bennett's esteem for this brave pilot that he dedicated his book to Cranswick's memory. This fine young airman ranks alongside Guy Gibson and Leonard Cheshire (who served with 35 Squadron during 1941) as a supreme bomber captain.

The squadron's long and meritorious war came to an end on 25th April 1945 when eight Lancasters were in action over the gun batteries at Wangerooge, but this was not before another bomber ace had been killed in action. Squadron Leader D. B. 'Danny' Everett, DFC 2 Bars, who had risen from a Sergeant pilot to Squadron Leader during 98 operations, had been forced to take a safe staff post. However, on the night of 7/8th March whilst at Graveley, he gathered a crew together and joined his old squadron attacking targets in eastern Germany. Sadly, Everett and his crew were posted missing.

In 468 operations, almost three quarters with the PFF, 35 Squadron had lost 126 aircraft. The Mosquito crews were in action for a little longer, not completing their war until 2/3rd May over Kiel. The squadron, which was disbanded in September, had undertaken 310 operations from Graveley, all for the loss of just 17 aircraft (0.5%) - another example of the value of this aircraft to the Pathfinder Force.

In July 1946, 35 Squadron under the command of another fine PFF leader, Wing Commander Alan J. L. Craig, DSO, DFC, who at 23 years was the youngest station commander, were chosen to make a goodwill

*35 Squadron led by Wing Commander A.J.L. Craig, DSO, DFC, on return from the USA, 29th August 1946. (RAF Museum)*

tour of the United States with their Lancasters. They left in their tropical livery - white on black - signifying they would form part of the Tiger Force. Whilst in the States, the squadron visited New York, St Louis, Los Angeles, San Antonio and Washington, as well as representing the RAF at the Army Air Forces Day.

Shortly after 35's return to Graveley in August, the airfield was closed to flying and placed under care and maintenance, though it would be another twelve years before it was finally closed. Standing on the perimeter road today and looking across the ploughed fields, it is easy to visualise a time when it throbbed and echoed to the sounds of Lancasters and Mosquitos taking off for enemy targets - the spirits of Lockhart, Cranswick *et al* live on.

# 13
# KIMBOLTON

Kimbolton is a large village set alongside the main A45 road some seven miles to the north-west of St Neots. Its wide High Street is lined by handsome old buildings and there is a gentle and quiet air about the place. It is rather difficult to visualise the time when it was thronged with American servicemen and its roads were filled with lorries and jeeps from the nearby airfield, Station 117, sited about a mile away on high land overlooking the village.

The airfield had been constructed by W. & C. French Ltd in 1941 for Bomber Command to act as a satellite for Molesworth, and the new concrete runways were first used towards the end of November. The aircraft were the fairly rare Wellington IVs; only 220 were ever produced and they served in just two squadrons. They were uniquely powered by two Pratt and Whitney Twin-Wasp engines that had slightly improved the aircraft's ceiling height, and operated by 460 (Australian) Squadron. The crews were engaged in training and familiarisation flights, but by early January 1942 had moved away to Breighton in Yorkshire.

Both Molesworth and Kimbolton were considered eminently suitable for USAAF use, and by July 1942 they were formally transferred to the Eighth Air Force. As has already been noted, the 91st Group moved in during September but stayed for only a month before leaving for the greater comforts provided by Bassingbourn. It was replaced by the ground personnel of the 17th Bomb Group, who were waiting for their move to North Africa. During the autumn and winter, building contractors returned to the airfield to enhance the facilities sufficiently to accommodate a Heavy Bomb Group. The runways were strengthened and extended, the number of hardstandings were increased and extra living quarters were erected closer to Kimbolton.

It was the 379th Bomb Group that had been allocated to the

*A splendid formation of B-17s of 379th Bomb Group returning to Kimbolton. (Smithsonian Institution)*

refurbished airfield. This Group had been activated in November 1942, and had trained in Utah and Sioux City, Iowa. When it was assigned to the Eighth Air Force in April 1943, the men began to prepare for their long overseas trip. The ground personnel left New York on the *Aquitania* on 10th May, arriving in the Clyde eight days later. The aircrews were, of course, required to fly their aircraft across, and they gathered at Bangor, Maine for the long and arduous flight. They flew via the Northern Ferry route - Gandar in Newfoundland to Iceland and then down to Prestwick in Scotland. The crossings were not without incident. One B-17 was lost over the Atlantic, one crashed in Iceland and another on landing at Prestwick. The first American airmen arrived at Kimbolton on 20th May, followed the next day by the arrival of the B-17Fs.

The 379th was one of five new B-17 Groups to join the Eighth Air Force during May, enabling it to exceed 1,000 bomber sorties in the month. It was perhaps fortunate in having one of the best Commanding Officers in the Eighth, Colonel Maurice A. Preston, who was known to his men as 'Big Moe', and had been in charge since its formation. The Group had been placed in the 1st Bomb Wing (later Division) and was the last of the newcomers to become operational when, on 29th May, 24 crews left for the U-boat pens at St Nazaire, known to the old hands as 'Flak City'. The mission proved to be a rather painful introduction into war. Three crews (30 airmen) were lost over the target, and another B-17 was written-off when it crash-landed on return to base.

The crews were given almost two weeks to train and reflect on this harsh mission, and no doubt Colonel Preston used the time to impress on them the basic principles of close formation flying, quoting the old adage, 'The tighter you fly, the lighter you fall'. Their next operation was detailed for 11th June, against the important German naval port and U-boat yards at Wilhelmshaven. The 31 crews were flying in the high wing position of the leading formation, and as the lead 'ship' was making its bomb run it received a direct hit from flak, which forced the following aircraft to take immediate evasive action to avoid collisions - a problem faced with close formation flying.

The aircraft became scattered and the Luftwaffe fighters attacked the leading bombers head-on, with the 379th taking the brunt of the assault. In next to no time, six B-17s 'disappeared out of the skies'. Most of the surviving aircraft sustained heavy damage, with 18 crewmen seriously injured. On one damaged B-17, *Dangerous Dan*, the pilot and co-pilot were injured so one of the gunners, Sergeant Cliff Erikson, took over the controls, and brought the aircraft back home, making his first ever landing under the instructions of the wounded pilot. Nine aircraft and 90 crew had been lost in the first two missions - equivalent to a full squadron. Few of the Eighth Air Force's Groups had such a torrid introduction into the war.

Although all 13 crews returned safely from Bremen on the 13th, the Group had not turned the corner by any stretch of the imagination. One aircraft was lost over Huls on the 22nd, then three days later Hamburg was the primary target but heavy cloud dogged the crews right across the North Sea, and they were ordered to seek 'targets of opportunity'. Of the 197 B-17s despatched, 15 were lost with six failing to make it back to Kimbolton - 30%, or six times the 'tolerable' loss rate. For a Group that was to develop into perhaps the most efficient and effective unit in the Eighth Bomber Command, it was a most distressing and dispiriting entrance into the air war. There was a blessed relief as eight missions were launched (including one recalled) without any further casualties. Then, on 25th July Hamburg was detailed and 15 B-17s

149

*Colonel M.M. Elliott of 379th Bomb Group made a perfect belly landing at Kimbolton –
all the crew survived. (Smithsonian Institution)*

failed to make it back (12%), of which two came from Kimbolton.

Three days later, when the 1st Wing's Groups were engaged in attacking the Fieseler Components works at Kassel in central Germany, two of the formations failed to get through to the target because of a weather front extending to 30,000 feet. As the B-17s were returning to meet up with their fighter escorts near the Dutch/German border, the Group's aircraft were attacked by Me 109s firing time-fused rocket projectiles from a distance of about 1,000 yards (out of the range of the B-17 gunners). None of the rockets made a direct hit, suggesting that they were not that accurate. The German fighters were Mark G-6s - known to their pilots as 'Gustavs' - carrying two rockets under their wings. Only two Luftwaffe units were known to have been equipped with them. It is interesting to note that the Fieseler works had only recently been retooled to make parts for the new Me 109Gs!

No Bomb Group would escape unscathed from the two Schweinfurt operations in August and October 1943 and the 379th lost a total of ten aircraft, four on the first raid and six on the second. The Group's losses continued to mount, including eight crews during September. Perhaps

*A party of children at Kimbolton, 2nd October 1943. (USAF)*

the most galling loss was over Nantes on the 16th, when four B-17s were destroyed, two of them brought down by bombs falling on them from a higher formation. In the Division's costly mission to Oschersleben on 11th January 1944, it survived with one aircraft lost, and along with the other Groups the 379th received its first Distinguished Unit Citation.

Despite its losses, the Group was gaining quite a reputation for the accuracy of its bombing as well as its low rate of aborted aircraft, and this had not passed unnoticed by Command headquarters. The bombing excellence of its crews spoke volumes for the technical expertise of the Group's Bombardier, Major Edwin Millson. And the fact that the Group managed consistently to get more aircraft over the target is a tribute to the hard-working ground crews who succeeded in keeping their B-17s operational despite heavy battle damage and various technical problems. One aircraft, *Ol' Gappy*, is thought to have completed 157 missions, a record for the Eighth Air Force, with another, *Birmingham Jewel* on its 128th mission when shot down over Berlin in January 1945 - a total then unsurpassed by a B-17.

Under the leadership of Colonel Preston, who was a fine tactician, the 379th was fast becoming a highly disciplined and professional outfit. Later its crews became expert in the use of Gee-H, as the Americans called it. It was the British beam radar device, and was particularly effective against small and precise targets such as airfields, road and rail bridges and junctions. These missions were of a relatively short range over the near Continent, which enabled the Group to mount over 10,000 sorties, the second highest total in the Eighth, and more than several Groups that had been in operation far longer. It also delivered over 24,000 tons of bombs, far in excess of other Groups, which averaged out at 2.33 tons for every aircraft that left Kimbolton.

*The crew of* Carol Dawn *of 379th Bomb Group arrive home tired but safe, February 1944. (USAF)*

It was perhaps with some acknowledgement of the Group's standing that the Commander of the Eighth, Lieutenant General James Doolittle, chose Kimbolton to witness the return of the aircraft engaged on the first Berlin mission on 6th March 1944. As he stood on the balcony of the control tower he must have been heartened, if only briefly, to watch all but one of the Group's aircraft return safely. One, *Dragon Lady*, was badly damaged with one dead engine, and as it landed with four injured crew, it careered across the runway towards the control tower. Luckily, the pilot managed to fully throttle to avoid hitting the tower and thus prevented a serious accident. Berlin was the ultimate test for all Groups, and in 15 operations in over twelve months the 379th lost only nine aircraft, another measure of its excellent performance.

In April 1944 the Eighth Air Force suffered its heaviest losses of the war, and although it was far from a happy state of affairs, such casualties were now sustainable because of the USAAF's massive resources. During the month the Group managed to mount 13 operations without losing a single aircraft in action. Included was a trip to Schweinfurt on the 13th, when the 41st Wing was led by Colonel Preston. During the operation the Wing sustained a heavy Luftwaffe frontal attack, which the Colonel, who had been combat flying since May 1943, thought 'the most severe fighter attack I have ever witnessed'. Fourteen B-17s were lost, which proved to be the Eighth's heaviest set-back since January. The Group's only loss in April came on the 11th when one aircraft crashed at Stow Bardolph during assembly, and nine of the crew were killed.

The assembly of heavily loaded bombers was a most precise and

THIS MEMORIAL PLAQUE IS DEDICATED TO
THE CREWS OF TWO B.17G FLYING FORTRESSES
OF
379TH BOMBER GROUP
8TH AIR FORCE
SOME OF WHOM
IN A MID AIR COLLISION OVER CANVEY ISLAND
ON 19TH JUNE 1944
GAVE THEIR LIVES IN THE DEFENCE OF FREEDOM
"WE WILL REMEMBER THEM"

*The memorial plaque on Canvey Island.*

involved operation even in good visibility, let alone in heavy and overcast conditions. The Group used an old B-17E, *Birmingham Blitzkrieg*, as its assembly aircraft, painted in white stripes for easy identification. To arrange the Groups into their agreed positions in the bomber formations needed highly disciplined flying, and it is really surprising that there were not more accidents. Nevertheless, more than one in six of the bombers lost during the war were as a result of accidents in one shape or form - training, on the ground, assembly and mid-air collisions during missions.

One of the Group's airmen recalled a collision which occurred when assembling in dense fog. He said that the resultant explosion, 'burned a clear hole in the fog that must have been at least a quarter of a mile in diameter.' On 19th June two of the Group's aircraft, one called *Heavenly Body II*, collided over the Thames Estuary near Canvey Point, when eleven airmen were killed and only three were rescued. Fifty-two years after this tragic accident a memorial plaque was dedicated, in November 1996, to the dead airmen, sited outside the Paddocks Community Centre on Canvey Island.

The V1 rocket sites in the Pas de Calais had become regular targets for the Eighth since December 1943 under Operation Crossbow, although they soon became known to American crews as Noball missions. After the first launching of the V1s in June 1944, these sites received far greater attention from all the Allied air forces, and the Group led several G-H operations during June and July (one of which resulted in the above mid-air collision).

On 27th June, the 379th was detailed to attack a rocket site at St Martin L'Hortier, and Brigadier General A. W. Vanaman, who was the head of Intelligence at the Eighth's headquarters, went along as an observer. Unfortunately, the B-17 in which he was travelling received a direct hit from flak and was set on fire. Along with four of the crew, the General baled out and was taken prisoner. Shortly afterwards the fire on board went out and the pilot, First Lieutenant Jamieson, succeeded in bringing his aircraft back to Kimbolton, though no doubt he had a lot of explaining to do of how he managed to 'lose' a General en route!

In August 1944 the 379th was awarded its second DUC for its excellent all-round performance since its entry into the war. Two months later the Group lost its popular CO, when Colonel Preston was promoted to command one of the Combat Bomb Wings. His replacement, Colonel Lewis E. Lyle, remained in charge until almost the end of the war.

On 30th November, the 379th incurred their heaviest loss for over 13 months, and again the destruction of the German oil industry was the cause. The Eighth had targeted the synthetic oil plants at Bohlen, Zeitz and Merseburg for a major operation, with the 1st Division detailed for Zeitz, about 20 miles to the south of Merseburg. Although this target was not so heavily defended as Merseburg, it was still surrounded by at least 90 heavy guns, which accounted for most of the eleven B-17s missing on this operation, six coming from Kimbolton. It was the New Year before any more aircraft were lost in action; one crew went missing on 6th January, followed by another two just four days later.

The Allied armies' airborne crossing of the Rhine on 24th March 1945 saw the greatest Allied air armada since D-Day, with the Eighth contributing over 1,700 heavy bombers in support of the operation, which was codenamed Varsity. Over one third of this force was supplied by the 1st Division, bombing airfields in western Germany, and of the four B-17s missing two came from the Group. Seventeen days later (on 10th April), the 379th suffered its last losses, two crews, whilst operating over the German Army headquarters at Orianienburg, and on 25th April it mounted its last and 330th mission. Although the Group had lost 141 aircraft in action, because of the high number of individual sorties flown, its percentage loss was 1.17, one of the lowest in the Eighth Air Force.

It is interesting to compare this Group's record with a major RAF bomber squadron, for example 156 Squadron. The RAF squadron entered the war slightly earlier than the 379th and completed 17 fewer operations, though its sorties were almost 6,000 less (this was because of the greater number of aircraft operating in an Eighth Bomb Group). The squadron's losses were 143 (almost the same as those of the 379th) but its percentage loss was far higher at 3.1 - which, in fact, was above average for a RAF heavy squadron. Of course, the two outfits flew largely different operations, and 156 spent much of its war with the Pathfinders. But what this rough and ready comparison does show is that Bomber Command's front-line heavy squadrons suffered proportionally heavier losses for a far longer period.

Unlike most Bomb Groups, the 379th did not go back to the USA straight away, but left for Casablanca in early June to ferry home US troops as part of the Green Project; the crews remained in North Africa for about a month before departing for the States. Their airfield at Kimbolton has long since disappeared under farmland and the Stow Langa trading estate. Colonel Lyle probably best captured the essence of all those brave American crews when he recalled: 'They came out of the wheatfields, out of the factories, from villages, small towns and from big cities. They were guys just off the streets. Some of them only had a few months of training at the most. As soon as the Commander said, "I think I can make it", they sent his Group out.' Over 350 of those 'guys' lost their lives whilst serving at Kimbolton, and they are remembered by the fine memorial set at the roadside close to the site of the old airfield, as well as in a memorial book on display at Kimbolton church.

# 14
# LITTLE
# STAUGHTON

Although the village of Little Staughton is in Bedfordshire, the airfield that bears its name is situated on an enclave of land to the south-east and surrounded on three sides by the present Cambridgeshire county boundary. It is probably the best surviving example of a wartime airfield in the County. The control tower, dispersal areas and runways remain, and light civil aircraft use the same runway where once, long ago, Lancasters and Mosquitos thundered off into the night sky. Little Staughton was operational for barely 13 months, yet it was an active Pathfinder station with the unique distinction of two Victoria Crosses awarded to airmen serving at the airfield.

Built during 1941/2, it was tentatively allocated to the USAAF in November 1941 and confirmed the following May as a bomber base. By September it was known as AAF Station 127 and earmarked for use as an air depôt. Traditionally all American bases were given a specific number, which was used in official reports and correspondence, though the airmen normally used the name of the nearest village to identify their base.

On 1st December 1942 some 500 or so American airmen arrived to establish an Advanced Air Depôt for 1st Bombardment Wing of the Eighth Air Force, mainly occupying airfields to the west and north of Little Staughton. The unit was responsible for the maintenance and repair of damaged B-17s of the Wing, as well as major overhauls and modifications. There was also a Reclamation Unit that visited American bases to identify serviceable items for repair at the depôt, and they established a close working relationship with Morris Motors at Cowley, which received scrap metal for melting down. During the latter months of 1943 the Americans knew their days at Little

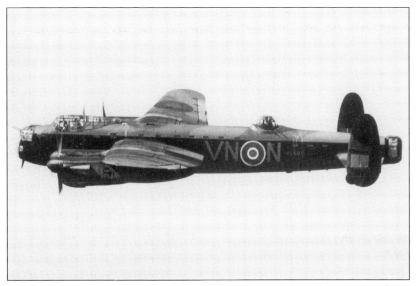

*582 Squadron operated Lancasters (although this Mark I belonged to 433 Squadron). (RAF Museum)*

Staughton were numbered, as a new depot was being constructed at Abbots Ripton, adjacent to Alconbury, and they moved there in late February 1944.

The airfield was formally transferred to RAF Bomber Command on 1st March, and was allocated to No 8 (PFF) Group. The decision to reduce all the Group's heavy squadrons to two Flights, resulted in a new Lancaster squadron being formed a month later. It was made up from the nucleus of B Flight of 7 Squadron and C Flight of 156 Squadron, both veteran PFF squadrons. The new squadron was numbered 582, and it became operational within days of its formation.

It was equipped with Avro Lancaster Is and IIIs. This famous wartime bomber had elicited high praise from Air Chief Marshal Harris: 'This emergency design turned out to be, without exception, the finest bomber of the war...its efficiency was almost incredible, both in performance and in the way it could be saddled with ever-increasing loads...The Lancaster surpassed all other types of heavy bomber... and I continually pressed for its production at the expense of other types.' Considering that its design came directly from the unsuccessful twin-engined Manchester, its universal success was somewhat surprising, not least to the Air Ministry, who very grudgingly agreed to a four-engined version in July 1940 with two prototypes to be built over the next twelve months.

The first prototype, Avro 683, powered by four Merlin X engines, flew on 9th January 1941 and the second followed five months later (13th May); both used the Manchester airframe. The performance was more than promising and 1,070 were ordered, with the first production aircraft reaching 44 Squadron in November. On 10/11th March 1942 two were used on a bombing operation to Essen - the Lancaster story had began.

The Mark I, now with Merlin XX or XXII engines, had a maximum speed of 287 mph and cruised at 210 mph at 20,000 feet with a ceiling service of 24,500 feet and a normal range of 1,660 miles. It remained in production throughout the war. The bomb bay originally held 4,000 pounds of bombs but this increased progressively up to 12,000 pounds and ultimately the aircraft was capable of carrying a 22,000 pound (Grand Slam) bomb. The Lancaster was armed with three Frazer Nash turrets with a total of eight .303 machine guns, requiring a crew of seven. In several marks, 7,377 Lancasters were produced by four different UK manufacturers and one in Canada; at the height of production 36 Lancasters were being completed weekly. The Mark Is and IIIs were the most numerous, accounting for over 87% of the production.

Of the three four-engined bombers, the Lancasters carried out the lion's share of the bombing, over two thirds, and achieved this with the lowest losses - 2.9%. By early 1945 there were 56 Lancaster squadrons in operations. It was a truly amazing bomber with a first class war record and was not finally retired from active service until October 1956.

The Lancasters of 582 Squadron were joined by the Mosquitos of 109 Squadron, which had been transferred from Marham in Norfolk. This was no ordinary Mosquito squadron, its crews had pioneered the use of Oboe into the PFF in January 1943, whilst operating from Wyton. For a squadron that was destined to fly more raids (522) than any other PFF squadron, it had an amazingly low casualty rate with just 18 aircraft (0.3%) lost in action, though the majority went missing whilst operating from Little Staughton.

On 4/5th April 1944 the Mosquito crews were in action over Cologne and other Ruhr targets, and, very unusually, one failed to come back. It had ditched in the North Sea. Five nights later, seven Lancasters left Little Staughton to join a force of 230 attacking the Déliverance railway yards at Lille - one of the Command's allotted targets in the Transportation Plan. Although the goods yards was damaged, so too was the suburb of Lomme and the bombing was so intense that 5,000 houses were damaged or destroyed with many of the French people feeling 'they were living their last hour'. Over 450 people were killed, the very reason that the 'Plan' had been so closely debated.

The following night the crews were active over marshalling yards at Laon but as the marking was not particularly accurate, the bombing was a little scattered. When a strong force returned to the same target on 22/23rd April, it attacked in two waves with quite devastating results, although 5% of the bombers were lost, including one from Little Staughton. By the end of the month the squadron had mounted 120 sorties with the Mosquito crews completing 70 more. The airfield was certainly now operational in a big way.

Both squadrons were very active in June. 109's crews would complete over 360 sorties, leading all the Command's attacks on Overlord targets - gun batteries, signals stations, ammunition and oil dumps - before concentrating on road and rail junctions, airfields and enemy troop positions. From the middle of the month, V1 rocket sites became a priority and the Oboe Mosquitos were ideal for marking such small sites. 582 Squadron lost crews over the Longues batteries on the eve of D-Day, as well as one on a raid to the railway yards at Etampes, south of Paris, four nights later. Three more Lancasters would be lost over rail targets during the month.

On the 30th, both squadrons were engaged in the daylight raid on a road junction at Villers-Bocage through which two German Panzer divisions were due to pass en route to the Normandy battlefields. This raid was very well-controlled by a Master Bomber, who ordered the crews to bomb from 4,000 feet to ensure greater accuracy. Over 1,000 tons were dropped and the planned Panzer movement did not take place. It was an impressive demonstration of PFF techniques.

In July 1944 the Lancasters were involved in the first major raid on a German city for over two months when, on the 23/24th, Kiel was attacked. The bombing lasted just 25 minutes and the city suffered its heaviest damage of the war. Only four Lancasters were lost but one came from 582 Squadron. During the month Stuttgart was raided three times in five nights. The third operation on the 28/29th proved to be rather costly for Bomber Command with 39 aircraft shot down, most of them to night-fighters on the outward leg over France. Again, a Lancaster was lost on this operation.

One of the most impressive displays of precision bombing occurred on the 11th, when 32 PFF Lancasters and Mosquitos made two separate attacks on a V1 rocket site at Gappenes. In this mission, the Lancasters

*Oboe Mosquito BIX LR504 of 109 Squadron. (RAF Museum)*

made the first 'heavy Oboe' strike of the war. A Lancaster of 582 Squadron had been fitted with Oboe and was flown by Wing Commander George F. Grant, DSO, DFC, of 109 Squadron, who directed the bombing. When Grant released his bombs, the other Lancasters followed suit. This system allowed a greater tonnage to be dropped directly on Oboe signals, and was ideal for finding small targets in cloudy conditions.

The month of August proved to be the busiest of the war for the squadron's Mosquito crews, when they mounted over 500 sorties against V1 rocket sites, rail targets, Ruhr oil plants, airfields, enemy troop positions and fuel dumps. On the 27th, Bomber Command launched their first major daylight operation against a German target since August 1941. The Rheinpreussen synthetic oil refinery near Homberg was the target, and the bombing was based on Oboe marking with eight of 109's Mosquitos in action. The heavy cloud cover produced difficult conditions, although some accurate bombing was claimed. Although the flak was most intense, fortunately not a single aircraft was lost. On the last night of the month the Mosquito crews were bombing and marking Ruhr targets - Düsseldorf, Cologne and Leverkusen - and two were lost in action with a third making a crash-landing at the emergency landing ground at Woodbridge. It was the squadron's worst night of the war.

One of the most successful missions undertaken from Little Staughton came on 3rd October 1944, when it was decided to attack the sea walls of Walcheren Island, whose coastal batteries dominated the approach to the port of Antwerp. The intention was to flood the

*Squadron Leader R.A.M. Palmer, VC, DFC and Bar, of 109 Squadron. (Imperial War Museum)*

island, much of which was below sea level. The operation was directed by a Master Bomber - Group Captain P. H. Cribb, DFC, flying a Lancaster from 582 Squadron.

The Lancasters were planned to attack in eight waves marked by Oboe Mosquitos and PFF Lancasters, and the specific target was Westkapelle, the most westerly part of the island. After the fifth wave had bombed, the wall was breached and a gap some 100 yards wide was made, with many of the batteries being submerged under sea-water. The Lancasters of 617 (Dambusters) Squadron carrying the 12,000 pound bombs (Tallboy) were not needed. It was a very successful operation without a single aircraft being lost.

On the night of 27/28th November, five Mosquito crews marked for over 300 Lancasters at Frieburg. It was not an industrial town and had never before been bombed, but intelligence sources had revealed that there were large concentrations of enemy troops in the town. The Oboe marking was directed from caravans situated in France and it proved to be deadly accurate with quite devastating bombing. It was considered the 'most outstanding attack of the year'. On the same night, other Mosquito crews were marking Neuss, near Düsseldorf, and one Mosquito failed to return from this operation. The following day, Squadron Leader J. B. Burt of 109 Squadron was the Master Bomber on a daylight raid to the Meiderich oil plant near Duisburg. This target was attacked on five more occasions during December.

Two days before Christmas, just 30 PFF Lancasters and Mosquitos were detailed to attack the Gremberg railway yards at Cologne. The force was split into three formations, each led by an Oboe Lancaster with an Oboe Mosquito in reserve. The Master Bomber was Squadron Leader Robert A. M. Palmer, DFC Bar, of 109 Squadron, who was on his third operational tour and 111th sortie. He was flying a Lancaster from 582 Squadron. The operation got off to a bad start with two Lancasters colliding over the French coast, and then over the target it was found the forecasted clouds had cleared so a message was sent to break formation and bomb visually.

Unfortunately, the message did not reach Palmer's aircraft, and he continued his Oboe run despite the fact that the Lancaster had already been hit. Smoke filled the nose and bomb bay, but Palmer kept the aircraft on a straight course, made a perfect approach and his bombs hit the target. The Lancaster was last seen spiralling to the earth in flames; only one member of the crew escaped. Palmer was posthumously awarded the Victoria Cross, for 'his record of prolonged and heroic endeavour is beyond praise'. It proved to be a costly operation for Little

*Captain Edwin Swales, VC, DFC, SAAF of 582 Squadron. (Imperial War Museum)*

Staughton, as five Lancasters and one Mosquito failed to return. One of the Lancaster pilots, Captain Edwin Swales of the South African Air Force, was awarded the DFC for his part in the raid.

February 1945 became an eventful month for the crews. On the 13/14th, nine Lancasters were engaged in the infamous Dresden operation, whilst six crews were detailed to attack a synthetic oil plant at Bohlen near Leipzig. This latter operation was not too successful due to heavy cloud cover, with severe icing experienced at 15,000 feet. Ten nights later Pforzheim, to the north-west of Stuttgart, was the target for the Command's first and only raid on this town.

The Master Bomber on this occasion was Captain Edwin Swales, DFC, of 582 Squadron, the only South African airman to serve in the PFF. Three hundred and eighty Lancasters and Mosquitos took part in what turned out to be a severe and destructive operation. Although Swales' Lancaster was hit twice over the target by night-fighters, he continued to direct the bombing (1,825 tons in 22 minutes!) from about 8,000 feet. It was thought that over 80% of the town was destroyed and 17,000 civilians were killed - the third heaviest toll after Dresden and Hamburg.

When Swales was satisfied that the attack had achieved its objectives he turned for home, but his Lancaster was severely damaged and it began to lose height and became difficult to control. Swales managed to keep it sufficiently steady to allow the crew to bale out but before he could make his escape the aircraft plunged to the ground, and Swales was found dead at the controls. This gallant South African airman was awarded the Victoria Cross and the citation read: 'Intrepid in the attack, courageous in the face of danger, he did his duty to the last, giving his life that his comrades might live.'

In April 1945 the two Oboe squadrons finally achieved their ambition. The ground stations had moved sufficiently forward to bring Berlin within the range of Oboe and on the 8/9th, three crews from 109 Squadron attacked the city for the first time. The squadron carried on doing so until the final RAF raid on the German capital, which was mounted on the 20/21st. It fell to a Mosquito XVI of 109 Squadron, crewed by Flying Officers A. C. Austin and P. Moorhead, to drop the last bombs on Berlin. The squadron's operational sorties ceased on 7th May 1945, when ten crews marked five different aiming points for aircraft dropping supplies to the Dutch people at The Hague, Gouda, Rotterdam and Leiden.

The contribution of the two Oboe squadrons to the air offensive was immeasurable, out of all proportion to the small number of crews engaged in their operations. Without doubt, they made it possible to achieve accurate and effective bombing, which became the hallmark of Bomber Command during the last twelve months of the war.

Four Lancaster crews were active on the same day, although they, too, had finished their bombing offensive almost two weeks earlier when 16 Lancasters bombed the gun batteries on the island of Wangerooge. In their brief time at Little Staughton the squadron had mounted over 2,100 sorties in 165 raids, losing 28 aircraft in action, with over 120 gallantry medals being awarded to its crews. The squadron was disbanded on 10th September and at the end of the month 109 Squadron officially ceased to exist, although another bomber squadron (No 627) was renumbered 109, thus ensuring the continuity of this famous squadron.

At the end of 1945 the airfield was placed under care and maintenance, but it was effectively closed to flying. In the village church is a tablet and a Book of Remembrance to commemorate more than 200 airmen lost whilst serving at the airfield, and a small airfield marker simply records the fact that Little Staughton was a Pathfinder station.

# 15
# MEPAL

Mepal is on the edge of the Fenlands and has been a peaceful backwater since the A142 road from Ely to Chatteris, or 'Ireton's Way', by-passed the village. This road was closed during much of the Second World War as it went through the middle of the airfield that had been built almost due south of Mepal. In the centre of the village is a rose garden containing a stone memorial to the only RAF squadron to operate from the airfield, its badge and Maori motto - 'Ake ake kia kaka' ('For ever and ever be strong') - proudly proclaiming its origins. No 75 (New Zealand) was the only night-bomber squadron from that country, and one of the most famous in Bomber Command, with a war record second to none.

The airfield opened in April 1943 as a sub-station for No 33 Base (Waterbeach) in No 3 Group. This base system had only recently been introduced. The sheer number of airfields coming into operational use had placed such strain on the Groups' administration that it was decided to link several airfields together to form a single base under the command of an Air Commodore, though this was not always so. The base airfield, invariably a pre-war permanent station, would undertake all the personnel functions as well as much of the overhaul work on the aircraft. The satellite stations became known as sub-stations, and nearby Witchford was the third member of No 33 Base.

On 23rd April, No 1665 Conversion Unit was formed at Mepal equipped with two dozen Stirling Is, but it only stayed for about a week before moving away to Waterbeach. There had been a general reappraisal of the airfields within the Group and Mepal had been set aside for an operational squadron. Two months would elapse before the Stirling IIIs of 75 (New Zealand) Squadron arrived from Newmarket Heath towards the end of June. Since April it had been made up to three Flights, giving it a complement of 24 aircraft with several more

*In June 1943, 75 (NZ) Squadron brought its Stirlings to Mepal.*

in reserve. Flights A and B were identified by the squadron's code AA, whereas C Flight had been allocated JN as its letters.

The squadron had been formed in April 1940 at Feltwell, predominantly from New Zealand airmen, and equipped with Wellingtons. It was the first Commonwealth squadron to enter Bomber Command. In July 1941 one of its pilots, Sergeant James Ward RNZAF, was awarded the Victoria Cross but he was killed in action two months later. One of its airmen, Pilot Officer Eric E. Williams, gained post-war fame. He was shot down in December 1942 over Duisburg, but later made an ingenious and successful escape from Stalag Luft III and on his return to England in early 1944 he was awarded the Military Cross. Williams recounted his experiences in the best-selling book *The Wooden Horse*, which was first published in 1949.

75 was an experienced and battle-hardened squadron, having already completed almost 3,500 sorties and lost over 100 aircraft in the process. It was now commanded by Wing Commander M. 'Mike' Wright, although he would shortly be replaced by a New Zealander, Wing Commander R. D. Max, DFC.

The first operation from Mepal was launched on the night of 3/4th July 1943 to Cologne and it passed without serious incident, the 13 Stirlings arriving back safely. Two nights later one aircraft failed to return from mine-laying off the Frisian Islands. The crews were well aware of the dangers of such missions, because on 28/29th April, whilst operating from Newmarket, four aircraft had gone missing on the biggest mine-laying operation of the war so far.

Mine-laying had become an increasingly important task for the Command, and it was now committed to drop at least 1,000 mines per month, so each Stirling squadron was required to take its share of the task. These operations were known as 'gardening' because each sea area was given a codename (130 of them!) of either fruit, vegetables or flowers - Artichoke (Lorient), Sweet Peas (West Baltic), Nectarines (Frisian Islands) and so on. The Admiralty later claimed that for every mine dropped, 50 tons of enemy shipping was sunk.

Gardening was no easy task, it called for great skill and resolution, but the loss rate was normally lower than on operations over Germany. Nevertheless, it was not too popular with crews as it only counted as one third of an operation. During the rest of the year, the squadron would lose another eight aircraft on mine-laying operations.

The major offensive over the Ruhr drew to a close with an attack on Remscheid on 30/31st July. This town had not been previously bombed, but it was expertly ground-marked by Oboe Mosquitos and the relatively small force of 273 aircraft created mayhem. Over 80% of the town was destroyed with considerable loss of life and industrial production. Of the 15 aircraft missing, eight were Stirlings with two from Mepal. With continuing higher losses than Lancasters and Halifaxes, the days of the Stirling as a main force bomber were becoming numbered. Two nights later the squadron lost another two Stirlings over Hamburg, and after raids to Nuremberg, Turin and Peenemunde during August, Berlin was the next big target.

The German capital already featured on the battle honours of the squadron, most recently on 1/2nd March, when the crews had returned unscathed. On 23/24th August 1943 it was somewhat different because three aircraft failed to return to Mepal, with the Stirling squadrons again bearing the heaviest losses. The second Berlin mission, on 31st August/1st September, saw the Stirling force suffering more grievously; 17 were lost in total (16%), five of which came from Mepal. Three were shot down by night-fighters, another crash-landed at Coltishall after coming under friendly fire, and one was struck by bombs over the target. The Stirling crews were always at risk from this type of accident because of the aircraft's lower operational ceiling.

After this, the Stirling squadrons were relieved from the next two Berlin operations, returning to the fray on 22/23rd November, when five out of 50 were shot down, two of which belonged to 75 Squadron. Air Chief Marshal Harris now ordered that the Stirlings would no longer operate over German targets. 75 Squadron had, in just three

Berlin raids, lost ten aircraft, or more than a Flight.

Some of the Group's Stirling squadrons were transferred into Transport Command. Others, including 75, started to convert to Lancasters, but the process proved to be agonisingly slow and protracted as most of the aircraft's production was needed to provide replacements for the Lancaster squadrons still engaged in the costly Berlin operations. Until the new bomber arrived at Mepal the bread and butter missions for the squadron's crews would be mine-laying and V1 rocket sites. In March 1944, the crews began to drop supplies to French Resistance units, but these clandestine missions were certainly not milk runs. Squadron Leader R. J. Watson, DFC Bar RNZAF, was lost on the 4/5th and only one of his crew survived.

The Lancasters arrived at Mepal during the month, but it was not until 9/10th April that the squadron launched its Lancaster operations - to the railway yards at Villeneuve St Georges. The first to be lost in action came on the 27/28th over Friedrichshafen. Railway yards in France became the priority targets for April and May although, on 21/22nd May, Duisburg was selected for its first major raid for almost twelve months. Heavy cloud obscured the target, but the marking was very accurate and considerable damage was inflicted.

Amongst the 25 Lancasters that left Mepal was NE181, making its first sortie with C Flight. Its identification letter was M and it quickly became known as *Mike*, later extended to *Mike, The Captain's Fancy*. This aircraft became the squadron's most famous Lancaster, finally completing 101 sorties on 2/3rd February 1945 before being retired from operations. As it was the only New Zealand heavy bomber to reach the magical ton, there were many post-war attempts to ship it to New Zealand as a museum exhibit, but to no avail and the aircraft was scrapped in September 1947.

In the early hours of D-Day, 26 Lancasters left Mepal to join an 86-strong Group force attacking the batteries at Ouistrehem, which guarded Sword Beach - part of the British landing sector. This was the tenth and last attack of the night (or early morning) by Bomber Command. The bombing was completed within 15 minutes and at about 5.15 am the Lancaster crews started back for their home bases without loss. The following night the Command turned its attention to enemy troop movements and road/rail junctions behind the battle-front. Nine likely areas had been located and the Group's Lancasters were detailed to bomb a road junction at Lisieux to the east of Caen; only one of the 97 Lancasters failed to return. More road and rail targets were bombed on the following nights but the first Lancasters

*ND 917 of C Flight of 75 (NZ) Squadron, the first Lancaster to land on an airstrip in France, 30th June 1944. (Imperial War Museum)*

lost by the squadron since D-Day fell on 10/11th June when the railway yards at Dreux were bombed. Another crew failed to return from a similar mission to Valenciennes near the French/Belgian border.

The squadron was responsible for a little bit of RAF history when on 30th June 1944 it was engaged in a daylight raid on a road junction at Villers-Bocage. One of its Lancasters, ND917 of C Flight, was damaged by flak and the pilot, Squadron Leader N. A. Williamson, RNZAF, made an emergency landing on a Normandy air-strip so that urgent medical attention could be given to his Flight Engineer. This was the first RAF heavy bomber to land in Normandy since D-Day, although a badly damaged B-24 of the Eighth Air Force had landed 18 days earlier. Squadron Leader Williamson would fly seven operations with *Mike, The Captain's Fancy.*

Like most of the Command's heavy squadrons, 75 would become fully involved in attacking V1 rocket sites and storage areas from the middle of June, and during the next two months in over 16,000 sorties, 59,000 tons of bombs were dropped on these targets. Some of the sites attacked by the squadron during this period were Linzieux, Bois de Jardine, L'Hey, Rimeux, Beauvoir and the large storage depôt at Watten. Because it was so involved in Operation Crossbow and continuing support for the Allied armies, Bomber Command made fewer major assaults on German targets. However, on 20/21st July, the Scholven-Buer synthetic oil refinery at Homberg, which provided the Luftwaffe with about 6,000 tons of aviation fuel daily, was the target for 147 Lancasters. It proved to be a disastrous night for the squadron.

A maximum effort had been called for and 26 Lancasters left Mepal. The target had been marked by Oboe Mosquitos and severe damage was inflicted, with the production of valuable oil greatly reduced. Unfortunately, the Luftwaffe night-fighters had a most successful night, accounting for most of the 20 Lancasters missing (13.6%). 75 Squadron lost seven crews (28%); 49 airmen missing or killed in action, over half of them from New Zealand with a fair sprinkling of Australians and Canadians. Four crews were lost in three raids to Stuttgart in the last week of the month, and with another Lancaster lost on the 30th, it brought the total to 13 crews missing in action - a costly month indeed.

In the last two weeks of August 1944, Russelsheim and its Opel Motor factory, which was making components for V1 rockets, was attacked on two separate nights. The first raid not only proved rather costly (8%) but the factory sustained only minor damage. The second operation, on the 25/26th, was well marked by PFF aircraft and the bombing, by over 400 Lancasters, was completed in just ten minutes with the factory being put out of action for at least one month. The losses on this occasion were relatively light - 15 Lancasters - but the squadron lost three crews in the two raids. During the month the squadron went out on several daylight operations, the first, on the 4th, to Bec D'Ambes oil depôt and all returned safely. From now on, daylight raids would increase markedly.

In the autumn, like other squadrons in the Group, some of 75's Lancasters were equipped with G-H, the blind bombing device, which enabled the force to bomb in almost any weather conditions. Air Vice-Marshal R. Harrison, DFC, AFC, the AOC of 3 Group, had been given a relatively free hand with his Lancaster force, but he mainly directed them at oil targets in the Ruhr. The main feature of these daylight operations was that they were small Lancaster formations, well escorted by fighters, and they bombed accurately on G-H leaders with quite minimal losses. The squadron did, however, lose one Lancaster on 4th November when Solingen, to the east of Düsseldorf, was attacked with not very satisfactory results. The following day the Lancasters returned and bombed through 'complete cloud cover', causing considerable damage.

Later in the month (the 20th) 28 crews returned to Homberg, the

*75 (NZ) Squadron's NE181 gets its 101st bomb symbol, 3rd February 1945. (RNZAF)*

scene of their worst disaster, but because of stormy weather there were problems maintaining formation behind the G-H aircraft on the bombing run, which resulted in scattered bombing. Five Lancasters

*Memorial to members of 75 (NZ) Squadron at Mepal.*

were lost, including three from Mepal. The following day the squadron despatched 21 crews to the same target and this time the oil refinery was heavily bombed with 'a vast sheet of yellow flame followed by black smoke rising to a great height.' No doubt a very satisfactory sight for the crews, considering their previous losses and especially as all returned safely.

The first operation of the New Year was to the railway yards at Vohwinkel. It was mounted because the previous day's operation had been rather unsuccessful when strong winds had carried the bombing away from the target. Twenty-one Lancasters left Mepal in the evening of 1/2nd January and only 20 returned; the Squadron Commander, Wing Commander R. J. Newton, DFC, RNZAF, and all his crew, were killed in action. He was replaced by Wing Commander C. H. Baigent, DSO, DFC Bar, who had been a Flight Commander in 1942 and had completed his second tour of operations in the previous November. He would lead the squadron until the end of the war, and also return to command it when it operated with the RNZAF back home.

During February and March 1945 eight crews were lost, and perhaps the most tragic were the three who went missing on 21st March. One hundred and sixty Lancasters were detailed to attack railway yards and a viaduct at Münster, but due to bad planning the two waves of bombers arrived over the target at the same time, and several of the aircraft were hit by bombs from above. Despite heavy flak only three Lancasters were lost in the operation, but they all came from 75 Squadron. One of the pilots was on his 29th operation, and one of his crew had completed over 30 missions. Over half of the missing airmen were New Zealanders, which showed that the squadron still retained strong links with the 'home country' even at this late stage of the war. These losses proved to be the last suffered by the squadron in the Second World War. It should be noted that 1,679 New Zealand airmen died whilst serving in Bomber Command - 3% of the total fatalities.

The squadron's final and 739th operation was mounted on 24th April 1945 when 20 Lancasters attacked the marshalling yards at Bad Oldersloe, between Hamburg and Lübeck, and all arrived home safely. From 29th April until 8th May they carried out 126 sorties dropping food supplies to the Dutch people at Delft, Rotterdam and The Hague. The squadron had flown 8,017 sorties, the highest total in Bomber Command, but at the cost of 193 aircraft, which was the second highest in the Command. The squadron left Mepal in July and was disbanded in October. The Air Ministry later suggested to the RNZAF that it should take over the squadron's number to perpetuate its proud wartime service and so 75 Squadron carried on, operating from New Zealand.

Like so many wartime airfields, Mepal was placed under care and maintenance, although it was not formally closed until 1963. The by-pass road now crosses the site and the Elan Business Park, close to Sutton, occupies part of the administration area of the old airfield.

# 16
# MOLESWORTH

When the USAAF moved into Molesworth in May 1942 it became one of the first RAF airfields to be occupied by the Eighth Air Force, and 55 years later the Stars and Stripes still flies over the airfield. Molesworth holds a special place in the history of the Eighth, as the airmen that arrived in the summer of 1942 were destined to open its bombing offensive, and they were followed by the airmen of a pioneer Bomb Group, the 303rd, who would set record upon record during their stay.

The airfield opened in May 1941, but it was another six months before the first aircraft arrived, Wellington IVs of 460 (Australian) Squadron. They quickly moved off to Kimbolton and were not replaced until February 1942, when Blenheims of No 17 OTU used the airfield whilst Upwood was out of commission. Molesworth had already been allocated to the Eighth Air Force and some improvements were necessary; the runways were extended, and extra hardstandings and accommodation provided. The American personnel of the 2nd Air Depôt arrived on 12th May, a mere handful compared with the veritable avalanche that would appear during the next three months.

Early in June the first operational unit moved in from Grafton Underwood. It was the 15th Bomb Squadron (Light), which had been sent to the United Kingdom to train as a night-fighter unit with Douglas A-20s. Since then its role had changed to daylight intruder bombing, and for this reason the crews were detached to Swanton Morley in Norfolk to work alongside the RAF crews of 226 Squadron, as they did not have any aircraft of their own. It fell to Captain Charles C. Kegelman and his crew to fly the Eighth's first bombing sortie of the war, when, on 29th June, they accompanied RAF Bostons attacking the marshalling yards at Hazebrouck. Two days later, two American airmen were killed at Molesworth as their Boston III crashed on its landing approach.

*A Boston III of No 15 Bomb Squadron. (USAF)*

*Crew of U.S. Engineers working on Molesworth Airfield in July 1943. (Smithsonian Institution)*

American Independence Day (4th July) appeared an appropriate date for the Eighth Air Force to formally commence its operations. Six American airmen manning RAF Bostons attacked several airfields in the Low Countries, along with crews of 226 Squadron. At De Kooy airfield, intense flak was encountered and one of the Bostons with an American crew was shot down in flames, whilst the other, flown by Captain Kegelman, was severely damaged. He managed to bring it back to base, but another two Bostons failed to return, one crewed by American airmen. Not a particularly auspicious start, but the RAF crews had to admit that it was one of the toughest operations they had flown.

These were the first fatalities in action for the Eighth, and the operation also resulted in the award of the first decorations of the war - three American DFCs, and the Distinguished Service Cross to Captain Kegelman: the second highest gallantry decoration and the first of 220 to Eighth Air Force airmen. Kegelman lost his life whilst serving in the Pacific during 1944.

Another mission was flown on 12th July 1942 without loss, and then the crews received their own aircraft. The first Eighth Air Force mission flown by aircraft carrying the famous American white star took place on 5th September to Le Havre, followed by an attack on Abbeville airfield. Both passed without incident. Six days later the Group moved to Podington, and would later serve with the Twelfth Air Force in North Africa.

The following day the ground and support personnel of the 303rd Bomb Group (Heavy) arrived by train from Greenock. They had ample time to settle in before their charges - B-17Fs - started to arrive at the airfield; the first landed in the late afternoon of 21st October. The Eighth was now growing in size, and when the 303rd became operational with the 1st Bomb Wing, General Eaker had seven Bomb Groups under his command, although he still considered it 'a piddling little force'!

The Group's first mission to St Nazaire, on 17th November, was an utter failure. All 16 crews returned without dropping a single bomb, although they survived quite a fierce flak attack. The next day they were sent to La Pallice, though they actually bombed St Nazaire, about 100 miles away, in error. St Nazaire became the bane of their lives in the early days. On the 23rd they were again briefed for this target, and the mission became significant for the Eighth because the Luftwaffe fighters changed their tactics. Hitherto, they had invariably attacked from the rear but now the Luftwaffe pilots realised that B-17s were relatively weak in forward firepower. On this mission about 50 FW 190s made determined frontal attacks and four B-17s were destroyed, with the 303rd suffering its first loss. Far worse was to befall the Group over the same target on 3rd January 1943, when four out of 17 aircraft failed to return, and another five went missing over Lorient towards the end of the month. Effectively, one third of the Group was lost in the month.

The ethos of the Eighth's daylight bombing offensive was that the massed firepower of a formation of B-17s or B-24s was a formidable obstacle to counter, but that meant that the formations had to be carefully planned and positions maintained during the operation to ensure the maximum protection. It was during the operations conducted in the winter of 1942/3 that the ultimate shape of the Eighth's bomber formations was developed from harsh battle experience. Bombing techniques were also refined, from individual aircraft releasing their bombs independently, to squadron bombing and ultimately to bombing on the sighting of the lead aircraft, determined by the Group Bombardier.

On 18th March 1943 the Group provided almost one third (22 aircraft) of the Wing's force attacking the U-boat yards at Vegesack, situated on the Weser about 30 miles from the North Sea. Lieutenant Colonel George Robinson, the Group Executive Officer, led the force and on the bomb run heavy and accurate flak was encountered. The Group's 359th Squadron, flying in the low box position, suffered the worst of the barrage, and its leading aircraft, *The Duchess*, received a direct hit within a minute of the bomb release point. The bombardier, First Lieutenant Jack W. Mathis, was hurled some nine feet to the rear of the nose compartment by the explosion. He was mortally wounded but managed to drag himself back to his position to release the bombs on time. Despite being heavily damaged, *The Duchess* was nursed back to base. Lieutenant Mathis was posthumously awarded the Congressional Medal of Honor, the first of only 14 Eighth airmen to receive this medal.

The raid was probably the Eighth's most successful so far, a number of U-boats were severely damaged and the shipyards were put out of action for about two months. At the time the operation was cited as a vindication of daylight precision bombing. The Group lost just one aircraft in action with another two being written off due to crash landings. It also produced a record claim of enemy fighters destroyed - 52. Throughout the war, overly high claims by the Eighth's gunners would be made. In the heat and fury of air battles several gunners

Eight Ball *comes to rest at Molesworth, 27th January 1943. (USAF)*

would often claim the same aircraft shot down, and many, in fact, that were not destroyed. Despite strenuous efforts by the Intelligence officers to accurately assess the gunners' claims, the figures were still greatly inflated, but it was acknowledged by the Eighth's chiefs that such claims were good for morale as they helped to counter the shock of the heavy losses that were being sustained.

The Group had already acquired the nickname 'Hell's Angels' and, in June 1943, a B-17 bearing that name would be the first Eighth Air Force heavy bomber to complete 25 missions. As was usual with Eighth Air Force Groups, the aircraft were given some rather strange and exotic names by their crews and pilots; some at Molesworth included *Bugs Bunny, Satan's Workshop, Tremblin' Gremlin, Old Glory, Flying Bison,* and *Knock-out Dropper.* The latter aircraft became the first B-17 to complete both 50 and 75 missions before being retired to the States to promote the sale of War Bonds. The names were usually accompanied by a pictorial representation painted on the nose, and this 'nose art' became famous, with many depicting scantily clothed young ladies in the style of Vargas, the 'pin-up' artist famed for his calendar drawings. Some were sexually quite explicit, just how much so depending on the attitude taken by the Group's commanding officer. RAF crews and pilots also personalised their aircraft but their illustrations tended to be more subdued and decorous.

On 28th June the Group, led by Major Glenn Hazenbach, returned to St Nazaire for the last time and the crews effectively bombed the lock entrance to the U-boat basin, which, according to the Major, was the best job of precision bombing he had seen in his 24 missions. In the following month the 303rd passed its half-century of operations and survived with just four B-17s lost in action. A most impressive performance considering that the last week of June became popularly known as 'Blitz Week', when targets in Norway, Kiel, Hamburg, Hanover and Kassel were attacked. It was a demonstration of the Eighth's growing might, but nearly 100 bombers were either lost in action or written off with severe battle damage. All crews were given a long and well-earned respite of 13 days free from operations, whilst aircraft were repaired, new ones delivered and fresh aircrews trained and assimilated into the Groups.

The 303rd went out again on 12th August 1943 and mounted another two missions before the first infamous Schweinfurt operation. Only two Groups (the 303rd and 306th) came back from Schweinfurt intact, and on the second operation in October, the 303rd lost just a single aircraft in action. This was the best record of any Group engaged in these two costly raids. It was Bremen rather than Schweinfurt that caused the Group some trauma. It had been first bombed in April and in a major mission on 29th November the 303rd lost four aircraft. During December another three operations were mounted, and on the last of these (on the 20th) the Group lost three aircraft. The formations were some 30 minutes late and slightly off course because of strong head winds, and the losses could have been heavier but for some sterling action by the fighter escorts.

One of the Group's aircraft, *Jersey Bounce Jr*, was struck by flak and the radio/gunner, T/Sergeant Forrest L. Vosler, was wounded in the legs but still continued to fire his gun. A second direct hit resulted in shell splinters injuring his face and chest, and he lost his sight. Vosler declined first aid and between bouts of unconsciousness, he attempted to repair his damaged radio by touch. The badly damaged B-17 finally ditched in the sea off the Norfolk coast and Vosler, despite his horrendous injuries, managed to drag another injured crewman out onto the wing of the aircraft, where they were both pulled into the dinghy. The crew were picked up by a passing coaster, and Vosler's courageous acts resulted in the award of a Medal of Honor. Vosler was only 20 years old, and after long hospital treatment in the States he eventually regained his sight.

The Group's heaviest loss of the war so far came on 11th January 1944 when the 1st Division was detailed to attack the FW 190 production plant at Oschersleben in central Germany. Brigadier General Robert F. Travis, the Commander of the Division, flew alongside Lieutenant General William Calthorn in the Group's lead aircraft *The Eight Ball*. The weather deteriorated quite dramatically after the formations passed the Dutch coast, and subsequently the other two

*B-17* Bad Check *at dispersal beside a cornfield, August 1943. It was lost on 11th January 1944. (Smithsonian Institution)*

Divisions engaged on the operation were recalled, but the First ploughed on regardless.

The Luftwaffe met the bombers in strength with several night-fighter units being pressed into action. Because of the inclement weather, only one P-51 Fighter Group - the 354th from Boxted in Essex - was around to give any protection. In the furious air battle, 34 of the 177 B-17s were shot down (19%). The 303rd lost eleven aircraft, although General Travis survived. Each Group was awarded a Distinguished Unit Citation, and Major James Howard, who was leading the Fighter Group, received a Medal of Honor after he single-handedly fought off about 30 Me 110s in a bravura performance that, according to one of the witnesses, was 'like something out of a Hollywood film'.

By the summer of 1944 the Eighth had reached its full strength, and the 'Hell's Angels' could lay claim to be known as a veteran group. In July it had passed the 200 missions mark, not long after several Bomb Groups had entered operations for only the first time. Nevertheless, it was a sobering fact that even such experienced Groups could still

*B-17s of 'Hell's Angels', the 303rd Bomb Group, flying over Molesworth. (Smithsonian Institution)*

sustain heavy operational losses, despite the toll taken of the Luftwaffe both in the air and on the ground. On 15th August, when the crews were engaged in bombing airfields in western Germany, 'suddenly out of nowhere' about two dozen FW 190s struck with speed and devastating accuracy. Eight B-17s went down in a matter of minutes, while another crashed on its approach to the airfield. As one of the veteran pilots commented, 'It wasn't as if it were a major target like Berlin or Merseburg'!

In the following month the 303rd again suffered at the hands of the Luftwaffe when attacking oil targets at Magdeburg. The crews faced a concentrated attack from FW 190s of the Sturmgruppen, a special bomber assault unit, operating their so-called 'Company Front' tactics, when streams of fighters flying three abreast attacked the B-17s head-on. On this occasion the Group lost eleven B-17s, equalling their heaviest single loss of the war. As one pilot recalled: 'About 50 Nazi fighters en masse coming at us in a solid bunch...they came again and again from all directions. These guys were like mad men - with but one idea - to knock us down in a suicidal attack.' After this nightmare mission the Group lost only seven crews up to the end of the year, despite being engaged in operations against oil targets at Pölitz, Merseburg and Zeitz, as well as Berlin and Schweinfurt.

Christmas 1944 was a time when many in the Eighth Air Force had genuinely expected to be 'back in the States with the job wrapped up'. Although this was never a realistic prospect, the Wehrmacht's major offensive through the Ardennes in mid-December certainly ended such a notion. The unfavourable weather that had precluded the Eighth playing a supporting role in the bitter battle, began to clear on Christmas Eve, and a maximum effort was called. Over 2,000 heavy bombers left for a variety of targets (mainly airfields and rail/road communication centres) in western Germany. The Eighth lost twelve bombers and ten fighters, with the 303rd losing one aircraft. However, the problems arose when the bombers returned home. Every airfield to the west of Cambridge was hidden under dense fog and the crews were diverted to American bases in Norfolk and Suffolk. One badly damaged B-17 came to grief whilst trying to land at Snetterton Heath in Norfolk. It took the rest of the festive season to get all the diverted aircraft back to their home bases.

The New Year brought some setbacks for the Group. Three crews were lost on the 13th whilst attacking rail bridges over the Rhine, and eight days later two were lost after a mission to rail marshalling yards to the north of the Ruhr. The following day (22nd January) Holten oil refinery at Sterkade, also in the Ruhr, was bombed by over 200 of the Division's B-17s. Five were lost, one of which came from Molesworth; Sterkade had been one of the first industrial targets to be bombed by the RAF, in May 1940. When the 303rd was sent out to Berlin on 3rd February, it was its 311th mission - a total unsurpassed by any Eighth Group. Although the Division lost 14 aircraft (3%), a high figure at this stage of the war, all returned safely to Molesworth.

Sadly, the Group had the misfortune to lose a crew on its final mission of the war on 25th April - its 364th. This was the highest number of missions by any B-17 Group, and for the loss of 165 aircraft. It had been a long, arduous and costly campaign waged by the 303rd, but all the 'Hell's Angels' are remembered on a plaque in All Saints' church at Brington close by. The Group left for North Africa in June, and on 1st July 1945 the airfield returned to the RAF. At the time of writing the airfield houses the 432nd Air Base Squadron, and the two Medal of Honor airmen, unique for an Eighth Air Force Group, have their memorial plaques in the airfield buildings.

# 17
# OAKINGTON

For the best part of 35 years, Oakington was a premier RAF station. It was a very active wartime airfield operating with Blenheims, Wellingtons, Stirlings, Lancasters and Mosquitos - a microcosm of Bomber Command - and for three years was a Pathfinder station. In the immediate post-war years the airfield was under the control of Transport Command, before it gained no small fame as a flying training station, with hundreds of RAF pilots gaining their 'wings' there. Nevertheless, Oakington has reserved a special niche in service history as the original home of the Short Stirling, the first four-engined heavy bomber to enter the service. The RAF station was handed over to the Army in March 1975, and is now the home of 1st Battalion of the Royal Anglia Regiment.

The airfield was built during 1939/40, and was one of the last to come out of the RAF Expansion schemes of the 1930s. When it opened on 1st July 1940 as part of No 2 Group, it was anything but complete. The first residents lived under canvas and the officers' and sergeants' messes were housed in large marquees until the permanent quarters were completed in the autumn. Despite this the first squadron, No 218 (Gold Coast), began to move in during the middle of the month and its Commanding Officer, Wing Commander L. B. Duggan, was temporarily appointed Station Commander, until Group Captain R. M. Field, CBE, arrived at the beginning of September.

The squadron had served in France since September 1939 and had experienced a torrid and costly time with its Fairey Battles. It had recently reformed at Mildenhall with Blenheim IVs. Before the squadron became operational, two crews were killed in a mid-air collision. On the following day (19th August), three Blenheims left to attack Dutch airfields, but only one was successful. The first loss in action came on 8th September 1940 when one crew failed to return

*A Stirling I of 7 Squadron. (via J. Adams)*

from a patrol of the Dutch coast.

During October some of the crews became engaged on 'roving commissions', which effectively allowed them freedom to attack targets as they thought fit. These were the forerunners of the later successful Mosquito intruder raids. In early November the squadron was transferred to No 3 Group and began to convert to Wellingtons, which soon played havoc with the airfield's grass runway, but by the end of the month they had moved to Marham in Norfolk.

On 29th October the first five Stirlings landed from Leeming in Yorkshire; 7 Squadron had arrived and it was destined to remain at Oakington for the rest of the war. The squadron dated back to May 1914, was reformed in 1923, and in the inter-war years won the coveted Laurence Minot bombing trophy on seven occasions. It would later add two more successes with its post-war Lincolns. The squadron's motto, 'Per diem per noctem', was to prove rather prophetic.

In November a new unit was formed at the airfield - No 3 Photographic Reconnaissance - under the command of Squadron Leader P. B. B. Ogilvie, who would later command XV Squadron. Its purpose was to photograph targets in order to assess the bombing accuracy and damage. Specially adapted Spitfires were used for daylight flights, with a couple of Wellingtons for experimental night photography. Some of the Spitfires were painted deep blue (known as 'PR blue') and others coloured pink in an attempt to gain maximum camouflage. In the New Year the unit moved away to Alconbury, but in July 1941 it left for a permanent base at Benson in Oxfordshire.

Oakington had become the centre of much attention because of the Stirlings, and a number of important visitors came to view the new heavy bomber, including HM King George VI on 16th January 1941. However, things were not going too well with the aircraft, there were several technical problems, as well as a number of modifications to be made, and the supply of the aircraft was rather slow.

It was not until 10/11th February that the squadron was able to mount its first operational sorties, when three aircraft bombed oil storage tanks at Rotterdam, and a fortnight later another three Stirlings joined the main bomber force attacking a warship in Brest. It was over this target a week later that a Stirling was lost to enemy action, the first of 625 (3.4%) - the highest proportional loss rate of the four main bombers.

The heavy aircraft (43,500 pounds unladen weight) had turned the airfield into a quagmire. The pre-war decision not to provide concrete runways for new airfields was now coming home to roost with a vengeance. The Air Ministry, in its wisdom, had maintained that 'there should be no difficulty operating bombers up to 40,000 pounds weight from properly prepared grass airfields', though the Stirling was the first bomber to exceed that weight. It is perhaps not surprising that Harold Balfour, the Under Secretary for Air should complain in March, 'I tried today to fly to Oakington but found it impossible to land there because the aerodrome is unserviceable... I found that they had to load up the Stirlings at Wyton, which are then sent on operations after struggling light off the sodden surface of Oakington...there we are with the first Stirlings, unable to function normally because of an untracked base!' By the middle of the month part of the squadron had been detached to Newmarket Heath, although towards the end of April all were back at Oakington. The construction of concrete runways began in late 1941 but even by the following March only the main one was completed.

During 1941 the squadron lost 37 Stirlings in action with many experienced crews missing, including three Flight Commanders. Berlin took the heaviest toll but, on 14/15th August, three aircraft returning from Magdeburg were written off in crash-landings with all the crews surviving. This was especially fortunate as two of the squadron's most experienced pilots were involved.

One was Wing Commander H. R. 'Jock' Graham, DSO, DFC, the CO, who had been described by the *Daily Express* as 'the best pilot in Bomber Command'. The other was Flying Officer Dennis M. Witt, DFC, DFM. He had already completed one tour when he joined 7

Squadron in November 1940 as a newly promoted officer. Dennis Witt successfully completed a second tour with the squadron, and by March 1944 had notched up 100 missions, over one third as a Pathfinder. He was awarded the DSO in 1945 for 'the highest standard of skill and bravery setting an example of a high order.' He retired in 1959 as a Group Captain and died four years later at the young age of 48 years.

Perhaps it was Bomber Command's attempts to destroy the elusive German battleships, *Scharnhorst* and *Gneisenau*, that provided the most taxing and onerous task for the squadron during the year. It all started with a daylight raid to Brest on 24th July and it reached a crescendo in late November and December, when eight operations were mounted, including one on 7/8th December when, along with XV Squadron, some of the crews made the first operational trial of Oboe. The daylight raid to Brest on the 18th involved 47 aircraft. Six were lost, half of which came from the squadron.

Since the previous July the squadron had shared the airfield with 101 Squadron, which had recently exchanged Blenheims for Wellington ICs. On 9th July the crews were in action over Osnabrück when the railway yards were claimed to have been bombed successfully, and in August they were in action over Hamburg, Kiel, Cologne, Hamm, Essen and Mannheim and five Wellingtons were lost. On 10/11th September they were detailed to attack the Fiat steelworks at Turin, a long and exhausting flight across the Alps.

One Wellington crash-landed in France, and four of the crew managed to escape capture. Nine nights earlier, another two crewmen had successfully evaded capture when they landed in Belgium. In two years (1940-1), 82 of the Command's airmen managed to avoid becoming prisoners; perhaps the two most famous 'evaders' were Basil Embry and Hal Bufton. Such escapes required a certain courage and determination, and, of course, assistance from hundreds of brave people in the occupied territories who risked torture and death to help some 1,970 Allied airmen evade capture during the war. Probably more than half this total came from Bomber Command.

During the autumn the Wellingtons began to use Bourn on a more regular basis, although on 30th November 1941 they set out from Oakington for the shipyards at Hamburg. It proved to be a most successful operation conducted in bright moonlight, but unhappily two Wellingtons ditched in the sea. One crew was quickly picked up off the Dutch coast and taken prisoner. Only two of the other crew survived, being rescued by a Danish fishing boat about 24 hours later. By February 1942 the squadron had moved to Bourn, though its Stirling

Conversion Flight, which had been formed earlier in the month, remained at Oakington until the autumn.

For most of January 1942, 7 Squadron was taken off major operations whilst GEE sets were fitted into their Stirlings, but nevertheless two aircraft were lost in training flights. Eight airmen were tragically killed when their Stirling collided with a Hurricane of No 56 OTU. Squadron Leader J. N. Mahler, who was on secondment from 218 Squadron, was killed in the accident. In a minor operation to Soesterburg airfield, one Stirling returning home was damaged by 'friendly' fire from an Allied convoy, and it crashed whilst trying to land at Oakington. Amongst the survivors was Lieutenant H. N. Denny of the Royal Artillery, one of several Army officers drafted into the RAF to act as air-gunners. Lt. Denny had escaped another crash-landing only three days earlier - his short experience of RAF life was anything but reassuring!

In the last week of March the Squadron's Commander, Wing Commander J. H. A. Chapman, was lost over Essen when the crews encountered heavy flak and strong Luftwaffe opposition, all for an operation that the Command admitted was 'a dismal failure'. He had been in charge for less than a month.

Quite undaunted by the Essen set-back, two nights later (28/29th) Bomber Command launched its first 'fire-raising' raid on the ancient city of Lübeck. Much of the centre was destroyed and three of the squadron's Stirlings went missing, a quarter of the total loss. In the following month the squadron mounted 106 sorties for the loss of just two aircraft; it was the first time a century had been exceeded.

August 1942 was quite an eventful month for 7 Squadron because it had been transferred to the new Pathfinder Force, and left on its first PFF mission on the 24/25th to Frankfurt. It was a costly operation with 16 aircraft lost, five of them Pathfinders; two came from the squadron, including one piloted by Wing Commander J. M. Shewell. During the month one of the most famous Pathfinders arrived at Oakington, T. G. 'Hamish' Mahaddie, DFC, AFC, who started his second operational tour with 7 Squadron and by the end of the year was acting Wing Commander. After he finished this tour he became a Group Captain at PFF headquarters, responsible for the recruitment of PFF crews. Mahaddie died in early 1997 at the age of 85 years.

By the end of January 1943, 13 Stirlings were equipped with H2S sets and, along with the Halifaxes of 35 Squadron, they would lead the marking for PFF operations until all the Group's squadrons were supplied with H2S. The Battle of the Ruhr proved costly for the squadron, especially on 21/22nd June over Krefeld, when four Stirlings were lost to night-fighters, and three nights later when three more crews failed to return from Wuppertal. On this night Wing Commander R. G. Barrell, DSO, DFC Bar, was flying a Lancaster III. Since May, the squadron had been converting to Lancasters but it was a slow business and the trusty Stirlings were not phased out until the end of August. Barrell was only 23 years old, and on his 60th mission when he was killed because his parachute failed to open.

So many experienced pilots and crews were lost over the Ruhr, well named the 'land of no return', including four squadron leaders, with another two missing over Milan on 12/13th August. By the end of the month the B Flight Commander, Squadron Leader C. J. Lofthouse, OBE, DFC, and Group Captain A. H. Willetts, the Station Commander were prisoners of war after a particularly costly mission to Berlin. The great difficulty for both the PFF and the squadron was to adequately replace such experienced pilots and leaders - a task Group Captain Mahaddie undertook with great enthusiasm.

The first Mosquito IVs appeared at Oakington on 1st April, to equip the newly formed No 1409 (Met) Flight, which undertook long distance weather reconnaissance patrols ('Pampas') over targets to be bombed by the main force. Later it made patrols on behalf of the USAAF. The first sortie left on the 2nd for Brittany prior to the Command's last operation to St Nazaire and Lorient that night. In May the Flight began to receive its first IXs, and on 14th June the first aircraft was lost in action over France, shot down at 28,000 feet by two FW 190s. Both crew members baled out and some months later the navigator, Pilot Officer R. Taylor, arrived back at Oakington - another successful evader. By this time Squadron Leader The Hon. P. I. Cunliffe-Lister, DSO, and his navigator were prisoners of war after being shot down on a patrol over Osnabrück on behalf of the Eighth Air Force. The Flight moved to Wyton in January to be closer to PFF headquarters.

In November 1943 a new Mosquito squadron was formed at Oakington under the command of Wing Commander R. P. Elliott, DSO, DFC. By the 24th the squadron, No 627, had five Mosquito IVs on charge, and three crews were detailed for Berlin on the same night. Two returned early because of severe weather but one made it to the target. The squadron worked in concert with 139 Squadron at Wyton and at the end of the year had completed 53 sorties. The New Year saw targets as diverse as Berlin, Leipzig, Düsseldorf, and Frankfurt, often delivering the 4,000 pound bombs. Before it was transferred to No 5 Group on 15th April, 73 raids had been mounted for the loss of four aircraft. Wing Commander Guy Gibson, VC, DSO, DFC, was flying a

*Mosquito BXVI, ML963:8K-K of 571 Squadron. (RAF Museum)*

Mosquito from 627 when he went missing in action on 19/20th September.

During the winter of 1943/4, 7 Squadron ploughed on relentlessly with the increasingly costly Berlin raids, and their luck had not changed for the better. In 19 Berlin operations, 26 aircraft were lost and 185 airmen killed or missing in action - the highest losses in the whole of Bomber Command. Other targets were also costly; the squadron's CO, Group Captain K. J. Rampling, DSO, DFC was lost on 22/23rd March when Frankfurt was bombed with devastating accuracy. He was replaced by the ebullient Wing Commander W. G. Lockhart, DSO, DFC, who lasted barely a month before failing to return after a raid to Friedrichshafen on 27/28th April. Air Vice-Marshal Bennett said of him, 'I never, throughout the entire war, met anybody so fanatically courageous and "press on" at all times and in all circumstances. Virtually nothing would stop him...his determination passed all bounds.'

His replacement was the brilliant young New Zealand pilot, Wing Commander J. Fraser Barron, DSO Bar, DFC, DFM, who had already completed two tours and was brought back from training duties to take charge of the squadron, although he was only 23 years old. On 19/20th May, Barron was Master Bomber on a raid to the railway yards at Le

*The village sign commemorates its RAF links, and especially 7 Squadron.*

Mans; it was his 79th operation. Over the target his Lancaster collided with that of the Deputy Master, Squadron Leader J. M. Dennis, DSO, DFC, and both airmen were killed. It was a staggering blow to the squadron to lose three commanders, all brilliant pilots and leaders, in a matter of months.

Another new addition to Bennett's Light Night Strike Force was formed in April, 571 Squadron, comprising at first just one Flight of Mosquito XIVs. Its first operational sorties were conducted from Graveley. Commanded by Wing Commander J. M. Birkin, DSO, DFC, AFC, it soon became deeply involved in the Mosquito night offensive and when 13 aircraft left for Kassel on 3rd October, the squadron had passed the 1,000 sorties mark in a very quick time.

Ten days later four Mosquitos left to mine the Kiel Canal. The hazardous nature of such operations, when the mines were dropped from a height of 50 to 250 feet, is shown by what happened to Squadron Leader E. J. Greenleaf's Mosquito. Just after the mine was released, a flak shell burst alongside the cockpit, which killed the navigator and severely injured one of Greenleaf's arms. He managed to bring the Mosquito back, literally flying it single-handed, some 400 miles, to make an emergency landing at Woodbridge. Greenleaf was immediately awarded the DSO for his brave actions.

The squadron mounted its first daylight operation on 29th November when a benzol plant at Duisburg was attacked, and this was quickly followed by another two daylight raids, with 50 sorties in total being flown. March 1945 proved to be the squadron's busiest month with 275 sorties being mounted to a variety of targets, with Berlin in the forefront. It was over the German capital that the squadron's most famous Mosquito, ML963:8KK, was lost on 10/11th April, after almost twelve months' continuous operations. Sixteen nights later, twelve crews left to bomb Grossenbrode airfield, bringing the squadron's short but impressive war to an end - 260 raids for the loss of eight aircraft.

On 25th April, ten crews of 7 Squadron bombed the batteries at Wangerooge and all returned safely. They now became involved in more pleasurable missions - dropping supplies to the starving Dutch, picking up British prisoners of war, and some 'Cook's tours', which were flights to show ground crews the damage inflicted by Bomber Command. The squadron was due to serve in the Far East but the war ended before the move could be made. After almost four years' service at Oakington, the squadron moved away to Mepal on 24th July 1945.

No mere statistics can convey the contribution and sacrifice made by 7 Squadron's crews during the war, which resulted in more than 500 gallantry awards. Five hundred and forty six operations were mounted and 165 aircraft lost - the most raids and losses for a PFF heavy squadron and the third highest losses in Bomber Command. It is a record that speaks for itself.

# 18
# SNAILWELL

For a small and relatively little known wartime airfield, Snailwell played host to a variety of fighters: Tomahawks, Airacobras, Whirl-winds, Hurricanes, Spitfires, Mustangs, Havocs and, last but not least, Typhoons - an impressive list! The airfield was sited on the northern edge of Newmarket, just over the boundary between Cambridgeshire and Suffolk, and despite the presence of a bomber station only a few miles to the west at Newmarket Heath, it became a satellite for Duxford some 18 miles away.

The airfield was established in early 1941 and the Army Co-operation Command quickly stepped in to claim it for one of its squadrons, No 268, which was using a smaller airfield at Westley near Bury St Edmunds. It was then operating Lysanders but they were being phased out of the Command and replaced by Curtiss Tomahawks. These American fighters required a far longer runway than Westley provided, so the move to Snailwell was inevitable. Even after their arrival in April, the two airfields worked closely together until well into 1942, with many aircraft using Westley for circuit training.

268 Squadron was commanded by Wing Commander A. F. Anderson, DFC, and in May his pilots began conversion training at the Army Co-operation School at Old Sarum in Wiltshire. Towards the end of the month they took part in an army exercise mounted from West Raynham in Norfolk, but it was not until the end of October 1941 that the first operational sorties were mounted, using Coltishall as a forward base. Hurricanes of 56 Squadron, then based at Duxford, had used the airfield briefly during August, as did Spitfires of 192 Squadron, whilst en route from Portreath to Swanton Morley. Then the Tomahawks were left in splendid isolation until March 1942 and the arrival of an unusual RAF wartime fighter, the Westland Whirl-

*137 Squadron was one of only two squadrons to be equipped with the Westland Whirlwind.*

wind. The squadron, No 137, had flown over from Matlaske in Norfolk to take part in affiliation exercises with the Tomahawks.

The Whirlwind was a twin-engined aircraft and only 112 were produced, mainly because of continual niggling problems with its engine, which made maintenance most difficult. It had a high landing speed, at least for its time, and several accidents occurred in training; the first squadron commander, Squadron Leader J. Sample, DFC, a Battle of Britain veteran, had been killed in a mid-air collision. The Whirlwind was fast at low altitudes (360 mph), strongly armed with four cannons in the nose, and had a longer range than most fighters, so in theory it should have made a welcome addition to the fighter force, but by December 1943 it was being phased out of service. Prior to its detachment at Snailwell, 137 Squadron had lost four out of six aircraft whilst engaged in the unsuccessful attempt to prevent the 'Channel Dash' of the three German battleships in February. The Whirlwinds returned to Snailwell in late August, staying for almost three weeks.

At the end of March 1942, Typhoons made their first appearance at Snailwell when 56 Squadron commanded by Squadron Leader Hugh Dundas, DFC, arrived from Duxford. The rather basic facilities did not appear to concern the pilots because Dundas later commented, 'although the amenities there were primitive, the move suited us well, for we enjoyed being on our own.' Over the next twelve months or so, Typhoons would become regular visitors to the airfield. From April, 56 began to train with the other Duxford squadrons as a Wing under

*Hawker Typhoons of 56 Squadron.*

Wing Commander Denys Gillam, DSO, DFC Bar.

Finally, on 30th May, the pilots went into action with their Typhoons, a notable first for these remarkable fighters. One Flight led by Dundas went to Westhampnett in Sussex, the other led by Gillam left for Manston in Kent. The intention was to intercept the frequent Luftwaffe attacks against coastal towns and targets. For the next six days the pilots patrolled daily but without seeing any action, except that two Typhoons were shot down by Spitfires, followed by a similar incident on 30th July. The Wing went into action for the first time in August 1942 over Dieppe and although several enemy aircraft were destroyed, the squadron's pilots drew a blank. When the Wing disbanded, 56 Squadron left for Matlaske on 25th August.

Meanwhile, 268 Squadron continued to operate from the airfield, although in April it had begun to convert to Mustangs. During the summer the pilots became engaged on Jim Crows - operational patrols to intercept intruder raids on coastal targets. In June a new Army Co-operation Command squadron, No 168, was formed at the airfield from a nucleus of 268's pilots, but within days they and their Tomahawks left for Bottisham. Early in October the first USAAF personnel arrived at the airfield - 347th squadron of 350th Fighter Group - with Bell P-400s (Airacobras). The Group was based at Duxford, but it was due to serve with the Twelfth Air Force in North Africa and left in December.

Within days of their departure another Typhoon squadron, No 181, moved in from Duxford, where it had recently been formed with Squadron Leader Dennis Crowley-Milling, DFC, as its Commanding Officer. Since his service with 242 Squadron during the Battle of Britain, 'Crow', as he was known, had been shot down over France but evaded

*A Mustang I, November 1941. (RAF Museum)*

capture, escaping to Spain, where he spent several months in a concentration camp before being released. Crowley-Milling later commanded No 124 Typhoon Wing of the Second Tactical Air Force and completed the war with eight victories to his name. He retired from the service at the rank of Air Marshal with a knighthood, and died in 1996.

Poor weather prevented much flying until well into the New Year, but in early February 1943 the squadron began mounting anti-shipping patrols along the Dutch coast and was later engaged in a major Army exercise codenamed Spartan. On 22nd March just six Typhoons left for Coltishall to take part in their first dive-bombing operation. The aircraft were loaded with a 500 pound bomb under each wing and their target was Alkmaar airfield in Holland; this was a role that ideally suited the aircraft. The Typhoons left for Gravesend in the last week of March.

They were replaced by Mustangs of 170 Squadron and during May the pilots began operating along the Dutch coast seeking out shipping targets. Unfortunately, the squadron's Commander, Squadron Leader St Aubyn, was lost over the North Sea on the 27th.

During the summer the airfield had its most active period of the war, especially when another Mustang squadron, No 309 (Polish), arrived in early June. It had been specially formed in October 1940 as the only

Polish Army Co-operation unit in the RAF, and was also known as the 'Land of Czerwien'. Polish airmen made a large contribution to the RAF during the war, far more than any other European country. There were 14 Polish squadrons with some 17,000 officers and men, of whom nearly 2,000 were killed.

During this period the airfield literally abounded with Mustangs. 613 (City of Manchester) Squadron operated from there from July to October, and within days of its arrival the pilots were engaged in shipping reconnaissance flights from Coltishall.

The days of the Army Co-operation Command were now numbered. The resident squadron, 268, had left the airfield by the end of May and two months later the Command was disbanded in advance of the formation of the Second Tactical Air Force later in the year. Snailwell was now transferred into No 12 Group of Fighter Command, although the Polish Mustangs remained until April 1944.

During the next few months two major army exercises were mounted in East Anglia and a number of squadrons from airfields in Kent and Surrey used Snailwell on a temporary basis. This period of intense activity proved to be the final fling for the airfield. During the winter of 1943/4 the Polish airmen experienced considerable problems with their troublesome Allison engines, and began to re-equip with Hurricane IICs and later IVs. The latter were the successful 'tank busters', supplied with the so-called 'universal wing' allowing the carriage of eight 60-pound rocket projectiles along with two heavy cannons and two machine guns.

After the Polish pilots had left towards the end of April 1944, there was a short breathing space before the influx of American personnel from Grove in Berkshire. They were members of the 33rd and 41st Mobile Repair and Reclamation Squadrons of the Ninth Air Force, although the 41st moved back to the Technical Air Depot after just a few weeks and was replaced by the 51st Squadron. For about two and a half months, Snailwell became known as Station 361 and was involved in the modification, maintenance and repair of A-20s (Havocs). The reason for the temporary move was that Grove had become a little overcrowded because of the intense activity in preparation for D-Day. The last vestiges of the Americans' sojourn had disappeared by the end of July.

Until the middle of October the airfield was quiet, when the RAF (Belgian) Initial Training School arrived from Snitterfield in Warwickshire. The school had been formed to produce both pilots and ground crews for a reformed Royal Belgian Air Force. Snailwell was now under the control of No 28 Group of Technical Training Command. Not many wartime airfields had passed through so many RAF Commands! The first training aircraft - Masters and Tiger Moths - began to arrive during February 1945 and flying training commenced, with Bottisham airfield also being used.

The school remained until October 1946 and when the Belgian airmen left, the airfield was closed down. Soon the land returned to farming and some land was used as paddocks for the nearby racehorse studs. Little now remains of the old airfield, and the Newmarket by-pass road has almost bisected its site.

# 19
# STEEPLE MORDEN

It might be argued that the most exciting incident in Steeple Morden's short existence as a wartime airfield occurred on the night of 16th February 1941, when an all-black Junkers 88A appeared and calmly landed. It was returning from a bombing mission over Birmingham, and although it was a bright moonlit night the crew had become completely disorientated. They were under the misapprehension that they were over France rather than southern Cambridgeshire! As the aircraft touched down, the undercarriage collapsed and it suffered serious damage as it slewed across the grass airfield. The four-man crew were captured and although the aircraft proved to be beyond repair, its equipment was intact, and was sent for evaluation by the radio experts from RAE at Farnborough.

Until that night, life had been a little humdrum at the small grass airfield situated north of the A505 road between the villages of Littlington and Steeple Morden. It opened in September 1940 as a satellite for nearby Bassingbourn, and was used by Wellington Is of No 11 OTU, mainly for circuits and practice landings. During the early months of 1941, when a German invasion remained a strong possibility, Fighter Command drew up elaborate plans for alternative airfields should a forced withdrawal from south-east England be necessary. Steeple Morden was selected to take the fighter squadrons based at Northolt.

Whether it was pure coincidence or an act of deliberate retaliation, eleven nights after the Junkers made its unscheduled landing the airfield was bombed. Nine high explosives straddled the field, damaging two Wellingtons. The Luftwaffe struck again in April 1941, this time a Wellington was shot down as it was making a night approach.

During the autumn the airfield became more involved with the

*A Junkers 88 at Steeple Morden, 16th February 1941. (Imperial War Museum)*

training unit and towards the end of the year, when concrete runways were being laid at Bassingbourn, the unit's complement of Wellingtons, Ansons and Lysanders was shared out between Steeple Morden and Tempsford. In the following spring many returned to Bassingbourn, but not before they had been involved in the three '1,000 bomber' raids in May /June. On the Bremen raid of 25/26th June 1942, three failed to return to Steeple Morden. Almost 12% of the training aircraft were lost on this raid - a far higher percentage than the main force's losses. By September the OTU had moved away to Westcott. The airfield had been allocated to the USAAF as a bomber station, which would entail a considerable amount of construction work.

The first American airmen arrived sooner than expected. On 2nd November 1942 the personnel of the 3rd Photographic Group, one of its squadrons, 15th, was commanded by Lt. Colonel Elliott Roosevelt, arrived with their F-4s; these were converted P-38Es (Lightnings) on which the armament had been removed from the nose, and cameras installed. The Group had already been transferred to the Twelfth Air Force serving in North Africa, so they were merely 'birds in passage'. Roosevelt, who was the US President's son, would be awarded a decoration whilst serving with the Twelfth Air Force. Meanwhile, Blenheims of D Flight of 17 OTU based at Upwood used the airfield during the early months of 1942.

*P-47 Wrie of the 355th Fighter Group with the new 108-gallon tank –'Baby'. (USAF)*

It was quickly realised that the site was not really suitable for the standard Class A bomber station, so in April 1943 the USAAF reallocated it to house one of their Fighter Groups - 355th - then nearing the end of its training at Philadelphia. They arrived on 8th July, commanded by Colonel William 'Bill' J. Cummings Jr. Under his leadership and drive, the 355th would develop into one of the most effective and successful fighter units in the whole of the Eighth Air Force. It was the fourth Group to join the Eighth Fighter Command and was placed in 65th Wing along with the two veteran Groups - the 4th and 56th. It would be equipped with P-47Ds but because there were considerable supply problems the pilots took quite a time to become operational.

Their first operational sorties were made on 14th September 1943 - a sweep of Dunkirk and the Dutch islands - nothing more than a gentle introduction into the war and mainly to allow the pilots to familiarise themselves with their area of operations. It was not until 4th October that they were detailed for their first escort mission, Frankfurt, which gave them their first taste of air combat and their first victory, but one pilot was killed when his aircraft crashed in Kent. This mission also saw the first use of drop-tanks; one was slung under the fuselage of the aircraft and they were dubbed 'babies' by the airmen. The tanks extended the aircraft's escort range to about 350 miles.

For a Group destined to complete the war with a high number of enemy aircraft destroyed, its pilots made a very slow start. At the year's end, just six enemy aircraft had been claimed and in the process 15 P-47s had been lost. Matters did not improve in the New Year, especially when four pilots went missing after another Frankfurt operation. So it probably came as a welcome relief to hear, in February 1944, that it would be the second of the Eighth's fighter units to change to P-51s. In their last complete P-47 operation, to Berlin on 6th March, all returned safely with eight 'kills'.

Two days later, on their second visit to Berlin, a composite force of P-47s and P-51s was sent, with just a single victory for the loss of two aircraft (each type). The P-51s dramatically changed the pilots' fortunes, and by the end of the month 47 victories had been chalked up. On the 28th the pilots strafed Longvic airfield and returned with claims of 30 aircraft destroyed on the ground. Thus commenced their very successful career as ground-strafers *par excellence*, earning them the deserved nickname of 'The Steeple Morden Strafers'.

With such a growing reputation, it is not surprising that the Group was asked to provide four experienced pilots to join a special squadron, led by Colonel Glenn Duncan at Metfield in Suffolk. Duncan, the CO of 353rd Group, was deeply concerned that more specialised tactics should be used for the strafing of airfields. He proposed that a squadron should be formed, manned by some of the Eighth's most experienced pilots, to develop and perfect new methods of attack. Major General William 'Bill' Kepner, the Commander of the Eighth's Fighter Command, approved Duncan's proposal and authorised him to set up the squadron to mount some experimental missions. The American habit of finding apt nicknames meant that it quickly became known as 'Bill's Buzz Boys'!

Metfield was used as the target airfield, and generally the pilots would dive from about 15,000 feet, levelling out within five miles of the target, then fly line abreast at a very low altitude in order to gain the maximum element of surprise. This also spread the area of targets for the defending flak batteries. It was emphasised that the pilots should make a thorough study of the enemy airfields at their briefings to ensure that they were fully conversant with the lay-out and landmarks of their targets. From 26th March to 10th April 1944 six trial missions were flown, and 14 aircraft and 36 trains destroyed for the loss of three pilots. At the end of the experiment the small group was disbanded and the pilots returned to their own bases. Sufficient evidence had been gathered to enable Fighter Command to draw up broad guidelines for ground-strafing on a larger scale.

At the end of March, Lieutenant General James H. Doolittle said in a broadcast to the United States: 'Our immediate goal is the destruction or neutralisation of the German Air Force...In our most recent operations the German fighters have shown little inclination to come up and fight, an indication that their losses are now exceeding their replacements and that they are conserving their forces.' In retrospect, it is now known that the German fighter production, although disrupted by the Allied bombing raids, was still meeting the Luftwaffe's demands. In fact, because of a vastly increased building programme in 1943, largely dictated by the growing might of Bomber Command and the Eighth Air Force, German fighter production was far higher than originally planned. The Luftwaffe's problems were not really a lack of aircraft but rather a shortage of trained pilots and severe fuel restrictions.

As if in direct response to Doolittle's speech, the Luftwaffe operated in far greater strength during April. By the end of the month the Eighth's fighter pilots had won that particular battle by a wide margin, although sterner tests still lay ahead for them. It also proved to be a most successful month for the 355th. On the 5th its pilots strafed six airfields in the Munich area, claiming 43 aircraft destroyed and another 81 damaged, as well as eight downed in air combat. Most of these victories were at the Dornier airfield at Oberfaffenhofen, and for this operation the Group was awarded a Distinguished Unit Citation. By the end of the month another 62 air victories had been added to their total, as well as almost 100 on the ground, for the loss of twelve aircraft.

In May 1944 the pilots escorted B-17s to oil targets at Pölitz in western Poland, a round trip of some 1,480 miles. It was the longest trip for P-51s to date, made possible by using British-made 108 gallon drop-tanks. It was an exhausting and demanding flight, no American fighter pilots having spent such a long time confined in a small cockpit.

The Group flew six missions on D-Day and on one its pilots happened to catch a formation of Junkers 87s sneaking up the English Channel. These once feared Stukas were no match for P-51s and at least nine were downed in quick succession, making the 355th the most successful unit on the big day. In the following month the pilots claimed over 110 aircraft destroyed in just four missions, bringing their total to an excess of 400. The strafing expert was Lieutenant Colonel Clairborne H. Kinnard Jr, who would later temporarily command 4th Group, and return to Steeple Morden to take over the 355th in February 1945.

The Group's personnel were more than a little delighted when the legendary Glenn Miller and his AEF band came to Steeple Morden in August to play for them. For Miller this was just one stop on a long and exhausting tour of Eighth Air Force bases throughout the country, which was undertaken from July to October 1944. Miller and his band

*Major Glenn Miller and his famous band entertain air force men at Steeple Morden, 18th August 1944. (Smithsonian Institution)*

flew in from Bentley Priory on the 18th and on the same day left for Attlebridge in Norfolk. For many of the airmen on the base who were fortunate enough to attend the concert, it would, perhaps, become their most abiding memory of their service in England.

Sixty-four P-51s left Steeple Morden early on the morning of 18th September 1944, and for the next few days the airfield was unusually quiet. They had departed on the last Frantic mission to be mounted by the Eighth Air Force. These were politically motivated operations mounted to placate Stalin, but they also enabled the Eighth Air Force to bomb targets in Poland, from whence the aircraft flew on eastward to land at Russian airfields. Frantic VII was a special mission to drop urgent supplies to the Polish Resistance fighters engaged in the Warsaw uprising. The pilots returned to Steeple on the 22nd, via Italy, and were given two days well-earned rest before it was 'back to business as normal'.

As the Eighth made longer strikes into Germany it was realised that there was an urgent need for current weather information. It had been found that forecasted conditions could often change quite dramatically during the course of an operation. It was decided to establish a 'scouting force' within each Fighter Wing, and Steeple Morden was selected to house one of the three forces, known as the Second Scouting Force. Eight aircraft from 354th Squadron were seconded and they were identified by a black bar above the squadron's code WR, with the upper half of the cowling painted bright green.

The scouting aircraft would seek out high cloud formations or other adverse climatic conditions along the planned flight path and, if necessary, plot a clearer route. This information would be transmitted back to the bomber leaders on a special frequency. The take-off was timed so that the P-51s would overtake the bombers en route and arrive over the target area about ten minutes before them, to report any smoke screens or changes in wind speeds. The scouting pilots were mostly experienced bomber pilots, who had completed a combat tour and had elected to retrain for fighters. It was found that they, better than fighter pilots, knew most of the problems that adverse weather could have on bomber formations. The force was commanded by Lieutenant Colonel John R. Brooks, who had previously flown B-24s with the 389th Bomb Group, and its first mission took place on 26th September.

On 3rd October, whilst on an escort mission to Nuremberg the Group lost two outstanding pilots in most unusual circumstances. Captain Henry W. Brown, its leading ace with 17 air and $14\frac{1}{2}$ ground victories, became the victim of ground flak, but he managed to crash-land in a field well outside the city. Major Charles W. Lenfest, 354th Squadron leader, realised that Brown was safe, so he decided to land to attempt to rescue him. Unfortunately, the field was soggy and try as he may, Lenfest was unable to get his P-51 off the ground again. Another pilot had also landed but failed to attract their attention. He managed to take off and returned to relate the fate of the two pilots. Both were captured. After several abortive attempts to escape from his POW camp, Lenfest finally succeeded and evaded recapture, but by then it was the middle of April 1945 when the war was almost ended.

The incident was not quite as foolhardy as it sounds, because in August exactly the same thing had happened in occupied France. On that occasion, the Group's P-51s had circled overhead keeping a German truck at bay whilst one of their P-51s landed and its pilot picked up his stranded colleague, who sat in his lap for their journey back to Steeple Morden! However, after October's ill-fated rescue attempt became known to Headquarters staff, a strict order was issued that in future no such risks should be taken.

*The Steeple Morden strafers in action. Me 110s being raked by fire. (Smithsonian Institution)*

The Group's mentor and guiding light over the previous two years, Colonel Cummings, left Steeple Morden on 4th November, and he was replaced by one of the Eighth's finest fighter commanders, Lieutenant Colonel Everett W. Stewart. He had previously served with 352nd Group at Bodney in Norfolk, and in February would be selected to command the 4th, the oldest Fighter Group in the Eighth.

After a month when the Luftwaffe was hardly seen in strength, November saw some of the fiercest air battles of the war with the Luftwaffe frequently operating in considerable numbers, proof that it was not yet a spent force by any stretch of the imagination. On the 26th, when it was estimated that over 500 enemy fighters were airborne, the Group's pilots scored 21 victories for the loss of just one pilot. This was followed by a successful mission over Berlin - another 13 victories for the loss of a P-51 missing in action.

The presence of another large USAAF base in the vicinity (at Bassingbourn about three miles away) meant that there had to be close air traffic control between the two bases, considering the sheer number of aircraft operating from the two airfields. Early on New Year's Day, 1945 a B-17 *Heat's On* of 91st Group at Bassingbourn suffered engine trouble shortly after take-off and it crashed onto one of the P-51

*The memorial to 355th Fighter Group.*

dispersal areas at Steeple Morden, seriously injuring a number of the ground crew. All in the B-17 crew were killed - a most distressing start to the New Year.

Up to the end of the war, the pilots were still ground-strafing, which did not become any less hazardous as was shown by the loss of four pilots on 16th April whilst attacking enemy airfields. They were the last to go missing from Steeple Morden during the war. Four days later the pilots attacked rail targets in southern Germany and Czechoslovakia, when four enemy aircraft were downed - the final tally to be claimed by the Group.

The 355th flew its last operational mission on 25th April 1945, ending up with a superb record of 868 victories in total, with over 500 of them on the ground, which was the highest ground-strafing total in the whole of the Eighth Air Force. These figures were achieved at no small cost - 175 aircraft lost in action. The pilots are remembered in a most impressive memorial, which stands on a minor road near the original airfield site.

The Group did not return to the United States like most Groups but in early July went on to serve at Gablingen airfield in Germany. About two weeks later the 4th Fighter Group moved in to Steeple Morden, a welcome return for Colonel Stewart, but slowly the P-51s disappeared to Air Depôts and at the beginning of November the American personnel left for the United States. The airfield closed the following year and was sold in the early 1960s.

# 20
# UPWOOD

Nowadays the only activity around the airfield is to be found at the 423rd Medical Flight of the USAF Medical Service. How times have changed! The architecture of Upwood's buildings loudly proclaim the fact that it was a pre-war RAF permanent station. The village sign has a representation of a Canberra bomber, recalling days now long gone, and the neat rows of married quarters lie empty and forlorn but yet still perfectly preserved, giving the eerie appearance of a ghost town.

The airfield opened in January 1937, and has suffered more highs and lows than most permanent stations of comparable vintage. Before it had celebrated its first anniversary, the rather outmoded Hawker Hinds and Audaxes (biplanes) of the two resident squadrons, Nos 52 and 63, were exchanged for Fairey Battles. Within three years these aircraft would also become obsolescent when their inferior performance and armament were harshly exposed in the French skies during May 1940.

Within days of the outbreak of the war the two Battle squadrons had left for 'safer' airfields in Oxfordshire. Their replacements were Blenheims, which would dominate the airfield for the next three years. The first squadron, No 90, arrived on 20th September 1939; it had ceased to be an operational unit and had been given a training commitment within No 6 Group. It would have a rather chequered wartime career, being disbanded and reformed twice before becoming an operational squadron in No 3 Group.

The training of new crews did not progress too smoothly. Several accidents in October and the particularly adverse weather conditions experienced during the winter of 1939/40, caused serious disruptions in the training programme, and it had to be extended from the normal six to ten weeks. Snow, and then a waterlogged airfield, made flying almost impossible even for the Flight of Avro Ansons that had been

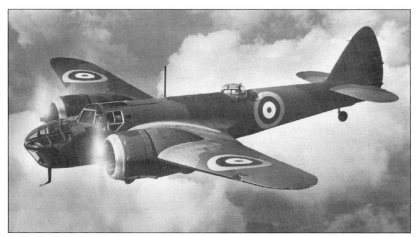

*No 17 OTU operated the Bristol Blenheim IV from Upwood.*

formed the previous October. Until concrete runways were laid the airfield often became unserviceable during the winter months. In February 1940 another Blenheim training squadron arrived at Upwood, No 35. Later it became a Halifax/Lancaster PFF unit operating from Graveley and, in the 1950s, would return to Upwood equipped with English Electric Canberras.

Early in April a new system of operational training was introduced with the result that the two squadrons lost their separate identities, and were merged to form 17 Operational Training Unit. The unit was commanded by Group Captain J. K. Summers, MC, and within a month it had expanded into four Flights - Conversion, Anson, Armament Flying and Operational Training. All OTUs had their fair share of accidents, but in about 30 days towards the end of the year five Blenheims crashed on cross-country flights, and in each case the crews were killed. During 1941 the total number of accidents reached 40, mainly Mark IVs.

In September another new unit was formed at the airfield - No 11 (later 1511) Beam Approach Training Flight. Its function was to instruct crews in the complexities of the Beam Approach system. Most airfields operated the Standard Beam Approach (SBA), which was based on short-distance radio beams providing an aid to night-landings or when weather conditions were unfavourable. Ultimately, there were a great number of these units throughout the country and they basically taught 'blind' flying techniques. Certainly in the early days (1940/1), many pilots distrusted the system and avoided it if at all possible, though when used correctly it was as near perfect as possible.

The aircraft used by the unit was the Airspeed Oxford I, more familiarly known as the 'Ox-box'. Over 8,500 were produced and they were in universal use with training units in Britain as well as those countries operating the Empire Training Scheme, and remained in the service until 1954. Training continued apace during 1942, with the incidence of accidents falling to 25. Two satelite airfields at Warboys and Molesworth were brought into use, as well as Steeple Morden when the airfield was, once again, under water.

By the end of the year the operational life of the Blenheim had been reached and the training units were being re-equipped with Wellingtons. In its present state the airfield could not cope with these far heavier aircraft, certainly not during the winter months, so it was decided to transfer the OTU to Silverstone, which was finally accomplished by the end of April 1943. The BAT Flight left for Greenham Common about the same time. The airfield was placed under care and maintenance, and a month later it was passed over to No 8 PFF Group. Four Airfield Construction Flights moved in to rapidly construct three concrete runways, and they were finally completed at the end of October.

It was not until the New Year that the airfield's first Pathfinder squadron arrived - No 139 (Jamaica). It had gained its name in 1941 when the colony provided sufficient funds for twelve Blenheims under the 'Bombers for Britain' scheme. 139 was one of the most famous Mosquito squadrons, only the second to be equipped with these remarkable aircraft, and it had been operating in the Pathfinders from Wyton since July 1943.

Within days of its arrival at Upwood (on 1st February 1944), Wing Commander G. H. Womersley, DSO, DFC, took over command of the squadron, which was operating a mixture of IVs, IXs, XVIs and XXs. On the same night, one crew left to mark Berlin for a small force of Mosquitos, and they used H2S equipment, which they had been trialling operationally since the beginning of the year. Two nights later, Cologne and Dortmund were marked with another two crews also bombing the latter target, which was the first wartime bombing operation mounted from Upwood. By the end of the month the crews had notched up 114 sorties to Frankfurt, Hanover, Mannheim and Brunswick, and in March they easily doubled this total with Berlin, Duisburg and Stuttgart figuring large.

In early March the airfield suddenly became crowded with Mosquitos and Lancasters; on the 5th of the month, 156 Squadron's

*Lancasters at dusk. (Imperial War Museum)*

Lancasters had trundled across from Warboys. The squadron's time at Warboys had been marked by heavy losses, and perhaps a change of station would also bring about a change in its fortunes? Two operations were cancelled, so it was not until the 15/16th that the crews left Upwood for the first time. Stuttgart was the target, the third mission in about three weeks, and the squadron was able to put up 24 aircraft. It was the last time it would operate in such strength, because in April C Flight left for Little Staughton to form the nucleus of a new Lancaster squadron. Although this third Stuttgart raid was not a spectacular success, as adverse winds had badly affected the marking, all the aircraft returned safely.

In the last major Berlin operation on 24/25th March, 18 crews were in action. The losses on the night amounted to 72 (8.9%); only one crew failed to return to Upwood, but they had been on the squadron for barely four weeks. The squadron had already paid a heavy toll over Berlin, losing 24 aircraft and 168 airmen killed - the highest losses in Bomber Command.

Unfortunately, the month ended with a disaster of some magnitude for both the Command and the squadron. On the ill-fated Nuremberg raid of the 30/31st, out of 110 PFF aircraft taking part, 156 Squadron contributed 17 and lost four of them, two of which were shot down side by side on the outward flight. Both were manned by experienced crews and the two pilots, Warrant Officer Jack A. Murphy and Captain Finn Johnsen of the Royal Norwegian Air Force, were on their 19th and 25th operation of a second tour respectively. Eleven Lancasters were forced to land at other airfields because of the severe weather conditions.

There was a welcome break from operations until 9th April 1944, when railway yards in France were bombed. These targets would occupy the crews for most of the month. The squadron was by then down to 16 Lancasters and four in reserve, and had suffered the loss of its Commanding Officer, Group Captain E. C. Eaton, DFC, and his experienced crew (five DFCs) over Friedrichshafen on the 27/28th. Also in the crew was the squadron's Bombing Leader, Squadron Leader L. H. Glasspool. The raid was undertaken in bright moonlight and entailed a long flight to southern Germany, which was a calculated risk considering the Nuremberg operation just a month earlier. The specific targets were important factories manufacturing engines and gearboxes for tanks. It was rated as 'an outstandingly successful attack' with excellent PFF marking; 18 of 322 Lancasters were lost.

Wing Commander T. L. Bingham-Hall, DFC, took over command of 156 Squadron, which since January had lost four COs in action. During May, 170 sorties were made. Although only three aircraft were lost, the crews were experienced airmen, including the squadron's Gunnery Officer, Squadron Leader J. F. Blair, DFC, DFM. However, the squadron still had a number of experienced pilots, many of them being called upon to undertake Master or Deputy Master Bomber duties, such as Squadron Leaders T. W. Godfrey, DFC; M. R. Attwater, DFC; T. E. 'Tiny' Ison, DFC; G. C. Davies, DSO; and Flight Lieutenant R. C. Wiseman, DFC.

In April 1944, the Mosquito crews of 139 Squadron were also very active with over 220 sorties flown. Ten crews left on the 13/14th for Berlin loaded with 4,000 pound bombs, the first occasion that Cookies were carried to Berlin by Mosquitos. Only five crews were able to bomb

*A Mosquito XX of 139 Squadron. (Imperial War Museum)*

because of heavy weather over the North Sea, and one of the squadron's Mosquitos was hit by flak, with the pilot forced to land at Coltishall.

Three crashes in May slightly marred the squadron's busiest month so far - 256 sorties - which included seven night raids on Berlin, as well as many targets in the Ruhr. On the night of D-Day, twelve crews marked Osnabrück for a large Mosquito force, and all returned safely.

On 21st June, 156 Squadron went out on its first daylight operation when the flying bomb site at St Martin l'Hortier was bombed through 10/10ths cloud with Squadron Leader Ison acting as Master Bomber. The two raids on the other V1 sites were abandoned because of the heavy cloud cover. During the next two months the squadron became increasingly engaged on V1 rocket targets, although the French railway system was still accorded a high priority. On 14/15th July the yards at Revigny and Villeneuve were attacked by a strong force of Lancasters and Mosquitos. Nine crews from Upwood were detailed for Revigny, which was a long flight into southern France, with Flight Lieutenant Wiseman, DFC and Squadron Leader G. C. Davies acting as Master and Deputy Bomber. Wiseman made three runs over the town but was still unable to locate the target so he decided to abandon the mission. Seven Lancasters were shot down by night-fighters, including Squadron Leader Davies.

A fortnight later (the 28/29th), the Command launched a major operation against Hamburg, the first for over twelve months. The 16 Lancasters returned safely and three experienced pilots completed their tours - Wiseman (70 operations), Godfrey (61) and Squadron Leader H. F. Slade, DSO, DFC, of the RAAF (58). Slade and his crew almost did not make it back. Their Lancaster had been severely damaged by flak but Slade managed to land at Woodbridge, and although the aircraft was a write-off, he and his crew survived.

Like many other Lancaster squadrons, 156 had one aircraft that managed to achieve the magical century of successful sorties - ND875 *Nuts*. This aircraft went out on its first operation on 24/25th April flown by (then) Flight Lieutenant Slade. Less than twelve months later, on 24th March, it was credited with its 100th sortie under the control of Squadron Leader P. F. Clayton, DFC. It is thought that the aircraft completed another eight sorties before being transferred to a Conversion Unit and it was finally scrapped in August 1947. Several of the squadron's top pilots flew this indestructible aircraft - Squadron Leaders Ison and 'Kiwi' Cochrane, as well as the CO.

During the autumn and winter the Mosquito crews of 139 Squadron were involved in a variety of tasks. These included dropping flares and target indicators, making diversionary or 'spoof' raids, dropping 'window' ahead of the main force, and trialling G-H radar, as well as straightforward bombing, with Berlin figuring large followed by mainly oil targets in the Ruhr. In the New Year they commenced official siren tours, those nuisance raids that caused such disruption to German industry. From 20/21st February to 27/28th March 1945, the squadron led 36 consecutive night raids on Berlin.

The most spectacular came on the night of the 21/22nd March when 142 Mosquitos bombed in two waves - the largest ever Mosquito strike against Berlin. Eight crews marked for the first wave, with another four leading the second wave, and all twelve arrived back safely at Upwood. Only one aircraft was lost on this most ambitious operation. The squadron was now led by Wing Commander J. R. G. 'Roy' Ralston, DSO Bar, DFM, AFC, another product of the Halton Apprentice School, who had gained a fine reputation as an expert Blenheim and Mosquito pilot. Ralston had previously served at Upwood in December 1941 as a trainer with 17 OTU and he completed a total of 91 operational sorties.

Meanwhile, 156's Lancasters had been active over a wide variety of targets - Duisburg, Kleve, Wanne Eickel, Essen, Gelsenkirchen, Wilhelmshaven and Bochum, to name but a few. Several operations were conducted by day. In an analysis of the bombing performance of Pathfinder squadrons, 156 came out on top, and perhaps as a reward for its expertise the crews were given a ten day rest from operations in November. The CO had left to command Oakington and he was replaced by Wing Commander D. B. Falconer DFC, AFC, who prior to joining the squadron had flown with 571 Mosquito Squadron at Oakington.

Two operations against targets not previously bombed showed the immense and awesome power of Bomber Command at this stage of the war. One was against Frieburg on 27/28th November and the other to Ulm on 17/18th December, when 1,900 tons and 1,550 tons of bombs were dropped respectively in less than 30 minutes. Both towns were severely damaged with high civilian casualty figures. Only three Lancasters were lost in the two raids, but one of 156's crews failed to return from Ulm.

Wing Commander Falconer had only been CO for five weeks when he and his crew went missing in the raid to the Kalk/Nord railway yards at Cologne on the penultimate night of the year. Although heavy cloud caused some problems with the marking, subsequent reports suggested that the railway yards had been severely damaged and at least two ammunition trains had been blown up.

In the New Year the crews, now commanded by Wing Commander 'Tiny' Ison, DSO, DFC, found themselves engaged in some rather long and exhausting missions. The raid on the synthetic oil plant at Zeitz near Leipzig on 16/17th January 1945 took over seven hours and Pölitz on 8/9th February lasted over eight and a half hours. It was on this latter mission that 156's Lancasters came under attack from the jet fighters - Me 262s - and one of the squadron's gunners claimed to have destroyed one, quite a kudos! Furthermore, both operations were achieved without a single loss. However, when the Blohm & Voss shipyards at Hamburg were attacked on 31st March, even at this late stage of the war the Luftwaffe still had sufficient day-fighters (including Me 262s) to account for eleven aircraft - the last time the Command's losses were in double figures for a single operation. Unfortunately, two of the eight missing Lancasters came from Upwood.

On 10th April 1945, the squadron had another new Commander, Wing Commander A. J. L. Craig, DSO, DFC, and it lost its last crew in action over the railway yards at Schwandorf six nights later. Squadron Leader Clayton acted as the Master Bomber on what proved to be a very effective operation. On 25th April, 16 crews left for the coastal batteries at Wangerooge. Rather appropriately, for this last heavy raid of the war 156 supplied both the Master Bomber and Deputy,

*The small and discreet memorial stone proudly displays the Pathfinder badge.*

Squadron Leader A. W. G. Cochrane, DSO, DFC 2 Bars and Flight Lieutenant H. G. Hughes. Six of the seven aircraft lost on the operation were involved in collisions, with over 40 airmen being killed - an unfortunate conclusion to Bomber Command's operations.

The Mosquito crews had to wait until 2/3rd May 1945 before their operations came to a close when 14 attacked Kiel. It was thought that the Germans were preparing vessels to take troops to Norway to continue the war from there. During its time in the Pathfinders, 139 Squadron completed 438 raids and lost 23 aircraft, the heaviest losses of any Mosquito PFF squadron. It remained at Upwood until February 1946.

How is it possible to convey the immense contribution made by the Pathfinder heavy crews to Bomber Command's offensive? 156 Squadron's total of 308 bombing raids (three-quarters with the PFF), 143 aircraft lost, and 913 airmen missing or killed, speaks volumes for their determination, bravery and sacrifice. The squadron flew more sorties, over 4,230, than any other Pathfinder heavy squadron, and certainly lived up to its motto, 'We lead the way'. Towards the end of June 1945 it moved away to Wyton, where it was disbanded.

Both PFF squadrons are remembered by the stone memorial set alongside the old main gate of the airfield. It proudly bears the famous Pathfinder badge and is small, discreet and without doubt, remarkably understated.

# 21
# WARBOYS

Warboys was one of a clutch of airfields situated in what became known as 'Pathfinder Country', with Upwood a stone's throw to the north-west and Wyton a short distance away down the road to Huntingdon, where No 8 Group's headquarters was finally sited.

Long before the Pathfinders were thought of, the airfield began to take shape. In 1940 it was a conventional bomber station in all respects, except that it was provided with an unusually long main runway of 6,290 feet, requiring the Huntingdon road to be closed. A new road was built giving access to the village from the east. The airfield was intended to act as a satellite for Upwood, then deeply engaged in operational training. At the end of July 1941 it was considered ready to receive the overflow of 17 Unit's Blenheims, but none actually appeared. The empty airfield was, however, heaven sent for nearby Wyton as it could be used by XV Squadron to relieve the pressure on the main station, and in late September some training flights and air tests took place from Warboys.

There was more than a little tension at the airfield on 28th September 1941, when a Stirling crashed whilst making a landing in poor visibility. At the controls was none other than XV's Commanding Officer, Wing Commander P. B. B. Ogilvie, DSO. Although the aircraft was a total write-off, fortunately there were no serious injuries. Most of the squadron arrived on 9th October, and almost immediately began to mount some operations from the airfield. On the 21st, one aircraft crashed at Methwold airfield in Norfolk when returning from Bremen. The crew had previously baled out, but one member was killed. On the evening of 15th November, a Stirling bound for Kiel failed to gain height after take off and it crashed beyond the airfield. The crew managed to scramble away before the bombs went up in a terrific explosion.

*A Lancaster crew of 156 Squadron at Warboys. (via Bronwen Wilkin)*

Ten days later, three Stirlings left to bomb targets in the Ruhr but all three were compelled to turn back. One was piloted by a young New Zealand airman, Flight Sergeant J. F. Barron. It crashed heavily at Warboys because of failing engines but all the crew escaped unharmed. It was a close shave for this brilliant airman, who would later reach Wing Commander, and be decorated with DSO Bar, DFC and DFM! By the middle of December the Stirlings had returned to Wyton and were replaced by the Blenheims of D Flight of No 17 Training Unit. For the next eight months the airfield would be given over to training.

The formation of the Pathfinder Force in August 1942 effectively sealed the future of the airfield. It became a Pathfinder station and remained so for the rest of the war. 156 Squadron was allocated to the new force, and during the first week of August its Wellington IIIs began to arrive at Warboys from Alconbury. Since its reformation the squadron had suffered heavy losses, and during its time at Warboys it would pay a high price for Bomber Command's offensives, especially over the Ruhr and Berlin. The nature of the Pathfinders' operational role meant that 156, like other PFF squadrons, would lose a high proportion of senior and experienced crews.

On the day the Pathfinder Force was officially formed, 15th August, eight crews left for Düsseldorf. Three returned early and of the remaining aircraft, one failed to return. Thus the squadron gained the dubious honour of losing the first PFF aircraft in action, although not on a PFF-led operation. This was mounted on the 17/18th, when Flensburg on the Baltic coast was selected. Eight Wellingtons left, two carrying flares, the rest loaded with incendiaries. The operation was not a conspicuous success but Bennett's men were in business. Two days later Group Captain Bennett visited Warboys to explain to his aircrews the aims and philosophy of the new force and the various PFF techniques that he was convinced would bring about an improvement in bombing accuracy.

The third PFF-led operation, to Kassel on 27/28th August, resulted in an improved performance with the Henschel aircraft factory suffering damage but the Luftwaffe had a successful night. Thirty-one aircraft were lost, with Wellingtons suffering more heavily in proportion - of the 14 lost, three were from 156. Two nights later Nuremberg was attacked and once again the Wellington crews suffered harshly. Another 14 went missing (34%!), with just a single loss for Warboys. In their first month of operations from Warboys, the squadron had lost nine crews in action.

Matters could be said to have improved over the next four months when 'only' 13 aircraft went missing, although many Ruhr targets were attacked as well as Kiel and Stuttgart. Several trips were made to Turin and Genoa. On 19/20th September a remarkable escape was made by a New Zealand airman, Squadron Leader A. Ashworth, DFC, AFC. He was returning from Saarbrücken when some flares ignited in the aircraft. They were notoriously volatile, and Ashworth ordered his crew to bale out. To his horror, Ashworth could not find his own parachute, but with some adroit flying he managed to put out the fire and successfully brought his aircraft back single-handed to land at West Malling. Almost two months later Squadron Leader B. V. Robinson would emulate this feat but from an even greater distance (see Graveley).

There were expectations that the squadron's fortunes in 1943 might change for the better, because on the last day of the year three Lancaster Is arrived at Warboys. For most of January the crews were engaged on conversion training. Their last Wellingtons were sent out on the 23/24th to the U-boat pens at Lorient, and three nights later four Lancasters left for the same target - the first of 230 Lancaster operations. Until the opening of the Battle of the Ruhr on 5/6th March, the squadron's losses were minimal with one Lancaster missing, and one written-off when it crashed on return to the airfield and burst into flames, although all the crew escaped.

The Ruhr would cost the squadron 13 crews. Duisburg and Essen brought the heaviest casualties, with eight crews failing to return from these important targets. On the fourth Duisburg operation, mounted on 12/13th May, the marking was excellent, resulting in heavy damage being inflicted, especially in the port area (the largest inland port in Germany). Of the ten Lancasters lost on the night, two came from Warboys. One was captained by Squadron Leader L. Verdon-Roe, who was related to the family that built the Lancaster. He was one of the last surviving veterans from the Wellington days, and the fifth squadron leader to go missing in two months, including the Squadron's Navigation leader.

Non-Ruhr targets also took their toll. The Command's attempt to bomb the Skoda armaments works at Pilsen in Czechoslovakia, in April 1943, proved to be a costly and dismal failure - 36 aircraft lost (11%), with two out of ten Lancasters failing to return to Warboys. Cologne, on 16/17th June, was marked by 16 H2S aircraft rather than by Oboe Mosquitos, and the operation was hampered by bad weather with half of the force turning back. Fourteen Lancasters were lost with three from 156. One of the missing pilots, Squadron Leader J. C. Mackintosh, had taken part in the very first raid over Germany in March 1940.

The four Hamburg raids during late July and early August involved over 3,000 aircraft with some 8,000 tons of bombs being dropped. 'Window' was used for the first time; this was thin strips of black paper with aluminium foil stuck to one side of the strips. When dropped in sufficient quantities it swamped the German radar defences, giving the bomber force a positive advantage. Eighty seven aircraft were lost in the four raids, representing a rate of 2.8%, very low for 1943 and an indication of the effectiveness of 'window'. The squadron despatched 83 aircraft. Four were lost, including one unfortunate crew on their first operation.

During May the squadron began to receive its first Lancasters fitted with H2S cupolas instead of the ventral turrets. These aircraft were coded Y, and as and when time was available the crews were involved on 'Y training', gaining experience of the new equipment. The H2S aircraft suffered more heavily than other PFF aircraft because the German flak defences concentrated on them, and the Germans had devised a method to home in onto H2S transmissions. The crews began to use H2S Lancasters on operations at the end of the month.

The squadron's losses (30 in five months) brought new crews to Warboys with a bewildering regularity - new faces, new flight

Commanders, as well as the appearance, in June, of a new Commanding Officer, Group Captain 'Ray' Collings, AFC, who also was given the job of Station Commander. The airfield had become a full station in January 1943.

In June, 24 Lancasters, Halifaxes and Stirlings of the Pathfinder Navigation Training Unit arrived at Warboys, and the airfield became rather crowded with heavy bombers. The Unit had recently been formed at Gransden Lodge and was commanded by Wing Commander R.P. Elliott, DSO, DFC. Within days of its arrival the unit started its three day courses in training crews on PFF techniques. As the PFF losses mounted, the Unit became more heavily engaged and reached a height in January 1944 when over 600 flying hours were accomplished. In this month it suffered its only really serious accident when a Halifax crashed on take-off, killing all ten crewmen.

August was a particularly active month for 156 Squadron with several long outings to Italian targets. Only two crews were lost in action, over Berlin and Nuremberg, both in the last week of the month. This respite from casualties was to prove all too brief because in just five days in early September, six Lancasters were lost; three from a Munich operation. The following month one of the squadron's last veterans (although he was only 21 years old!), Squadron Leader A. S. 'Syd' Cook, DFC, DFM failed to return from Frankfurt.

But it was the Command's long and harrowing winter offensive against Berlin that brought the squadron's darkest hour. Wing Commander John H. White, DFC, along with his all-decorated crew, failed to return from Berlin on 18/19th November. Although it was not unique, it was unusual to find each member of the crew decorated. White had acted as the second Deputy Master Bomber on the Peenemunde raid in August.

From now on, right through the winter the squadron would suffer horrendous losses with many familiar faces missing around the messes, mostly lost in action. One crew that went missing on 20/21st December comprised four Australians, one New Zealander and two British airmen, all decorated, an example of how 'mixed' crews operated so successfully in Bomber Command.

The New Year brought tragedy for the squadron when on two successive raids to Berlin on the nights of 1/2nd and 2/3rd January, nine Lancasters were lost - over 60 airmen missing! Twelve nights later when the Command made its first major raid on Brunswick, 21 Lancasters left Warboys. The whole force suffered a torrid time at the hands of the Luftwaffe's night-fighters, with 38 Lancasters (7.6%)

*HM The King and Queen Elizabeth inspect crews of 156 Squadron at Warboys, February 1944. (Imperial War Museum)*

missing. Eleven were PFF aircraft, of which five came from Warboys. All were experienced crews and one of the pilots, Wing Commander Mansfield, DFC was a Flight Commander. During January 1944 the squadron lost 17 aircraft in nine operations, and it was getting the reputation as the PFF 'chop' squadron. New crews were hurriedly drafted in to bring it back to strength. Another senior leader, Wing Commander C. L. G. Deane, DSO, DFC, left to command 83 Squadron at Wyton, and Wing Commander E. C. Eaton, DFC, moved in to take over the squadron to allow Group Captain Collings to concentrate on station matters.

The squadron was effectively stood down from operations for 15 days, and during this period The King and Queen visited Warboys to help to bolster morale. The crews were back on operations on 15/16th February, when six went to Frankfurt and 15 to Berlin. The latter again proved the downfall of another experienced crew; the pilot, Flight Lieutenant Simpson, DFC, had been at Warboys since July 1943 - a long time in Pathfinder terms. It was estimated that during the winter of 1943/4 a PFF crew stood about a 15% chance of survival.

*No 1665 Mosquito Training Unit, No 8 (PFF) Group was based at Warboys.*

From 20th to 25th February 1944 the Allied Air Forces launched a major offensive against the German aircraft industry, with Leipzig, Stuttgart, Augsburg and Schweinfurt being attacked in a space of seven nights. One hundred and forty-four RAF aircraft were lost, with the Leipzig raid providing almost a half of this total. On this long flight (seven hours) across Germany, the bomber crews were under constant fighter attack, both on the way over and their return. In the four operations, 156 lost seven crews, including a Wing Commander and two Squadron Leaders. Two months of operations had resulted in 25 aircraft lost - the equivalent to a three Flight squadron.

By the end of February it became known that the squadron would be moving to a new station. The last operation from Warboys took place on 1/2nd March when 18 Lancasters left for Stuttgart. It turned out to be a successful operation, with the Daimler-Benz motor factory being seriously damaged. Losses were light, but one aircraft failed to make it back to Warboys. Three days later 156 Squadron made the short journey to Upwood; the 18 months it had spent at the airfield had been a most costly and traumatic time.

Henceforth, Warboys would be a training station, its operational days over. The NTU became complete with the movement of its headquarters staff from Upwood. Early in March 1944 it was joined by No 1655 (Mosquito) Training Unit from Marham, specially formed to train the two-man crews for the growing PFF Mosquito squadrons. It

*The fine stained glass window in St Mary Magdalene's church at Warboys.*

was commanded by Wing Commander J. R. G. 'Roy' Ralston, DSO, DFC, who would later command 139 Squadron. Besides Mosquitos, the Unit also used Airspeed Oxfords, the twin-engine advanced trainers familiarly known as 'Ox-boxes'. They had first flown in 1937, and most bomber pilots had trained on them. Their handling qualities were designed to be as close as possible to those experienced on heavier aircraft, though they were far easier to control. During the Unit's relatively short stay at Warboys it expanded into five Flights with specialist training in H2S and Oboe. It suffered several unfortunate accidents during the summer of 1944, with a sad loss of lives.

Perhaps the most tragic accident occurred in April when the Navigation Unit lost one of its most popular and talented pilots, Flight Lieutenant John L. Sloper, DFC Bar. He was killed in a Lancaster crash in Wales whilst on a cross-country flight. Sloper had joined 156 Squadron in May 1943 as a Sergeant pilot, and just before Christmas completed his tour. He was posted to the Unit to act as a trainer, like several of the squadron's tour-expired airmen. There is a memorial tablet to Sloper in the delightful church at Warboys.

During the summer of 1944 the main tarmac runway began to break up and required urgent remedial action. In October, Group Captain T. G. 'Hamish' Mahaddie, DSO, DFC, AFC, arrived to take over command of the station from another PFF airman, Group Captain John Searby, DSO, DFC. Mahaddie's enthusiasm and drive resulted in some improvements in the facilities at the airfield, most notably a swimming pool built 'in-house'! However, the days of the airfield were now numbered. In December the Mosquito unit moved away to Upper Heyford, leaving the Navigation Unit in sole occupation. The airfield was anything but quiet, though, as the Unit's strength had grown to 45 aircraft - Lancasters, Mosquitos and Oxfords, with the odd Hurricane detached from Bourn for fighter affiliation exercises.

Before the airfield was placed under care and maintenance at the end of 1945, two PFF Mosquito squadrons, Nos 128 and 571, arrived during the summer, and the latter was disbanded at Warboys. The airfield became a base for the Bloodhound air-defence system in 1960, with the crews living at nearby Upwood, but they were withdrawn at the end of 1963 and the airfield finally closed. There are two memorial stones in the village to the PFF units, and in St Mary Magdalene's church is a fine stained glass window in memory of 'The members of the Pathfinder Force 1942 - 1945'. It incorporates 156 Squadron's badge, and the words, 'If I spread my wings towards the morning your hand shall lead me.'

# 22
# WATERBEACH

Waterbeach was among the last permanent stations to be planned and developed before the Second World War, one of 16 airfields to be approved under the expansion of the RAF during the late 1930s. Of the three East Anglian airfields included in this final group (with Oakington and Swanton Morley), Waterbeach was the last to open on 11th January 1941. It was very much in the Fens, situated about six miles north-east of Cambridge alongside the A10 road to Ely. The site did not appear ideal, being only 17 feet above sea level, but the Air Ministry's surveyors had chosen well. The land was blessed with good drainage, and the airfield suffered far fewer problems with mud and surface water than others in the County.

The airfield had been allocated to No 3 Group of Bomber Command and, for the next ten months, it became the home of one of its premier squadrons. 99 (Madras Presidency) Squadron dated back to the First World War, and had been the first to receive Wellingtons in October 1938. Since the first week of the war it had operated from Newmarket Heath, making its first bombing raid in April 1940.

The squadron moved into Waterbeach in March, and lost its first aircraft on 9/10th April when 80 aircraft - Wellingtons, Hampdens, Whitleys and Stirlings - bombed Berlin. Three Wellingtons were lost, one of which failed to make it back to Waterbeach. It was captained by Squadron Leader D. C. Torrens, an ex-fighter pilot, and he and his crew were taken prisoner. On the same night another of the squadron's Wellingtons failed to return from Vegesack. Ten nights later a Wellington, returning from Cologne, collided with a barrage balloon over Harwich harbour. It burst into flames and crashed into the sea just offshore, with a complete loss of life.

In early March 1940, Bomber Command had been directed to concentrate its efforts on U-boat yards and the FW Kondor aircraft factories. As Winston Churchill stated, 'We must take the offensive against the U-boat and the Focke-Wulf wherever we can and whenever we can...the U-boat in the building yard or in dock must be bombed. The Focke-Wulf, and other bombers employed against our shipping, must be attacked in the air and in their nests.' Thus it was, on 29/30th April, that Mannheim, about 130 miles south of the Ruhr, was the target, and more specifically its important marine diesel engine plant. Of the 71-strong force despatched, only 15 crews managed to locate and bomb Mannheim, causing slight damage.

This operation highlighted the major problem that faced Bomber Command during the early war years - the identification of targets at night. Without the benefits of sophisticated navigational aids such as Gee or H2S, the crews navigated by 'dead or deduced reckoning'. This was basically a technique of calculating the aircraft's position by reference to its course and direction, in relation to the speed it had been travelling from a known point - its home base. Although the principle sounded simple in theory, it was prone to error, the margins of which became accumulative and increased the longer the flight lasted. The accuracy of the aircraft's magnetic compass and its air speed indicator could be at fault, and as the latter operated on the outside air pressure, this could vary quite considerably. Often the expected wind speeds were inaccurate, having a material effect on the navigator's pre-plotted course. The inaccuracy of the Command's bombing was starkly revealed by the famous Butt report published later in the year.

Just a single aircraft was lost on the Mannheim operation and it came from 99 Squadron. The crew had the misfortune to be attacked by a Junkers 88 just off the East Coast as they were almost home. Any losses were hard to bear, but for two crews to perish within sight of England was uncommonly bad luck. Later, in September, Pilot Officer G. S. Eccles was diverted to Mildenhall after a Cologne raid. He mistimed his first approach to the airfield and whilst the aircraft was on a second circuit it was shot down by a Junkers 88. Only one crew member survived.

The squadron had received a few Mark II Wellingtons at the end of March. This mark had first flown in May 1939 but its production was delayed as priority was given to the Mark ICs. It was powered by Merlin X engines, which gave some improvements in speed and service ceiling, and it was this mark that was modified to take the 4,000 pound ('Blockbuster' or 'Cookie') bomb. First used over Emden on 31st March, this became one of Bomber Command's main weapons for the rest of the war, ultimately used very effectively by the Mosquito force.

*Stirlings of 1651 CU in April 1942. (Imperial War Museum)*

During the year the airfield was one of 20 to be selected for an unusual experiment. There had been considerable concern at the Air Ministry about the number of aircraft that overshot the runways. Indeed, the so-called 'approved' runways' length left little margin for error. It was decided to trial arrestor gear - similar to that used on aircraft carriers, but more robust. The system effectively consisted of two steel cables, some 400 feet in length, which were stretched across the runway about 100 feet apart. They were connected to a hydraulic braking system set in a pit at the side of the runway, and six sets were installed to all three runways. The project was abandoned in the summer of 1943 on financial grounds, since it involved modifying all the Lancasters and Halifaxes and 'improved pilot training'!

The squadron lost 32 aircraft during 1941, and over a third went missing in just seven weeks during the autumn. On 28/29th September four Wellingtons failed to return from Frankfurt, two of which crashed in Suffolk. When Berlin was targeted, on 7/8th November, the squadron sent eight crews and not one managed to identify the target because of heavy cloud and severe icing. Three aircraft were lost over Germany. It was a harsh night for the Command with 21 aircraft missing (12.4%), all probably due to the heavy storms that were encountered. This would be the last time the German capital was bombed for almost 14 months.

Not a single sortie was flown by Bomber Command from 10th to 15th November because of severe weather, but on the 15/16th both Kiel and Emden were attacked. Two crews failed to return from Kiel. One Wellington bound for Emden returned early because of the weather; it crash-landed at Wilburton near the airfield but all the crew survived.

In the previous month the first Stirling Is had arrived at the airfield. These aircraft would become synonymous with Waterbeach for the next two years. No 26 Conversion Flight was formed in the month, followed by No 106 Flight in December, positive signs that Wellingtons were on their way out and the Group was changing to the four-engined bombers. Early in 1942 the two Flights merged to become No 1651 Conversion Unit, and another two Conversion Flights would appear during the year - Nos 15 and 214. Each would ultimately merge into the main Unit, with Waterbeach completely given over to conversion training.

99 Squadron was preparing for its move overseas, to India. On 3/4th January 1942 a crew went missing over Brest, and ten nights later the 43rd, and last, aircraft to be lost by the squadron in the European air war crash-landed near Honington airfield in Suffolk on return from Emden. Only one member of the crew was severely injured, but he had completed his 30 operations. In the previous two years and more, the squadron had mounted 228 bombing raids and had been in the forefront of the Command's nascent bombing offensive. It still carried on as a bomber squadron in the Far East, operating Liberators right up to VJ Day. There is a splendid propellor memorial to the squadron at Newmarket Heath racecourse.

Although solely devoted to training, Waterbeach's operational days were not quite over. During the summer of 1942, the trainee crews and their instructors were engaged in several operations. The first training Stirling was lost in action on the '1,000' raid to Bremen on 25/26th June. Actually 'only' 960 aircraft took part, but never before and never again would Bomber Command put up such a mixed force. Ten different bombers were in action on the night - Whitleys, Hampdens, Wellingtons, Stirlings, Manchesters, Lancasters, Halifaxes, Blenheims, Bostons and four Mosquitos! The operation also brought the Command's heaviest losses of the war so far - 48 aircraft.

Sadly, on the Unit's next operational outing to Hamburg on 28/29th July, four Stirlings were lost. Two experienced pilots, Pilot Officer G. C. Bayley, DFC, and Flight Lieutenant D. A. Parkins, DFC, were killed along with another 23 crewmen, and five were taken prisoner. On

*A Lancaster II of 514 Squadron. (Imperial War Museum)*

13/14th September, No 15 Conversion Flight, which had arrived from Wyton in May, lost a Stirling after a Bremen operation. It crash-landed at Feltwell in Norfolk due to loss of power in three of its engines, but all the crew escaped unharmed.

Besides these operational losses, a number of aircraft were written off in a variety of training accidents - 30 in 1942, with a marked improvement in the following year when 16 were lost. In September 1943 the station became the headquarters for No 33 Base, with the nearby airfield at Witchford coming under its control, and soon Waterbeach would resume as an operational station. On 20th November the Conversion Unit left for Wratting Common, to be replaced three days later by a Lancaster Conversion Unit, No 1678, from Foulsham in Norfolk.

On the same day most of the personnel of 514 Squadron also moved in. The squadron had only been formed on 1st September with Lancaster IIs, a rather rare version of the famous bomber of which only 300 were produced. 514 Squadron became operational in November, and on the evening of its move the aircrews left Foulsham on their first Berlin operation. All returned safely to land at Waterbeach. In another four Berlin missions that year the squadron lost four Lancasters, one being forced to ditch in the North Sea due to heavy battle damage, but all the crew were rescued.

For such a celebrated bombing Group, No 3 now found itself in a rather invidious position. It had been 'caught out' operating mainly Stirling squadrons, an aircraft which, on Air Chief Marshal Harris's orders, was being phased out of the main force and relegated to other tasks - mine-laying and V1 rocket sites. The Group would not become a major strike force until its squadrons were re-equipped with Lancasters, but their conversion was slow. At the end of 1943 there were only two Lancaster squadrons in the Group - 514, and 115 at Witchford.

January 1944 was almost exclusively devoted to Berlin operations (six), but with the inclusion of the first major RAF raids on Brunswick and Magdeburg. Like all the main force squadrons the crews at Waterbeach had a break from operations for the first two weeks of February before the battles over Stuttgart (three), Frankfurt (twice), Schweinfurt, Augsburg and Essen. The last major Berlin raid was mounted on 24/25th March. In 15 raids on the German capital, 514 Squadron had lost seven aircraft, which was the lowest in No 3 Group and near enough the best record in the whole of the Command. The squadron had, however, suffered heavier losses over other German targets.

Its worst night came on 30/31st March when the target was Nuremberg. This operation, codenamed Grayling, proved to be Bomber Command's biggest disaster of the war. A 'maximum effort' was called for and finally 795 crews took part, with 514 Squadron despatching 19 Lancaster IIs. A couple of these were loaded with massive 8,000 pound bombs, in the bomb bays specially modified to take this weapon. The round trip was about 1,300 miles and of some seven hours duration. It turned out to be a nightmare journey.

The crews soon found out what kind of operation it would be, as close to the Belgian border they faced severe and concentrated fighter attacks right up to and over the target area. Eighty-two aircraft were shot down on the outward flight. The city was covered with heavy cloud and a strong cross-wind greatly hampered accurate marking. The subsequent bombing was far from effective; about one sixth of the force bombed Schweinfurt, some 50 miles to the north-east.

The total losses on the night were 95 aircraft (12%), when the average loss-rate for 1944 was 1.7%! Five hundred and forty-five airmen were killed, a tragedy for Bomber Command on a grand scale. 514 Squadron lost four Lancasters to night-fighters. One of the crews, led by Pilot Officer G. S. Hughes, DFC, was on its 19th operation. Two other Lancasters crash-landed, one at the airfield and the other near

*Lancaster IIs of 514 Squadron at Waterbeach.*

Sawbridgeworth in Hertfordshire. Another badly damaged Lancaster survived five separate fighter attacks and its Australian pilot, Pilot Officer D. A. Woods managed to bring it back safely to Woodbridge. It was a bitter blow for the squadron to endure, 7.5% of their total losses of the war sustained on a single operation.

During the next few months the crews' attentions were mainly directed to French railway yards at Laon, Rouen, Tergnier, Chambly, Le Mans and Angers. Chambly, a major railway depôt and repair yard for northern France, was attacked on 1/2nd May, by 120 aircraft, mainly Lancasters, and marked by Oboe Mosquitos. The resultant bombing was quite devastating, with over 500 high explosives falling inside the railway depôt, putting it out of action for almost two weeks. No 33 Base had sent over half the Lancaster force (56) and only one H2S Lancaster from 514 Squadron was lost.

As D-Day approached, the coastal batteries along the Channel coast were attacked, with those in the Pas de Calais coming in for special attention. On the night of D-Day, No 3 Group's squadrons were detailed to bomb the gun positions at Ouistrehem, with 514 Squadron sending out 21 Lancasters. The following night it attacked the road junction at Lisieux, about 25 miles east of Caen, and then the V1 rocket sites occupied the crews until 28th August. By now the squadron had begun to receive Mark I and III Lancasters. The latter were powered by American Packard Merlin engines, adding about 1,500 feet to its ceiling and a minimal increase in speed.

In August 1944, 514 became a 'proper' squadron when HM The King authorised its official badge. The design was a cloud pierced by a sword, to signify the squadron's main function as a G-H equipped blind-bombing unit. In its very first operation, in November 1943, G-H had been trialled over the Mannesman steel works at Düsseldorf with moderate success, but its general use was postponed until a more powerful G-H force could be assembled.

By the late summer Air Vice-Marshal R. Harrison, AOC of No 3 Group, had such a force at his command, with almost one third of his Lancasters being equipped with the accurate device. The Group proceeded to develop into a most effective and destructive bomber force, mounting many daylight precision raids with the Group's Lancasters bombing through clouds and 514's crews spearheading the assault, its G-H Lancasters prominently marked on their tail fins with yellow stripes. Because they operated mainly in daylight, they were escorted by Mustangs and Spitfires and losses were minimal.

The daylight operation against Bonn on 18th October demonstrated the effectiveness of the G-H force, when much of the town centre was destroyed for the loss of a single aircraft. Neuss, Essen, Leverskusen, Bottrup, Solingen, Homberg and Dortmund (all oil targets) were attacked in the following two months. However, the G-H force was limited to within about 250 miles of the ground beacon stations, although some had now been established in France and Belgium. As a trial, the railway junction at Fulda in central Germany, some 160 miles from the frontier, was attacked on 26th November, although it was beyond the range of G-H. The operation proved to be not too successful with very scattered bombing. The crews continued to attack Ruhr targets in the New Year but were also engaged in the Dresden and Chemnitz operations in February.

The squadron's last operation of the war left Waterbeach on 24th April 1945, when 13 Lancasters bombed Bad Oldersloe. All returned safely. During the first week of May, like so many other squadrons, the crews were engaged in dropping supplies to the Dutch, and they also found themselves dropping unwanted incendiary bombs into the North Sea! After mounting 218 bombing raids and dropping over 14,600 tons of bombs, 514 Squadron finished its rather short war, and was disbanded in August 1945. Waterbeach was passed over to No 47 Group of Transport Command and the first Liberators landed at the airfield.

The days of RAF Waterbeach have long since passed and the airfield is now occupied by the 39th Battalion of the Royal Engineers. There is a small wartime museum just inside the main gates which, at the time of writing, is being refurbished and can only be visited by prior appointment.

# 23
# WITCHFORD

This was a wartime RAF station, pure and simple, opening in June 1943 and closing less than three years later. Its brief, but not inconsequential, wartime existence has not passed unregarded. The road leading into the industrial estate which occupies part of the airfield site is called Lancaster Way, after the numerous Lancasters that flew from Witchford during the last 18 months of the war. The men based there during this period have not been forgotten either, because nearby is a fine memorial to 115 Squadron, standing on what was once a runway. This famous squadron fully deserves to be remembered, as it waged a long, arduous and costly war.

The airfield was situated about two miles to the south-west of Ely and allocated to No 3 Group, becoming a sub-station of No 33 Base. It was not until the third week of July 1943 that its first operational squadron arrived, No 196, which had previously been operating Wellington Xs from Leconfield, Yorkshire under the aegis of No 4 Group. The crews were in the process of converting to Stirling IIIs, perhaps a little belatedly considering that the aircraft was nearing the end of its life as a bomber.

The first Stirling was lost on 24th August when it ditched in the sea some 70 miles off the Danish coast, whilst engaged in an air-sea rescue search. The unfortunate crew now found themselves at the other end of the search and were a trifle lucky to be picked up by a Danish fishing boat, which had seen the aircraft come down. All of the crew were saved and had to spend the rest of the war in a POW camp.

The Stirlings left for a raid on Berlin on 31st August/1st September and one was shot down over Holland on its return. Four of the crew survived but one of the fatalities, Sergeant C. P. Pierce, RCAF, was only 18 years old, and the youngest navigator in Bomber Command as well as one of the youngest airmen to be killed in action during 1943.

Five nights later Mannheim, along with Ludwigshafen, was attacked. Eight out of the 111 Stirlings taking part were lost (7.2%). One came from Witchford and another, flown by Squadron Leader D. M. Edmundson, had one of its engines shot away by flak. Edmundson managed to nurse it back to Witchford and accomplish a crash-landing without any injuries. It was said that he had steered the Stirling through the London balloon barrage, flying at less than 2,000 feet, as well as attracting some attention from 'friendly' AA batteries!

In the following week (the 16/17th) Modane, close to the French/ Italian border and a major rail junction, was the target for a PFF-led force. The town was situated in a steep valley on the edge of the French Alps, and it proved difficult to mark accurately with the result that the bombing was rather ineffective. One crew failed to return to Witchford. Their aircraft had been heavily damaged by flak and finally crashed in northern France near Caen. Bomber Command returned to the target about two months later with greater success.

During September a new Stirling squadron was formed at Witchford - No 513 - under the command of Wing Commander G. E. Harrison, DFC, but it was disbanded in December without ever becoming operational. There was no doubt that Stirlings were now rather passé as a main force bomber. In fact, 196's last bombing raid was mounted on 8/9th October when seven Stirlings were despatched to Bremen. Three aircraft aborted and one of these ditched in the North Sea off the Norfolk coast with all the crew being rescued. From now on the crews were either engaged on 'gardening' or mine-laying, and two crews left Witchford for the last time on 10/11th November to mine the Deodars (Bordeaux) area. Before the month was out the Stirlings had moved away to Leicester East and No 38 Group of Transport Command, to be engaged on transport and glider-towing duties.

In advance of the formation of No 100 (Bomber Support) Group on 3rd December, there was a general rearrangement of airfields in East Anglia as a result of the decision to concentrate the Group's squadrons in Norfolk. Thus Little Snoring airfield, which had only opened in August, was transferred out of No 3 Group and its premier Lancaster squadron, No 115, moved into Witchford on 26th November. It was a First World War bomber squadron that reformed at Marham in June 1937, and from there 115 had commenced its war with Wellingtons. From October 1939 it operated virtually continuously as a front-line bomber squadron right up to VE Day, mounting more Wellington raids than any other squadron in Bomber Command and suffering the heaviest losses in the process.

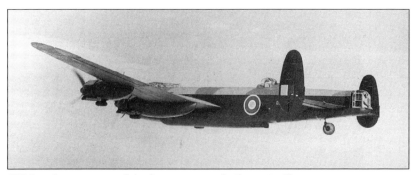

*115 Squadron was one of the few to operate the Lancaster II.*

During August 1941 it was entrusted with the first operational trials of GEE, and in February 1943 it began to give up its trusty Wellingtons to receive Lancasters - the rare Mark IIs. They were transferred from 61 Squadron, which had conducted the first service trials with the new mark. The IIs were powered by Hercules engines rather than Merlins and were produced by Armstrong Whitworth instead of A. V. Roe. They were slightly slower with a lower service ceiling and a smaller bomb load, but at least they could carry the 8,000 pound bomb.

The crews were delighted with their 'fine aircraft...able to penetrate to the most distant as well as the most heavily defended targets with a man-sized bomb-load and come back with good photographic evidence'. Also, their loss rate was far better than those in the Group's Stirling squadrons. Along with the Group's other Lancaster II squadron at Waterbeach, 115 pioneered the G-H operations that would prove so effective in late 1944.

The crews had already been blooded over Berlin whilst serving at Little Snoring, so it was no surprise that their first operation from Witchford should be to the 'Big B'. One Lancaster went missing on the night and by the end of the year another three crews would fall over Berlin. However, the squadron dropped the first 8,000 pound bombs on the German capital on 2/3rd December 1943. Certainly, the squadron paid dearly for Air Chief Marshal Harris's Berlin offensive and lost four crews in the final operation on 24/25th March 1944. In 19 raids, 259 Lancaster IIs were despatched with 21 missing (8%) - the highest loss of any Lancaster squadron in Bomber Command. 115 Squadron was a good example of the make-up of bomber crews at the end of 1943. Although the majority were British crews, there was more than a fair sprinkling of Australian, New Zealand and Canadian airmen.

*A Lancaster III being bombed up with an 8,000 pound bomb.*

The squadron had been made up to three Flights in November, but it was only able to muster ten Lancasters for the tragic Nuremburg raid on 30/31st March 1944. Sadly, two crews failed to return and one was on their first operation. Perhaps one reason for the squadron's short-fall was that it was exchanging its Mark IIs for 'normal' Lancaster Is and IIIs. They took them out on their first operation to the Lille/Deliverance railway yards on 9/10th April, but continued to operate a mixed force until the beginning of May when the Mark IIs left Witchford for the last time, which was the most successful operation to the railway yards at Chambly.

Ten nights later (19/20th), the Le Mans railway yards were successfully attacked by a 100-plus force of Lancasters. One of the squadron's aircraft was lost on this mission. Its most famous Lancaster I, ME803 *L for Love*, arrived at Witchford during May and was attached to C Flight. It proved to be a most durable aircraft, despite being damaged several times by flak. The aircraft seemed to live on borrowed time and completed 100 operations eleven months later.

In April, two Mark IIs had been lost in most unfortunate circumstances. Early in the morning of the 19th, the crews were returning from a successful operation over Rouen and were in the holding circuit, which merged with that of nearby Mepal and was used by both squadrons. Suddenly a solitary Me 410 joined the circuit and in a matter of seconds two Lancasters had been shot down. This twin-engined fighter/bomber had entered the Luftwaffe in April 1943, and was the Luftwaffe's closest equivalent to the Mosquito - a fast, heavily-armed night intruder, which could operate at high or low altitudes with equal facility. Me 410s had caused considerable problems over East Anglia from the summer of 1943.

The month of June 1944 was a very intense time for all bomber crews, and it proved rather costly for 115 Squadron. Coastal batteries were attacked on three consecutive nights immediately before D-Day, and on the next night (6/7th) the squadron lost the only aircraft shot down over Lisieux. For the next four nights French railway targets were detailed. The first were the railway yards at Massey-Palaiseau to the north of Paris. Seventeen Lancasters were lost on this night along with eleven Halifaxes (8.3%), mostly to night-fighters. It was a costly night for Bomber Command, and more so for 115 Squadron as six of the Lancasters came from Witchford. Another crew went missing about a week later over the rail centre at Valenciennes. However, the crews had been involved in a most successful Oboe-led daylight operation to the Nordstern synthetic oil plant at Gelsenkirchen, a major producer of aviation fuel. Such was the accuracy and ferocity of the bombing that production was halted for several weeks.

The last ten days of June saw V1 rocket sites becoming a priority, and on the 24/25th another Lancaster was lost over Rimeux. The Luftwaffe night-fighters struck with a vengeance. They operated closely and successfully with the searchlight batteries and managed to bring down 22 Lancasters, but the Halifaxes returned unscathed, which was quite unusual as normally the Halifax squadrons suffered heavier losses.

The month's operations concluded with a daylight raid on an important road junction at Villers Bocage, and although the bombing attack was made from about 4,000 feet only two aircraft were lost, neither from Witchford. Nevertheless, 115 Squadron had lost ten crews during June, the equivalent to more than a Flight.

During August the squadron was involved in two impressive operations. On the 26/27th, Kiel was heavily bombed by a strong force of Lancasters (375) and considerable damage was sustained despite the fact that accurate marking had been hampered by the thick smoke screens put up by the German defences. Seventeen Lancasters failed to return, and unfortunately two came from 115.

Three nights later the port of Stettin, some 600 miles distant, was detailed for the second raid in the month. This port had been on the

Command's list of targets since September 1940 but because of the distance and the fact that it was out of the range of radar aids, it had only received its first major attack in January 1944. In the second raid, several vessels were either sunk or heavily damaged, and the town centre came in for some brutal treatment. It proved to be a relatively costly mission with 23 Lancasters missing, but only one crew failed to make it back to Witchford.

In October, C Flight of 115 Squadron was hived off to form the nucleus of a reformed squadron, No 195. This had previously been formed at Duxford in November 1942 as an Army support squadron equipped with Typhoons. The new squadron was able to send out ten Lancasters on 26th October to bomb the large chemical complex of I. G. Farben at Leverkusen. All the 105 Lancasters from No 3 Group returned safely. By November, 195 Squadron had moved away to Wratting Common.

It was in October 1944 that No 3 Group set in motion its powerful and very effective G-H force, when, on the 19th, the ancient city of Bonn was bombed. Oil targets in the Ruhr would now become the priority for this all-Lancaster force, though in the middle of December with the onset of the major German counter-offensive in the Ardennes, the G-H squadrons were diverted to railway targets, which were essential supply lines for the German forces. On the 16th (the day the battle commenced), the yards at Siegen were attacked by 108 Lancasters, but although the town was heavily damaged, the specific target escaped almost unscathed. There was just one Lancaster lost and this belonged to 115. The weather then closed in and it was not until three days later that the next operation could be mounted. This was on another railway junction, at Trier, which was just behind the front-line. It was bombed on three separate days. The most successful raid was on the 23rd when 153 Lancasters bombed through thick cloud - a potent demonstration of the excellence of G-H.

In the New Year the Group continued its strikes against the German oil industry interspersed with attacks on railway targets. Dortmund, Bochum, Wanne Eickel, Duisburg, Krefeld, Saarbrücken, Cologne and Neuss figured large during January 1945. All the attacks were conducted by day, well and strongly escorted by Fighter Command with very low losses. In the following month, 115 Squadron was engaged in most of Bomber Command's famous operations - Wiesbaden, Dresden, Chemnitz, and three raids on Wesel in the middle of the month, which left the town devastated and brought a generous message from General Montgomery, who considered it 'a

*A Lancaster being loaded with food supplies during Operation Manna. (Imperial War Museum)*

masterpiece of bombing'.

In the first week of April, 115 Squadron's crews gave a demonstration of low-flying to a gathering of Air Ministry officials and the Command's 'top brass'. They came over the airfield at a height of about 500 feet to drop small bomb canisters filled with food. This was to demonstrate how food drops could be made without the use of parachutes, which were then in short supply. This flying exercise was a prelude to Operation Manna, the airborne supply of food to starving people in western Holland. The local German Commander ultimately agreed to a truce to allow food supplies to be dropped at certain nominated airfields and on the racecourse at The Hague. The first Manna operation was mounted on 29th April when 115 led the Lancasters in over The Hague, and continued until 7th May. Over 2,800 Lancaster crews were involved in the operation, dropping some 6,600 tons of food, sweets and tobacco.

The squadron had completed its long war on 24th April with one of the finest records of service in Bomber Command – 678 operations during which over 7,750 Wellington and Lancaster crews had dropped more than 23,000 tons of bombs from five different airfields. This was

*The fine memorial to 115 Squadron at Witchford.*

the second highest number of sorties in Bomber Command, only surpassed by their near neighbours, 75 (NZ) Squadron at Mepal. 115 was the only squadron in Bomber Command to lose over 200 aircraft in action. On a more pleasant note, the crews were engaged in Operation Exodus, picking up Allied POWs from Juvincourt airfield from 10th to 12th May.

In September 1945 the squadron moved away to Graveley, and retained its Lancasters until late 1949 before converting to Lincolns. The airfield did not last so long, it was closed down in March 1946.

# 24
# WITTERING

Wittering is the most northerly airfield in the County and owes its origins to the First World War. From December 1916 it housed a Flight of the Home Defence Force, and was known as Stamford from the nearby town. After the war it was placed under care and maintenance until the summer of 1926 when the Central Flying School moved in from Upavon, completing its move in October. Since that time the airfield has been in continuous service and many famous aircraft have operated from there - Blenheims, Hurricanes, Spitfires, Beaufighters, Mosquitos, Canberras, Valiants, and Tornados. It was as 'the Home of the Harrier' that Wittering gained its most recent fame.

In September 1939, Wittering was Sector station in No 12 Group of Fighter Command with two squadrons in residence, Nos 23 and 213, operating Blenheim Ifs and Hurricane Is respectively. In October they were joined by a Spitfire squadron - No 610 (County of Chester). In 1940 Wing Commander Harry Broadhurst, DFC, AFC, the first of many famous wartime airmen to serve at Wittering, arrived as Station Commander. Never content to sit behind a desk, Broadhurst frequently flew with his squadrons. On 30th June, he led the 'Wittering Wing', two squadrons of Spitfires and Hurricanes, several months before the 'Wing concept' became such a contentious issue. Just before Christmas 1940, Broadhurst left to take over Hornchurch. He had a most distinguished service career, retiring in 1961 as a much decorated Air Chief Marshal.

Wittering was too far north to become directly involved in the Battle of Britain. Various squadrons left for action in the south, sometimes with the Duxford Wing, whilst others came for a rest and regrouping.

*Flying Officer A.V. Clowes, DFM, with his Hurricane of 1 Squadron at Wittering, October 1940. (RAF Museum)*

The only permanent residents were Blenheims of 23 Squadron, and its crews accounted for three enemy aircraft on 18/19th June 1940 for the loss of two aircraft. They did, at times, share the airfield with Spitfires of 266 (Rhodesia) Squadron, which returned to Wittering in September 1940 for a prolonged stay of almost ten months.

On 9th September, the Hurricanes of 1 Squadron arrived. This was one of the oldest RAF squadrons, first formed as a balloon unit in May 1912. The squadron had earlier served in France and had been fully engaged in the Battle of Britain from Tangmere and Northolt. Its leading pilot, Flying Officer Arthur Clowes, DFC, had at least eight victories to his name. Although the squadron moved back to Northolt at the end of the year, almost 30 years later it would return to Wittering to become the first to be equipped with the famous Hawker Siddeley Harrier VSTOL ('Jump Jet').

Since the early summer the small grassed airfield at Collyweston, just to the south-west of Wittering, had been used as a satellite, with several squadrons based at Wittering dispersing their aircraft there. After the departure of 23 Squadron, a detachment of Blenheims from 29 Squadron at Digby came down to act as night stand-bys. During the autumn of 1941 a second satellite airfield at King's Cliffe, about five miles to the south-west of Wittering, came into use by squadrons based at the parent station, which was moving inexorably towards becoming a specialist night-fighter station.

The heavy bombing raids during the autumn of 1940 highlighted the desperate need for a properly co-ordinated night defence system. Wittering was designated a sector control station, with its own radar stations at Orby and Lancroft in Lincolnshire, linked to the station's operations room. In late November, 25 Squadron arrived from Debden with the new night-fighter, the Bristol Beaufighter. Its crews had already claimed their first victory.

The Beaufighter was another wartime aircraft that owed its origins to a private venture. It was developed by the Bristol Aeroplane Company from its Beaufort torpedo bomber as a long-range fighter. A prototype flew in July 1939 and just twelve months later the first aircraft was delivered to the Fighter Interception Unit. From there it was rushed into service as a stop-gap and much needed night-fighter. The Beaufighter was then the only fighter capable of taking the heavy and rather cumbersome AI Mark IV radar set. It was immensely robust, with an armament of four Hispano cannons and six .303 machine guns, and a top speed in excess of 300 mph. It proved to be a most effective night-fighter, serving Fighter Command well until the arrival of the Mosquito, but perhaps its most successful wartime role was with Coastal Command as an anti-shipping strike aircraft.

In the middle of December 1940, the Hurricanes and Defiants of 151 Squadron arrived after a spell of night-fighting training at Bramcote. One of its pilots, Pilot Officer Richard P. Stevens DFC, became the most successful Hurricane night-fighter pilot in the service. Although operating without the advantage of AI radar, Stevens still managed to account for 14 enemy aircraft during 1941 with another six probables. On the night of January 15/16th, Stevens shot down both a Dornier 215 and Heinkel 111, only the third time a pilot had downed two enemy aircraft in one night. He later repeated the feat, gaining himself a Bar to his DFC. Stevens was killed in action on 15th December 1941, when attached to 253 Squadron at Manston. He was then an acting Flight Lieutenant and had been further decorated with the DSO.

One of the legendary wartime figures arrived to take over command of Wittering - Group Captain Basil Embry, DSO, DFC, AFC. Embry had not long returned to the country after being shot down over France leading his Blenheim squadron, and successfully evading capture. For the previous two months he had commanded Rochford in Essex, where he endeavoured to establish a night-fighter wing. Indeed, 151

*A Boston III modified with a Turbinlite and used by 1453 Flight.*

Squadron had been destined to be part of this wing. However, Embry was unconvinced of the suitability of the airfield for night-flying, and was also rather uncomplimentary about the qualities of the Defiant as a night-fighter! By December 1940 the project had been dropped, and he moved to Wittering to command its night-fighting force.

Wittering was still a grass airfield with a runway about 1,400 yards long, of which the last 150 yards, on the eastern boundary, 'sloped steeply to the Great North Road'. Embry was concerned about the number of accidents that had occurred, so he conceived a plan to extend the runway by joining it with the satellite airfield at Collyweston. The Air Ministry Works engineers came to look at his proposal, and they estimated that the work would take about nine months. In typical style Embry decided to complete the project 'in house'. He negotiated with the Marquess of Exeter, the landowner, to allow his land to be requisitioned providing the RAF purchased the potato crop that had already been planted! Within three weeks the work had been completed, including a flarepath made from locally purchased cable.

Wittering now boasted an extremely long and well lighted runway strip, and within a couple of months over 70 damaged aircraft had used the runway for emergency landings. This extended runway ultimately led to the completion of three Emergency Landing Grounds or 'Prangdromes' on the coast at Carnaby, Woodbridge and Manston, each provided with a single concrete runway 3,000 yards long and 250 yards wide.

The night-fighting squadrons achieved some modest success during

*A Spitfire of 266 Squadron at Wittering. Note the pre-war control tower. (RAF Museum)*

the spring of 1941. In the heavy raids suffered by Birmingham and Coventry in early April, they accounted for seven enemy aircraft on the 10/11th. The Spitfire IIbs of 266 Squadron were also getting into the action by flying 'Fighter Nights'. The Luftwaffe were well aware of the growing importance of the airfield's night-fighting force, as it was bombed on New Year's Day, followed by another attack in March and three consecutive raids in early May.

Two months later one of ten Turbinlite Flights in Fighter Command was formed at Wittering - No 1453. The concept was that a relatively large aircraft would be equipped with AI equipment operating under Ground Control Interception. It also carried a large searchlight in the nose. These aircraft would be accompanied by a single-seat fighter (normally a Hurricane), which would move into the attack once the enemy aircraft had been intercepted and illuminated with the searchlight. The flight was equipped with Douglas Havocs, and the first Turbinlite operation was mounted on 22nd October.

Some problems were experienced with this unusual method of night interception. Frequently, the Hurricanes lost touch with their Havocs in heavy cloud or bad visibility, and there were drawbacks in using the searchlights in bad weather. Although the flights were upgraded to squadrons in September 1942, all were disbanded early in 1943, and sadly there was little success to show for all the hard work and effort of their crews and fighter pilots.

When 266 Squadron returned from Martlesham Heath in October 1941, it was relegated to the satellite airfield at King's Cliffe. It was now operating Spitfire Vbs, which, powered by the new Merlin 45 engines, gave them a top speed of 374 mph. This was still inferior in performance to the Luftwaffe's FW 190s, which were beginning to appear in greater numbers. In the New Year the squadron moved down to Duxford and was replaced by 616 (South Yorkshire) Squadron, also flying Spitfires and commanded by a famous Battle of Britain pilot, Squadron Leader Colin Gray, DFC Bar. He was a New Zealand airman and ended the war with $27\frac{1}{2}$ victories.

This was just one of the several changes at Wittering. Group Captain Embry had been seconded to the Middle East as an adviser to the Desert Air Force, and the Beaufighters of 25 Squadron moved out to Northern Ireland. By the end of 1941 the Luftwaffe's heavy night raids were petering out, and it is interesting to note that during the whole of its night offensive the Luftwaffe lost about 600 aircraft (1.5%) - a rate that Bomber Command would have found more than acceptable!

The airfield was left with 151 as its only operational squadron, still equipped with Defiants and Hurricanes though it had been selected as one of two squadrons to be equipped with the new Mosquito II night-fighters. In March 1942 Group Captain Embry returned and he immediately urged the Air Ministry to supply his squadron with the scarce aircraft. He considered the Mosquito to be 'the finest aeroplane, without exception, that has been ever built in this country', and when he was in charge of No 2 Group of Bomber Command, he encouraged and authorised some of the daring and successful low-level Mosquito raids that so captured the imagination of the public. The first Mosquito arrived at the airfield on 6th April for A Flight and at the end of the month the first Mosquito sorties were mounted. The first success was on 24/25th June - two Dornier 217Es, followed a night later by a Heinkel 111.

Wittering and its satellite airfields had almost become a New Zealand enclave. The Commander of 151 Squadron, Wing Commander Irving S. Smith, DFC Bar, was a New Zealander and a most experienced pilot, who had served with the squadron since July 1940 and had claimed its first Mosquito victories. No sooner had Colin Gray's squadron left, in April, than it was replaced by the Hurricanes of 486, the second New Zealand fighter squadron to be formed. Three months later its first fighter squadron, 485, moved into King's Cliffe

248

*Bristol Beaufighter If, NG-F, of 604 Squadron.*

and would remain there, other than for breaks of detachment, until January 1943.

The sole RAF occupant of Wittering was 151 and its crews claimed their first victory of the New Year on 15/16th January - a Dornier 217E over Lincoln. For a short while the Mosquitos shared the airfield with P-47s of the 63rd Squadron of the 56th Fighter Group, which had recently moved into King's Cliffe.

In late March 1943 the Air Fighting Development Unit, along with its Enemy Aircraft Flight, arrived from Duxford, and used both Wittering and Collyweston. After almost two and a half years service at Wittering, 151 Squadron left for Colerne in Wiltshire at the end of April. Almost immediately it was replaced by a Beaufighter squadron, No 141, commanded by one of the most successful pilots of the Second World War, Wing Commander J. R. D. 'Bob' Braham, DSO, DFC. He was only 22 years old and in the words of a colleague, '[his] 100% dedication and commitment to the task, whatever it may be, set him apart from other people and lesser mortals.' When he was shot down over Denmark in June 1944, his total stood at 29 (mostly at night) confirmed victories.

The Beaufighter VIfs were higher powered and had a Vickers gun placed to the aft of the navigator's hatch. The crews were also engaged in trialling a new interception device, codenamed 'Serrate'. This electronic device enabled fighters to home in on the enemy's fighter radar emissions from as far away as 100 miles, and allied to AI MkVI produced accurate range indications. It was said to have gained its name from the serrated image portrayed on the screens.

During early June 1943, 141 Squadron was detached to Drem in Scotland for training exercises and when it returned to Wittering the crews began intruder raids over the Continent. The first one took place on the 14th and Braham, along with his regular AI operator, 'Sticks' Gregory, claimed a Me 110. The squadron became involved in the Peenemunde operation on 17/18th August. Braham led three Beaufighters ahead of the main bombing force and headed for northern Holland with the express purpose of tempting the Luftwaffe night-fighters into the air. The ploy succeeded, with Braham claiming two Me 110s. The other flight also made a kill, and all nine aircraft returned safely to Wittering.

Towards the end of their stay at the airfield the pilots began converting to Mosquitos, but with the establishment of No 100 (Special Duties) Group of Bomber Command in November, 141 Squadron was transferred into the Group and left for West Raynham in December.

The only operational aircraft using the airfield now were American fighters, P-38Hs (Lockheed Lightnings). They belonged to the 55th Squadron of the Eighth Air Force's 20th Fighter Group, based at nearby King's Cliffe. These were quite rare American fighters - at least in British skies - as the Eighth had only four P-38 Groups. It was a large twin-boom and twin-engined fighter, which had first seen the light of day back in 1937, but due to a prolonged development programme it had not come into service until 1941. The fighter was rather quick, about 410 mph at 25,000 feet, and heavily armed, but its great advantage was its range - with extra tanks it could exceed 600 miles. It was the first American fighter to fly over the German capital.

In April 1944, the Fighter Interception Unit arrived from Ford in Sussex. This had long been engaged in the development and trialling of new aircraft and various radar interception devices. Wittering was now the home for testing and experimental work, and it was no surprise that when Sir Roderic M. Hill, AOC-in-C of Fighter Command, proposed the establishment of a Central Fighter Establishment in August 1944, it should be first based at Wittering. This was really an amalgamation of the various training and development units into one centre of excellence for advanced fighter training, tactics and technical enhancements. The CFE was to have an important influence on service flying in the post-war years, but by February 1945 it had moved to Tangmere.

For a brief few weeks Mosquitos of 68 Squadron used the airfield, and when they departed for Coltishall at the end of the month, Wittering was transferred into No 21 Group of Flying Training Command. A year later the airfield returned to Fighter Command, ushering in a glorious era as a premier fighter station...but that is another story!

# 25

# WRATTING

# COMMON

This airfield was sited in the East Anglian Heights, and close to the boundary with Suffolk. At almost 400 feet above sea level it was not a particularly hospitable spot, especially in the winter months. It gained its first name, West Wickham, from the nearby village, and when it opened, in May 1943, the airfield was allocated as a sub-station of No 31 Base at Stradishall in Suffolk, under the control of No 3 Group. In those days that meant Short Stirling bombers.

It was 90 Squadron that arrived to occupy the airfield on the last day of May. This squadron had experienced a rather peripatetic wartime existence, serving at Upwood, Watton, West Raynham, Polebrook, Bottesford and latterly Ridgewell in Essex. It had been forced to move out of Ridgewell by the impending arrival of an Eighth Air Force Bomb Group (the 381st). Its wartime fame, until then, resided in the fact that it had been the only RAF squadron to be equipped with Flying Fortresses. Just 52 sorties had been flown and their operations were not cloaked in success. With this sad chapter behind it, the squadron had been operating Stirling Is and IIIs since January 1943 and its crews were well experienced, especially over the Ruhr and Berlin.

Bomber Command was deeply engaged in the Battle of the Ruhr when 90 moved into West Wickham, although the first crew to go missing in operations from the airfield was lost on 21/22nd June in a raid over Krefeld. This operation had been conducted in bright moonlight and the night-fighters took a heavy toll of the bomber force - 44 aircraft (6.3%) were shot down and nine of them were Stirlings. This night's operation ushered in an unfortunate period for the squadron because in just three raids it lost another five crews. Two went down over Mülheim on the following night, when this town was bombed for the first time, and although heavy damage was inflicted, 35 (6.2%) aircraft were lost.

Two nights later, Wuppertal was attacked for the second time in a matter of three weeks. Although on this operation the losses were slightly lower, ten out of 98 Stirlings were still lost, two of which came from 90 Squadron. On the 25/26th, the synthetic oil plant at Gelsenkirchen was attacked for the first time since 1941. The operation was not a great success as, unusually, the Oboe Mosquitos were inaccurate in their ground marking. Of the six Stirlings lost on the night, one came from West Wickham. In just five nights the squadron had lost 46 airmen in action, with only four surviving as prisoners of war.

Just a week later (3/4th July), the squadron experienced further losses on a mission to Cologne. Over 650 aircraft took part and substantial damage was inflicted on industrial buildings, which were mostly sited on the east bank of the Rhine. The Luftwaffe employed a new tactic on the night, which became known as the *wilde sau* or 'Wild Boar'. Hitherto, the German night-fighters had normally operated under strict radar ground control, attacking the bombers well in advance of the Ruhr targets. Now they appeared over the target area itself, with each fighter pilot operating individually using the light of the searchlights, RAF flares and the fires burning below to identify their targets. A new Jagdgeschwader, No 300, operating FW 190s was active for the first time and its pilots claimed twelve bombers. Actually, 30 aircraft were lost to a mixture of night-fighters and flak. Two Stirlings from 90 Squadron went missing and a third was written off when it overshot the runway on its return. One of the aircraft came down near Aalst in Belgium and the crew were buried locally; in 1992 the local historical society unveiled a memorial stone to them.

During July 1943 the squadron was engaged in the three devastating 'firestorm' raids on Hamburg in the last week of the month. Sixty-eight individual sorties were mounted for the loss of one aircraft, which was written off after a crash-landing at Stradishall. On the third raid (the 29/30th), one of the squadron's crews claimed the destruction of a Me 110.

The squadron's performance over Hamburg was one of the best in No 3 Group, and certainly, at this time, the crews felt a great sense of pride and achievement. They considered that they belonged to, 'a Rolls-Royce squadron as opposed to the mass produced Lancs and Hallies'! Sadly, the losses sustained by these Stirling squadrons over

*Stirlings of 90 Squadron line up at Wratting Common, August 1943. (Imperial War Museum)*

Berlin in the coming months would somewhat belie that view. In the devastating attack on the Krupps factory at Essen on 25/26th July, the squadron lost a Flight Commander, Squadron Leader J. Dugdale, DFC. His Stirling was lost over the North Sea and the bodies of three of the crew were washed ashore near Great Yarmouth.

Nevertheless the month ended with one of the most successful operations of 1943. A small force of 273 bombers attacked Remscheid on the southern edge of the Ruhr, a target that had not previously attracted Bomber Command's attention. The ground marking by only nine Oboe Mosquitos was nigh on perfect, a copybook exercise. Although only a relatively small tonnage of bombs was dropped (870 tons), untold damage was inflicted on the town. It was estimated that about 80% was destroyed, and industrial production virtually stopped for three months and really never recovered from the bombardment. Fifteen aircraft were lost, with eight Stirlings in this total, of which one belonged to 90 Squadron. The average age of the crew was 22 years. This operation marked the end of the Command's Battle of the Ruhr.

August brought a change of name for the airfield. There had obviously been some confusion with the name of another airfield so, from the 21st, it was renamed Wratting Common. During this month the crews were engaged over Hamburg (again), Nuremberg, Turin (twice) and Peenemunde; in this famous operation the squadron despatched 15 Stirlings, all of which returned safely. The two Berlin operations mounted in the month proved to be far different affairs. Thirty-eight crews took part and three failed to return (7.9%), although it should be pointed out that this loss-rate was considerably less than other Stirling squadrons in the Group. One of the crews in the first operation ditched in the North Sea not far from the German coast, but six of the crew survived for seven days in their dinghy before being picked up by a German vessel.

There was some relief from further casualties until the last ten days of September when missions to Hanover and Mannheim brought more losses in their wake. On the 22/23rd three aircraft were lost, one shortly after take-off, a second shot down by a night-fighter near the target area, and a third crash-landing at Lakenheath on return. There was a similar incident five nights later when a damaged Stirling crashed into trees near Horseheath, a couple of miles south-west of the airfield. Sadly, five of the crew were killed, including the pilot, Squadron Leader M. I. Freeman.

The squadron was shortly to pack its bags once again - it was the most travelled squadron in Bomber Command. Before the crews left Wratting Common for Tuddenham in Suffolk on 13th October, six were killed and another injured in a landing accident at the airfield.

It would be another month and more before the airfield once again resounded to the thunder of Stirlings, when No 1651 Heavy Conversion Unit moved in from Waterbeach on 20th November. The Unit had been in the business of training crews for a long time - almost two years. These Conversion Units filled the gap between the training of crews at Operational Training Units, where all the aircraft were twin-engined, and operational squadrons. The course now lasted five weeks, with a week at a ground station followed by at least 40 hours of flying, covering such aspects as bombing, air firing, fighter affiliation, navigation and radar training.

By the end of 1943 there were 20 such Units operating, each carrying a complement of 36 aircraft. Most were equipped with Halifaxes and Lancasters with just three operating Stirlings. Should the crews be posted to one of the few Lancaster squadrons in No 3 Group, they were sent on a twelve hour course at No 3 Lancaster Finishing School at Feltwell in Norfolk. The training commitment within Bomber Command was considerable, especially during the winter of 1943/4 when the Berlin operations were taking their toll of aircrews. It was estimated that almost 20% of the flying time in the Command was

*Lancasters of 195 Squadron operated from Wratting Common from November 1944 onwards.*

devoted to conversion training with hundreds of tour-expired and experienced pilots and crewmen acting as instructors.

The Conversion Unit remained at Wratting Common until 20th November 1944 when it moved away to Woolfax Lodge. Just eight days earlier, the only Lancaster squadron to operate from the airfield arrived from Witchford, No 195, which had reformed there at the beginning of October. It was one of six new Lancaster squadrons to be reformed in that month and was the penultimate squadron to join the Group's G-H force. The crews had already become operational, at first using some of 115's Lancasters in their early sorties, and shortly after their arrival at Wratting Common 195 became a three-flight squadron.

In its relatively short wartime existence as a bomber squadron, 87 bombing raids were mounted, over 1,380 Lancaster sorties, with the majority leaving from Wratting Common. Only 14 (1%) were lost in action, but 195 Squadron had entered operations at a time when No 3 Group had become a potent strike force. In the last two weeks of November the Group's Lancasters attacked nine targets, all but one by day, with 15 aircraft being lost (1.08%). The oil plant at Homberg caused the downfall of eight crews on two successive days - the 21st and 22nd. The following month started even more impressively with Dortmund, Oberhausen, Hamm and Osterfeld being bombed by day and the Leuna oil refinery at Merseberg in eastern Germany on the night of 6/7th December. Just two Lancasters failed to return from these operations.

The daylight raid on 12th December proved to be rather costly, at least compared with normal operational losses. The Ruhrstahl steel-works and the Mannesmann tube factory at Witten were the targets for 140 Lancasters. Witten was situated to the south-west of Dortmund and this would be its first major raid of the war. All went well until the force was close to the target area when a strong Luftwaffe force suddenly appeared, and in the fierce attack eight Lancasters were shot down (5.7%), the Group's heaviest loss with its G-H force. The main targets escaped unscathed, most of the bombing being scattered across the town.

195 Squadron had despatched 18 Lancasters. Three were shot down, and another badly damaged aircraft force-landed in Belgium. Of the remaining 14 crews, eleven were diverted to other airfields on their return because of the low cloud and mist that closed down their home base. It had been a traumatic day, not soon forgotten at Wratting Common. Three months later (18/19th March), Bomber Command successfully destroyed the steelworks. From then until the end of the year oil targets in the Ruhr along with railway yards at Gremburg, Coblenz, Trier and Vohwinkel were attacked by the Group with the loss, in total, of one fewer Lancaster than the ill-fated Witten operation.

In the New Year the Group's Lancasters went from strength to strength. In January 1945, eleven daylight operations were mounted against Ruhr oil targets and railway yards for a loss-rate of 0.82%. The following month another ten daylight raids were completed for the loss of ten Lancasters (0.69%). No other Group in Bomber Command managed to operate so effectively and with such low fatalities; the average number of Lancasters taking part in these operations was 145. It was certainly a most impressive performance. During these two months there were also night operations to Neuss, Munich, Duisburg, Dortmund, and the famous raids on Dresden and Chemnitz.

By the second week of March the G-H force invariably operated by day, with the notable exceptions of Kiel on the 9/10th and 13/14th April, and the following night when the army barracks at Potsdam to the south-west of Berlin was targeted. This was the RAF's last major raid on a German city and the first time that the heavies had returned to the Berlin area since March 1944. Only one of the 500 Lancasters was lost - what a change from twelve months earlier.

Like most of the Group's squadrons, 195 launched its last bombing operation on 24th April when 21 Lancasters left to bomb Bad Oldersloe. The crews then became engaged on Operation Exodus - the pick-up of British prisoners of war recently liberated from their camps. In total,

*The memorial at Wratting Common.*

the Command made 470 flights and returned with over 75,000 prisoners. The squadron's final operation left Wratting Common on 7th May when 16 Lancasters departed with food supplies for the Dutch, which were dropped on The Hague racecourse. In the middle of August 1945 the squadron was disbanded and eight months later the airfield was closed.

Although the airfield had a relatively short operational life, it has not been forgotten. On 28th May 1989 Air Marshal Sir Ivor Broom, KCB, CBE, DSO, DFC, AFC, unveiled a small memorial stone at the side of an unclassified road on the site of the old airfield. It is dedicated to the memory of members of 'XC Squadron, 1651 HCU and 195 Squadron'.

# 26
# WYTON

Wyton has been a major RAF station since July 1936. Its wartime fame rested first with Bristol Blenheims, then it became the home for XV Squadron's Stirlings, before accommodating the initial headquarters of the Pathfinder Force and several of its squadrons of Lancasters and Mosquitos. It is perhaps fitting that this celebrated airfield should bring this story of the County's main wartime airfields to a close, as Wyton was the scene of the first operational sortie of the Second World War.

The Blenheim originated as a private venture at the behest of Lord Rothermere, the newspaper proprietor, and he magnanimously presented the first aircraft, which he named *British First*, to the Air Council. The light bomber or Mark I came into service with 114 Squadron at Wyton in March 1937, and the RAF thought that they had a world-beater on their hands. It was capable of out-pacing the current fighters. In the following year a new version was developed, the so-called 'long-nosed' or Mark IV. Its Mercury XV engines gave it a maximum speed in excess of 260 mph, it carried 1,000 pounds of bombs and was armed with five .303 machine guns.

The Blenheim IVs proved to be doughty and pugnacious aircraft, greatly admired by their crews. Their brave exploits in the early war years have become legendary, when despite fearsome losses they prosecuted their daylight low-level raids over the near Continent. Although the aircraft was considered, 'slow, under-armed and totally unsuitable', they continued to operate as bombers until August 1942, with over 70 squadrons operating Mark IVs.

In 1939 both Wyton squadrons were equipped with IVs, but by December 114 and 139 Squadrons had moved to France. They were replaced by XV and 40 Squadrons, which had returned from France to convert to Blenheims. Little action was seen until May 1940 when both squadrons were engaged on the 10th; 40 Squadron lost five aircraft from a raid on Ypenburg airfield, with a sixth being written-off on its

*Blenheim IVs of 40 Squadron at Wyton, the summer of 1940. (Imperial War Museum)*

return to Wyton. In a matter of eight days the squadron lost two Commanding Officers, Wing Commanders E. C. Barlow and J. C. Llewellyn. During Operation Dynamo - the Dunkirk evacuation - the crews were engaged daily and by 3rd June, No 2 Group had lost 56 Blenheims in action with another ten lost to severe battle damage. There was a fearful loss of experienced crews.

The Blenheim squadrons returned to road and rail targets in France, as well as oil refineries in the Ruhr – or at least, when cloud cover gave them adequate protection (that was the theory!). In August and September, when the Battle of Britain raged overhead, the squadrons attacked airfields in France and the Low Countries both by day and night. Early in September the night campaign against invasion barges in the Channel ports began in earnest and continued throughout the month. The final Blenheim operation was mounted on 29th October 1940 when fuel tanks near Hamburg were bombed. Wyton and its squadrons were transferred into No 3 Group on 1st November, and their conversion to Wellingtons was not completed until the middle of December.

XV Squadron entered a different kind of warfare when its Wellingtons went operational on 21/22nd December over Bremen. On the same night, 40 Squadron attacked Antwerp. 40 lost its first crew for four months when one failed to return from Wilhelmshaven on 16/17th January 1941, before moving into Alconbury in February.

XV did not operate Wellingtons for very long, because in April the first Stirlings arrived at Wyton - the second squadron to receive the new four-engined bomber. One hundred and seventy-three Wellington sorties were made for the loss of three aircraft. Along with No 7, it became one of the famous Stirling squadrons, mounting more operations (over 350) than any other squadron.

Their first operation with Stirlings was to Berlin, but only three out of the ten crews managed to locate the target. It was over Berlin that Wing Commander H. R. Dale went missing; he had been in charge since December. His replacement, Wing Commander P. B. B. Ogilivie, DSO, DFC, arrived five days later (16th May) and remained until the end of the year.

During July 1941, the Stirlings were used uniquely in several Circus operations, which were daylight raids to specific targets under heavy fighter escort, with the real intention of attracting the Luftwaffe into the air. Hitherto, Blenheims had been used. In May one famous pilot and Blenheim veteran, Squadron Leader Stewart Menaul, DFC, AFC, completed his first tour and left for Group headquarters. He later returned to command the squadron.

The squadron operated perhaps the most famous Stirling - N6086 LS-F *MacRobert's Reply*, which had been provided by Lady MacRobert in memory of her two sons killed on active service with the RAF. The aircraft carried the crest and badge of the MacRobert family and survived twelve operations until it was heavily damaged in January 1942. It served in a Conversion Unit until March 1943. A second Stirling, W7531 LS-F, also bore the name, and this aircraft was lost whilst laying mines in the Danish Sound on 17/18th May 1942. All but one of the nine-man crew were killed when the aircraft crashed in Denmark after being severely damaged by flak. The pilot was Squadron Leader J. C. Hall, DFC, MiD, and one of the crew, Flying Officer J. F. Ryan, a New Zealander serving with the RCAF, had been visiting Wyton and, although not a member of XV Squadron, went along for the ride! In the winter of 1941/2 the squadron, along with No 7, was engaged in the trials of Trinity, which was a rudimentary form of Oboe.

The '1,000' raids of the early summer of 1942 engaged every heavy squadron crew in the Command, and on the first, mounted against Cologne on 30/31st May, XV was one of the lead squadrons. When Wing Commander J. C. MacDonald, DFC, AFC, and Squadron Leader

R. S. Gilmour, DFC, took off from Wyton at 10.30 pm, they were the first to leave on this historic operation. At 47 minutes past midnight, the two Stirlings were over the target, and although they were eight minutes early the pilots saw no reason to tarry and dropped their incendiaries on the aiming point - the Neumarkt in the centre of the old town - to act as a beacon for the following armada. The early squadrons fared well, and XV returned unscathed. During July, when Essen was attacked five times and Emden and Bremen each sustained four raids, the squadron lost only three Stirlings.

The squadron's long sojourn at Wyton was nearing its end; on two successive nights, 11th and 12th August, the ancient town of Mainz brought XV Squadron's operations from Wyton to a close. A Stirling was lost on each night; two crews that would not make the move to Bourn on the following day.

The airfield had been chosen to house the headquarters staff of the new Pathfinder force, along with two of its original squadrons. On 7th August, 109 Squadron moved in from Stradishall with a mixture of Wellingtons, Ansons and the odd Mosquito. For the previous two years it had been engaged on the development of various radio counter-measures as well as radar aids, especially Oboe. It was commanded by Wing Commander H. E. 'Hal' Bufton, the younger brother of the officer who was so influential in the formation of the Pathfinders. Bufton had been involved in the early research work of the Wireless Investigation Development Unit that ultimately provided the nucleus of the reformed squadron.

The squadron's task was to introduce Oboe into the PFF, and for the next three months its crews logged many hours ironing out the technical problems and perfecting techniques, whilst waiting patiently for more precious Mosquitos to arrive, all under the close and watchful eye of Group Captain Bennett.

The heavy PFF squadron, No 83, arrived on the 15th from Scampton, where it had been stationed since 1938. It had been 'loaned' by No 5 Group, and was the only Lancaster squadron in the nascent force. It had been operational since the beginning of the war. One of its airmen had been awarded a VC in September 1940 and the crews had only recently exchanged their unsuccessful Manchesters for Lancaster Is. One of these was destined to become the most famous of the war - R5868 *Queenie*. It flew over 60 operations from Wyton before moving to Bottesford, where with 467 (RAAF) Squadron, it became known as *S for Sugar*, finally completing in excess of 130 operations. The Lancaster is now on display at the RAF Museum at Hendon.

*Lancaster R5868 completed in excess of 60 operations from Wyton. It is now in the RAF Museum at Hendon. (via J. Adams)*

The squadron was quickly into its PFF role. Two crews were lost over Frankfurt on the 24/25th, and another went missing on 10/11th September on the Düsseldorf operation when 'Pink Pansies' were used for the first time. These were rather crude target marker bombs - chemicals and inflammable material packed in 4,000 pound bomb casings - that produced a coloured incendiary to burn on the ground as a marker. Italian targets were attacked on eleven nights during the late autumn; Genoa received six raids, Turin four, and Milan was bombed on 24/25th October. Although flak was a lesser problem, the weather and fatigue were more so, with flights lasting upwards of ten hours. On 6/7th November two Lancasters were lost over Genoa and a third crashed whilst attempting to land at Mildenhall, killing all the crew.

On 20/21st December 1942 six Mosquitos left on an historic mission for Bomber Command - the first Oboe bombing operation. The target was Lutterwade power station at Wittard, a small Dutch town on the German border. Bufton and two other crews were able to bomb with Oboe but technical problems affected the other three aircraft. On the last night of the year, two Mosquitos led eight of the squadron's Lancasters to Düsseldorf but with only moderate success. From now on the Oboe squadron would be essential to the Command's major operations against Ruhr targets, and not until 26/27th March would an Oboe Mosquito be lost in action.

The squadron's Mosquitos became deeply involved in the Battle of the Ruhr, earning high praise from Air Chief Marshal Harris, who considered them 'an indispensible pathfinder'. The massive Krupps munitions complex at Essen was the target on 5/6th March 1943 as the opening salvo of the major offensive. It had been bombed on 21 previous occasions but without any conspicuous success. Eight Oboe Mosquitos, along with the same number of Lancasters, left Wyton. This night saw Bomber Command's 100,000th sortie of the war.

Three Mosquitos had to return early because of technical faults but the rest marked the target with red ground indicators, on time and accurately despite the thick ground haze. The attack, in three waves, was over in 40 minutes and it proved to be the most successful and effective raid delivered on Essen so far. The squadron lost one Lancaster. In subsequent Essen operations another four crews would go missing, but 83 Squadron would suffer fewer losses than other Lancaster squadrons despite its PFF role. For two months during the summer of 1943 it survived many operations without a single casualty.

During June, 109 flew its first operations with Mark BIXs, enabling the crews to attack from 30,000 feet, which increased the operational range of Oboe. The Pathfinder Force now had a second Oboe squadron (No 105) operating from Marham and, on 4th July, 109 left Wyton to join it there.

In its place came another PFF Mosquito squadron, No 139, under the command of Wing Commander R.W. Reynolds, DSO Bar, DFC, a famous 'Mossie' pilot. It was a welcome return to Wyton for the squadron, which had flown the first operational sortie of the war from the airfield. The crews had been tasked with flying nuisance or 'spoof' raids in an attempt to confuse the enemy as to the main force's intentions. They also pioneered the bombing operations made famous by the Group's LNSF.

On 9th May 1943, Group Captain John Searby, DFC, had arrived to take over command of 83. It was a matter of the return of a local hero, as he was born at Whittlesey. Searby had been flying since 1935 and was a product of the Halton Apprentice School. He would control one of the most important and impressive bombing operations of the war - Peenemunde. Searby remained with the squadron until November 1943 and ultimately became Bomber Command's Navigation Officer, retiring as Air Commodore. During the month the squadron, along with 156, received its first H2S Lancasters and used them over

Wuppertal on the 29/30th.

Two devastating raids took place towards the end of July. On the 25/26th, Essen and the Krupps works were severely damaged, and it was said that the destruction caused Doktar Gustav Krupps to have a stroke from which he never recovered. Two nights later Hamburg was the target for the first of four operations. As the crews were waiting for their take-off signals, one of the Lancasters blew up, killing several ground personnel as well as three of the crew. Despite this tragic accident all but one of the aircraft left, and later Air Vice-Marshal Bennett praised the crews for carrying on with the mission. In the four Hamburg raids, 83 was the only heavy PFF squadron not to lose a single aircraft to enemy action, although one was written off after crash-landing at Wittering.

The attack on Turin on 7/8th August proved to be a dry run for the Peenemunde operation, with Group Captain Searby acting as Master of Ceremonies (later Master Bomber). Ten days later, the attack on the German V2 rocket research establishment on the Baltic coast was noteworthy for several reasons. It would be the first time Bomber Command had attempted a major precision raid at night on a small target. Also, it would be the first time a Master Bomber controlled a full-scale operation, and furthermore, as there were three specific aiming points, the PFF would attempt to move the marking whilst the raid was in progress. 139's Mosquitos were sent to Berlin to attract the Luftwaffe away from the main force. Searby would control almost 600 bombers and the importance of the operation was impressed on all the crews at their briefings by the threat, 'If you don't knock out this target tonight, it will be laid on again tomorrow and every night until the job is done.'

Fifteen Lancasters and eight Mosquitos left Wyton under the command of two Group Captains - the Mosquito leader was L. C. Slee, DFC. Searby remained over the target throughout the raid, issuing crisp instructions to the crews as they arrived, and much of the success was due to his calm and careful handling of the proceedings. Over 18,000 tons of bombs were dropped and much of the research station was destroyed, with the experimental work put back by over two months and the scale of the enemy's V2 rocket operation reduced. Forty aircraft were lost (6.7%), most of them in the third wave, several falling to the new 'Schräge Musik' Me 110s equipped with twin upward-firing cannons fitted in the cockpits. Two Mosquitos failed to make it back to Wyton; one crashed at Swanton Morley but the crew escaped. Only two PFF aircraft were lost from the main operation, but

*Mosquito ML897 of No 1409 (Met) Flight.*

83 Squadron survived intact. Searby was awarded the DSO, and the Master Bomber method of control later became standard practice.

At the end of 1943, the Mosquitos of 139 Squadron had completed 730 sorties for the loss of 15 aircraft (2%). Berlin had figured large on its itinerary, 41 occasions, with Cologne, Duisburg, Düsseldorf, Dortmund and Krefeld also featuring. The crews had also 'windowed' in front of the main force, as well as marking on many operations. By the beginning of February the squadron had moved away to Upwood.

The German capital took a heavy toll on 83 Squadron's experienced crews. On 23/24th August 1943, Flight Lieutenant Brian Slade, DFC was lost. He was on his 59th operation and his crew, despite an average age of 21 years, had amassed 330 PFF operations between them. Two Commanding Officers were lost during the bitter battle. Wing Commander R. Hilton, DSO, DFC, who had been in charge for three weeks, went missing on 23/24th November, and his replacement, Wing Commander W. Abercromby, DFC Bar, was lost on the first night of the New Year. Towards the end of March 1944 there were moves afoot to reduce the size of the PFF, and as a result the squadron moved back into No 5 Group in April. It had conducted 167 PFF raids and lost 56 aircraft (3.2%), the highest Lancaster losses amongst the four original PFF squadrons.

The airfield now became the sole preserve of Mosquitos. No 1409 (Met) Flight had been in residence since 8th January. Its crews had invariably completed at least one operational tour before being accepted in the Flight, and in late 1944 the average number of operations of the crews was 87!

One pilot, Squadron Leader Jack Currie, DFC, gained post-war fame with his best selling books, *Lancaster Target* and *Mosquito Victory*. As he described in the latter book: 'The Met Flight made their sorties - four or five a day - to hunt down all the weather in the European skies. Not the smallest cloud, from the Russian front to the Atlantic, from Norway to the Alps, from MSL [Mean Sea Level] to 40,000 feet, was left to live its life in privacy. A blue Mosquito would be sniffing around it, seeking out its secrets and running home to tell - to Bomber, Fighter, Transport, 2nd TAF and USAF [sic] - to anyone prepared to listen.' The Flight's long trips out into the Atlantic to seek out weather fronts prior to D-Day were critical in deciding the exact day for the invasion. The Flight remained at Wyton for the rest of the war and completed over 1,360 sorties for the loss of three aircraft.

In September the airfield saw the reformation of another squadron, No 128, becoming the latest addition to the LNSF. Its first BXXs arrived on the 8th of the month. Two days later one crew left to attack Berlin, actually several days before the squadron was officially formed. One Mosquito was lost on the 16th when engaged over Brunswick, and despite having only a handful of aircraft the squadron still managed to mount 22 sorties in the month. This figure increased dramatically in October with the crews operating on 21 nights, with some flying BXXVs.

The following month the Mosquito force made its first daylight raid, and on the last day of the month five crews attacked an oil plant at Meiderich, outside Duisburg. This proved to be a most effective strike with 'black smoke rising to a height of 10,000 feet' - another spectacular success for the 'wooden wonders'!

One of the most impressive operations came on 1st January 1945, when 17 Mosquitos attacked 14 railway tunnels in the Eifel region between the Rhine and the Ardennes. This was an attempt to block valuable supplies getting through to Von Runstedt's forces in the Ardennes. The operation started tragically at Wyton when a Mosquito crashed on take-off, killing its crew. The other five led by Wing Commander R. J. Burroughs, DFC, attacked tunnels in the Koblenz area. They were required to place their time-fused 4,000 pound bombs into the tunnel entrances from a height of about 200 feet. One Mosquito was brought down by light flak whilst attacking the Kochem tunnel.

Before the month was out another Mosquito squadron was formed at Wyton, No 163, the last to join the Strike Force. The first BXXVs were received on the 26th and two nights later four crews were in action

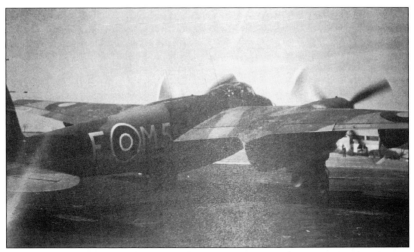

*Mosquito BXVI RV-297 of 128 Squadron at Wyton, March 1945.*

over Mainz. At the end of the month the Hansa benzol oil plant at Dortmund was attacked and, on 1/2nd February, the crews made the first of many trips to Berlin, with some of the Mosquitos going out for a second time on the same night. From the 21/22nd, the German capital was attacked on 36 consecutive nights, with the last big raid coming on 21/22nd March when 128 Squadron sent 14 crews in the first wave and 163 supplied twelve. Each squadron sent out four crews on the second wave. Only one Mosquito was lost from a total of 140 sorties on the night.

Both Mosquito squadrons finished operations on the same night - 2/ 3rd May 1945 - each putting out 16 aircraft to bomb Kiel in two waves. After VE Day each received a Lancaster on loan, and they proceeded to fly 'Cook's tours', enabling the ground staff at Wyton to view the destruction that had been wrought on German cities and towns. 163 Squadron was disbanded on 19th August, whilst in the following month, 128 left for Warboys. Already, in June, another famous PFF squadron, 156, had brought its Lancasters from Upwood and it, too, was disbanded towards the end of September. The airfield was ominously quiet after six continuous years of war.

# 27
# MINOR AIRFIELDS

Besides the wartime operational airfields there were five small landing grounds in Cambridgeshire which require a brief mention - Caxton Gibbet, Lord's Bridge, Peterborough, Sibson and Somersham.

The airfield at Caxton Gibbet was situated close to the village at the junction of the A428 and A1198 roads. It was shown in a Bomber Command return of September 1939 as an 'available satellite for Bassingbourn', but there is no evidence that it was used as such. From the summer of 1940 a landing area, to the right of the A14 (A1198) road, was intended to act as a relief landing ground for the Tiger Moths of No 22 Elementary Flying Training School based at Marshall's at Cambridge. Ultimately there were seven small blister hangars with temporary accommodation for about 80 persons. The school tended to use the small grass airfield mainly for night-flying circuits and landings, though from June 1941, F Flight operated from the airfield until well into 1942.

For such a small and rather inconspicuous airfield, the Luftwaffe seemed unusually attracted to Caxton Gibbet. Their first attack came in February 1941 when the Moths were busily engaged in their night-flying. Then, in July, when a Tiger Moth was in the landing circuit it was shot at but escaped without any serious damage. This incident only appeared to encourage the Luftwaffe because in the following month (6th August) two Moths were damaged by the blast from some ten high explosives that were dropped. Later in the same month (the 23/24th) the airfield came under a further attack, and sadly two civilian workers from Marshall's were killed. Ten days later a solitary German raider dropped a few HE and incendiaries after making two abortive approaches to the airfield. It is difficult to understand why the Luftwaffe thought the airfield deserved such treatment!

The airfield's last raid came in October 1943, on the night of the

*A de Havilland Tiger Moth II, 1942. (RAF Museum)*

3/4th, when four or five bombs fell close to the airfield without causing any damage. Perhaps this final attack was a case of mistaken identity because on the same night, nearby Gransden Lodge was also bombed. The occasional Wellington managed to make an emergency landing despite the restricted grass runway. During 1944 some of the accommodation huts, set at the northern end of the airfield, were used by airmen from Bourn, just a short distance to the south-east.

Lord's Bridge was a small relief landing ground to the north of the A1603 at the village of Barton. It was never really developed and was only used by the trainee pilots of 22 EFTS, just across the city at Cambridge airfield. Many airmen serving at operational stations in the area remember it as a large bomb store, and they made frequent visits to collect bombs. It would have seemed to be a prime target, which either the Luftwaffe ignored or were unaware of!

Peterborough, or Westwood as it was originally known, was about two miles to the north-west of the city, and has now disappeared under an industrial estate. For about 20 years virtually all of the service's training aircraft flew from the airfield: Hawker Harts and Audaxes, de Havilland Tiger Moths, Airspeed Oxfords, Miles Masters, Avro Ansons, and American Harvards with the odd Hurricane and Spitfire thrown in for good measure.

The airfield came into prominence in December 1935 when No 7

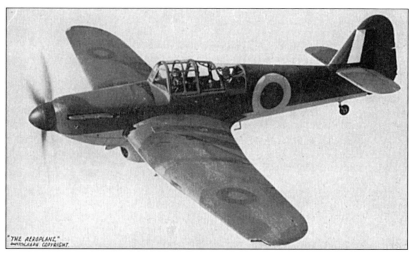

*A Miles Master I Advanced Trainer, as used by No 7 (Pilots) Advanced Flying Unit at Peterborough.*

Service Flying Training School was formed, with the first course commencing in the following January. These schools were one step up the ladder from the EFTSs, providing advanced flying practice where the student pilots had to complete at least 22 hours of dual flying along with 20 hours solo, before passing on to the Operational Training Units. By the summer of 1939 the school was training pilots for the Fleet Air Arm using Oxfords, and the course had been extended from 16 to 20 weeks. Twelve months later it was decided to transfer this stage of flying training to Commonwealth countries and by the end of 1940 7 SFTS was moved out to Ontario, Canada, with the last completed course passing out in January 1941. For the next 18 months Tiger Moths of several training schools used the airfield.

On 1st June 1942, 7 (Pilots) Advanced Flying Unit was formed at Peterborough under the control of No 21 Group of Technical Training Command. The Unit ultimately comprised four Flights operating in Masters (over 130) and a handful of Ansons. The intake of pilots rose dramatically from some 90 to over 200, and in March 1944 a Flight of Hurricanes were added to the complement. The Masters had a top speed of about 250 mph and offered a new experience for the embryo pilots. The unit was reorganised in August 1944 into two advanced Flights and by the end of the year 7 SFTS had been reactivated with Oxfords and Harvards, mainly to train French pilots for their new air force. The school left Peterborough in early April 1946, and it was then placed on a care and maintenance basis. In post-war years, British European Airways used the airfield as a helicopter base.

Sibson, to the south of Wansford, is the only airfield of these five that has survived. It first came into use in July 1940 as a relief landing ground for Peterborough, but by January it had passed to the control of Cranfield in Bedfordshire. Oxfords of 14 SFTS used the airfield for night flying and landings. Tiger Moths from two EFT Schools also used Sibson quite regularly. When the Advanced Flying Unit was formed at Peterborough, two Flights were soon based at the airfield on a permanent basis. Slowly the basic facilities began to improve with the provision of hangars, extra accommodation, flight offices and a lecture room. After the reorganisation of the Unit in August 1944, flying at Sibson slowly petered out, and the airfield was formally closed in October 1946. Since the early 1960s, Sibson has become the centre of civilian flying in the area, and is known as Peterborough Business Airport.

Somersham airfield was sited to the south-west of the village, and the rudimentary grass airfield was designed during 1941 to be the Q site for Wyton. It was effectively a sham airfield, and the sites were named after the decoy 'Q' vessels used during the First World War. There were a fair number of them dotted about East Anglia and their purpose was to confound the enemy and thus hopefully draw air attacks away from the operational airfields. This necessitated the construction of dummy hangars, living quarters and even mock aircraft to make the site look realistic from aerial photographs. In many cases they were also provided with flare path lighting.

Towards the end of 1942 it was felt that the threat from air attack had sufficiently receded, and most were closed down. Somersham was still used by Lysanders and Hudsons of 138 and 161 Squadrons at Tempsford, which were engaged on secret SOE operations. The small and secluded airfield was ideally suited to practise night-landings and take-offs. There is no record of the airfield being bombed, although in March 1945 a V2 rocket landed close by.

# 28

# CIVILIANS
# AT WAR

At six o'clock on the first evening of the war, HM King George VI made a broadcast to the Nation. His distressing stammer seemed to give his words greater moment and sincerity: 'There may be dark days ahead, and war can no longer be confined to the battlefield. But we can only do right as we see right, and reverently commit our cause to God...ready for whatever service and sacrifice it may demand, then with God's help, we shall prevail.'

A copy of the King's short speech was sent to every household in the country, but most people little realised just how heavy their trials and burdens would be in the coming war. These six years would dramatically change the lives of every man, woman and child in the country. The conflict would soon become known as the 'People's War' or, as Winston Churchill called it, in the summer of 1940, 'a war of the unknown warriors'.

Already the public had been inculcated into the possible horrors of a future war. In April 1937 the Air Raid Warden Service had been created, and during the Munich crisis of the following year half a million volunteers had come forward. The universally detested gas masks had been issued (38 million) with the warning that in the event of war, they should be carried at all times, though most ignored this edict. Posters regarding their use were prominently displayed and the tops of GPO post boxes were coated with yellow gas detector paint.

Thousands upon thousands of sandbags had been filled, and now surrounded important buildings as well as the anti-aircraft machine gun posts that had sprung up in the towns, along with air raid warden posts and emergency static water tanks in suburban streets. Air raid slit trenches had been dug in Old Chesterton in Cambridge, with other concrete shelters being built around the city, although by 1942 there was still only sufficient public shelter accommodation for 30% of its population. The famous Anderson shelters, constructed of corrugated steel sheets and designed for domestic gardens, were made available free to those with incomes of less than £250 per year, otherwise a charge of £7 was levied. The indoor 'tabletop' Morrison shelter appeared in 1941.

During September 1939 the National Register was established, enabling the issue of National Identity cards to every person, followed closely by ration books - the two most important documents of wartime Britain. Petrol rationing was introduced and the blackout regulations strictly enforced, at times by over-zealous wardens! The blackout transformed civilian conditions of life more than any other single feature of the war, and it was this that the majority found most irksome and inconvenient, food rationing included. In September, road accidents increased by 100% and during the war there were thousands of minor injuries to pedestrians as a result of the lighting restrictions.

The first week of the month saw the mass evacuation of children. The County was classified as a 'reception area', with Cambridge expecting 24,000, but only receiving 6,700. By the middle of November over half of these had returned home. Seven months later less than 2,000 children remained.

The winter of 1939/40 was the most severe of the century. Although coal was not rationed supplies were scarce, not because of the war but rather as a result of delivery problems due to the adverse weather. Throughout the war, the public were continually exhorted to save fuel. Food rationing was introduced on 8th January 1940 with the Government's intention, 'To begin it gently'. Four ounces of bacon per person per week and the same quantity of butter were allowed, followed by rationing of cheese, meat, sugar, preserves and, in July, by tea (two ounces!). The first wartime winter was a hard and difficult time for all. The extreme weather, the blackout, bus and train problems, food rationing and queuing, all added to the misery. Queuing became a wartime necessity and the habit was so engrained on the public that it almost became automatic. The cynical would say, 'If you see a queue join it'!

The uncertainty of what the future held brought about a general malaise, with the 'Phoney' or 'Strange War' only adding further unease, as everybody waited for the 'war to start and get it over with'. The BBC was the chief solace during these dark winter nights, and the favourite show was *ITMA* (It's That Man Again) with Tommy Handley and a talented team of mimics producing much needed humour and bringing many catch-phrases into everyday speech. The nine o'clock evening news almost became essential listening, although in the early days two out of three listeners admitted to tuning in to Lord Haw Haw (William Joyce) on Radio Hamburg to hear his biased view of the progress of the war!

Suddenly, winter gave way to an early brilliant spring and at Easter (the end of March) people flocked to the coasts. It would prove to be the last 'peaceful' holiday of the war. On 4th April the Prime Minister, Neville Chamberlain, made a most ill-considered speech: 'After seven months of war I feel ten times as confident of victory as I did at the beginning...one thing is certain, Hitler has missed the bus.' Four days later Denmark and Norway were invaded, and the 'Phoney War' had come to a sudden end. By early May, Neville Chamberlain was forced to resign and an all-party Coalition Government was formed with Winston Churchill at its head. In his first speech as Prime Minister, on 13th May, he said that he had nothing to offer but 'blood, toil, sweat and tears'. Within a month Britain found itself on its own, and the 'People's War' was about to begin.

On 14th May 1940 Anthony Eden, the Secretary of State for War, made a radio appeal for men between the ages of 17 and 65 years to enlist for a new force to be known as the Local Defence Volunteers. They would be given a uniform and armed. Within 24 hours a quarter of a million men had come forward. At Peterborough 400 enrolled in two days with the average age of recruits being 35 years, and a fair percentage of First World War veterans. By the end of June the total numbers had grown to one and a half million, and in July the name of the new force was changed to 'The Home Guard' at Churchill's insistence.

The original and primary function of the Home Guard was to deal with enemy parachutists, but they also manned road blocks as well as patrolling regularly at night. Weapons were rather scarce, although one million First World War rifles were purchased from America. Over 8,000 arrived at the Corn Exchange at Cambridge in July, but they were so heavily covered in thick grease that 250 women volunteered to clean the rifles, a task which took them about two weeks. The comic images created by the television series *Dad's Army* are a little unfair on a force that ultimately became quite professional, and many Home Guards- men manned anti-aircraft batteries as well as undertaking regular army duties later in the war. However, the official issue of specially manufactured pikes in September 1941 did little to improve its image!

*Bomb damage to houses in Vicarage Terrace, Cambridge in June 1940. (Cambridge-shire Collection)*

During the summer of 1943 there were over 1,100 battalions comprising some one and three quarter million men, with an average age of under 30 years. Now, less than 7% were 'old sweats'!

It was not until June 1940 that the County suffered its first air raids. On the 5/6th some bombs fell around Peterborough and the first incendiaries to be dropped on Britain landed near Duxford airfield. But it was the Luftwaffe's first major raid on the 18/19th that brought the first fatalities. Seventy enemy bombers attacked targets in eastern England with bombs falling around Huntingdon, March, North Witchford and St Neots. At Cambridge only two bombs fell but they severely damaged eight houses in Vicarage Terrace, killing nine persons. Ten more were admitted to hospital with injuries, and there was also one fatality at West Fen, Ely. This air raid was the most severe of the war so far, at least in terms of civilian casualties, and there was a shocked reaction in Cambridge. Many had felt that, 'It would never happen to anywhere as lovely as Cambridge...too beautiful to bomb.'

More raids occurred during the summer and the autumn, and, on 15/16th October, a 500 kg bomb landed at Berrow Road in Cambridge, the heaviest bomb to fall on the city. Further sporadic raids continued during early 1941 and through to 1944. In total there were over 320 alerts in Cambridge with 39 civilians killed and another 71 injured, although Cambridgeshire did not suffer as many air raids as other East Anglian counties. Ed Murrow, the American commentator on wartime Britain, was amazed at the people's reaction to bombing. He marvelled at their 'sang-froid' under the frightening and terrible bombardment. Indeed, most viewed air raids with a grim fatalism, 'If your number's on it, the bomb'll get you.' After visiting bombed-out civilians Winston Churchill remarked, 'I see the spirit of an unconquerable people.'

But 'Death from the Air' also took another form, the additional hazard of crashes of friendly (and enemy) aircraft. As the number of airfields in the County increased, the threat heightened each year, especially from 1942 when the number of aircraft using the County's airspace escalated. In 1941 there were at least 16 crashes. The most serious occurred on 11/12th February when a badly damaged Wellington was abandoned and it came down onto a house in Histon Road, Cambridge, killing three elderly ladies with another two seriously injured. On the same night, another Wellington crashed about five miles south of Wisbech. In the following year another Wellington, which was on fire, crashed into cottages at Somersham on 5/6th October, and in the tremendous blaze seven cottages were destroyed and eleven villagers lost their lives.

Although there were more incidents in 1944, most aircraft came down in open land but in September one civilian and four US servicemen were killed when a RAF aircraft crashed at Pampisford. On 6th February 1945, two B-17s crashed whilst assembling and they came down at Prickwillow and Wicken, with two civilians killed. On a more mundane note, there were frequent complaints about low-flying aircraft, especially at dusk, 'waking up children or tired workers, who had just gone to sleep.' Roads and lanes crowded with service vehicles and the 'continual din of planes' were things that had to be borne with stoicism and patience.

With the fall of France in June 1940 the threat of invasion became a distinct and frightening possibility. Most were convinced of its inevitability, a view that was fuelled by the distribution to every household of a pamphlet entitled *Rules for Civilians in case of Invasion*. The ringing of church bells was forbidden, in future this would denote that an invasion had taken place. Signposts were removed, milestones obliterated, the names of railway stations taken down and guide books and maps were withdrawn from sale. A spy mania gripped the country. The carrying of cameras could lead to arrest, and posters exhorting the public to be careful in their speech, with slogans such as,

*The Cambridge Airport Home Guard unit, 1945. (Marshall of Cambridge Aerospace Ltd)*

'Careless talk costs lives' and 'Be like Dad keep Mum', becoming popular. Well into 1941 the threat of invasion was still real and in March, parish invasion committees were formed under the control of the East Anglian Regional Commissioner in Cambridge, Sir Will Spens.

In June 1940 a Regional War Room had been set up in Montague Road, Cambridge. The Regional Commission would take on 'absolute powers' to govern East Anglia, should the area be invaded and isolated from the Government in Whitehall. The gravity of the situation was only heightened by the deployment of more troops into the area, a night curfew being imposed, and the appearance of 'strong nodal points' - pill boxes - at road junctions and in the surrounding fields. Many have survived to this day.

At the height of the Battle of Britain the first National Savings week was launched to provide money for the Spitfire Fund - each aircraft priced at £5,000. The public's response was magnificent, and throughout the war National Savings reached an unprecedented level. It was estimated that by 1943 over a quarter of the public's disposable income (after tax) was being saved, compared with 5% pre-war. Over 300,000 National Savings groups were formed in factories, offices, schools and in streets. Quite frankly, there were few consumer goods available and the odd luxury, if it could be obtained, was purchased furtively as it would be considered against the 'war effort'. By November 1941 the citizens of Cambridge had saved over £5 million. Considering that the war was costing £12 million *a day*, National Savings was a mere drop in the ocean, but the Government viewed it as a valuable safety valve to prevent rampant inflation. The BBC news programme announced details of each week's donations, such was the importance attached to National Savings.

In addition to the normal on-going weekly savings, each year a special drive was mounted for a specific cause: War Weapons, Warship Week, Wings for Victory and Salute the Soldier. In Wings for Victory Weeks in the spring and summer of 1943, Cambridge set a target of £750,000 and almost reached £1 million. Stirlings and Lancasters were put on display in city and town centres to encourage public interest. These weeks were just part of the savings mania that gripped the country during the war years when the watchwords were, 'Waste Not Want Not'. Almost every conceivable item was salvaged. Iron railings disappeared from parks, cemeteries and houses, and there were salvage drives for waste paper, rags, bones, gramophone records, jam pots, aluminium pots and pans, tins and books. Salvage shops were opened throughout the country and many streets had their own 'salvage stewards'. Any kitchen waste was saved to feed pigs, and newspapers and magazines ran salvage competitions with prizes for the best hints. The nation had become dedicated to a 'saving regime'.

National self-sufficiency became the keynote of the Home Front, and if saving had become a national obsession then 'Dig for Victory' became a serious and universal enterprise. The famous slogan had first appeared at the outbreak of the war and every available open space was commandeered for cultivation. Gardens were turned over to vegetable plots and the number of allotments increased from 800,000 in 1938 to one and a half million in 1943. The Ministry of Information launched a massive propaganda programme in 1942 with posters on hoardings and over ten million leaflets being issued on the subject.

The cultivation of home produce was considered one of the most important civilian tasks of the war. Many back gardens housed chicken coops to provide their own supply of eggs, which were always in desperately short supply. By 1944 these domestic hens were providing over a quarter of the nation's fresh eggs. The short-fall had been supplemented by the packets of dried egg, which was imported in great quantities from the USA. The public was exhorted to spend their holidays working on the land at one of the many 'harvest camps'. Even

*A publicity shot for the Women's Land Army. It was not always so happy and sunny! (via G. Thomas)*

schoolchildren attended during their summer holidays, although there were some disquieting reports about children being used as 'slave labourers...working in excess of 60 hours a week.'

The most famous farm workers were the voluntary members of the Women's Land Army. It had briefly existed at the end of the First World War, and was reformed in June 1939 by Lady Denman. By the end of the war it numbered close to 100,000 young women. They were drawn from all walks of life but mainly from the towns, and were enticed by the visions of 'a healthy and happy job' in some rural arcadia, as portrayed in the various recruitment posters for the WLA. The reality was often vastly different; long, hard, dirty and back-breaking work in all weathers, suspicious farmers, low wages and inadequate accommodation with concern expressed over their moral welfare! Nevertheless, they proved to be excellent workers and ultimately gained grudging respect and even praise from the farming community.

In June 1942 groups of land girls were inspected by the King and Queen when they visited the County to view the extensive reclamation work completed in the Fenlands. Most of the girls had been engaged on the reclamation work and this was an official acknowledgement of their war efforts. In July 1943, Land Army girls paraded in Cambridge on Farm Sunday and many were presented with merit awards.

In December 1941 women between the ages of 21 and 24 (later extended to 31) were required to register for National Service. Already many had volunteered for the three armed services, and there were members of the Women's Auxiliary Air Force (formed in June 1939) at most of the airfields in the county. Perhaps the most numerous body of women wartime workers was the Women's Voluntary Service (WVS), over a million of whom had been engaged in a variety of tasks since the outbreak of the war - civil defence, mobile canteens, reception and rest centres, evacuation, distribution of clothes etc. The majority of women worked in factories, offices, canteens, on trains and buses, or undertaking maintenance works and some were employed as labourers in the construction of airfields.

By 1943 it was estimated that seven million women were engaged in war work of some description or other. In April HM The Queen made a broadcast for the country's women, when she told them, 'In these years of tragedy and glory, you have earned the gratitude and admiration of all mankind.' The mass employment of women was perhaps the major social change brought about by the war.

For the civilians, 1941 and most of 1942 were the nadir of the war years. Another two harsh winters had to be endured, at a time when it was reckoned that the country's diet was at its poorest. Rationing had been extended to soap, sweets and tinned foods by a points system, buying clothes and footwear was restricted by coupons, and petrol was now available only for 'essential users'. White bread had disappeared, and only 'national wheatmeal' bread was available, described as 'nasty, dirty, dark, coarse, and indigestible.' There was an acute shortage of even the essentials of life, let alone beer and cigarettes, and any complaint was greeted with the reply, 'Don't you know there's a war on?' The black market and profiteering flourished, and the word 'spiv' entered the country's vocabulary.

Two years of war had taken a heavy toll of supplies, and had greatly strained the public's tolerance and patience; all the sacrifices they had made and all the hardships that had been endured had brought scant results. In Cambridge, where the population had increased from 50,000 to 80,000, there were many instances of homeless women sleeping in air raid and bus shelters, and more hostels had to be set up. In rural areas the massive programme of airfield construction, then reaching a height, had brought an invasion of workers with the roads and lanes choked by heavy vehicles. The incessant noise and omnipresent mud made living conditions in the villages almost intolerable.

Air raids still continued although with less frequency or severity but, in 1942, the bombardment of cathedral cities and towns brought fresh and added hardship and misery. The war news from abroad was dismal and depressing to say the least, disaster upon disaster with only the RAF taking the offensive to the enemy. Many expressed the view that there appeared to be no end in sight to the war. It seemed to have lasted for an eternity and the morale of the country was at its lowest ebb. They were dark days indeed. The sole consolation came at the end of 1941 when the country was no longer on its own, America had entered the war.

The *Cambridge Daily News* of 1st August 1942 carried a headline, 'Glad to see you, Americans' - the first acknowledgement of the 'Friendly Invasion' of US servicemen into the area. Over the next twelve months, and until the end of the war, Cambridge, Peterborough and most towns and villages in the County would be thronged with American airmen. They had been issued with a pamphlet called *Over There*, which gave them information on the British people. It was larded with comments such as, '[they] are reserved but not unfriendly...are a tough strong people and good allies.' There were also many 'don'ts'. 'Don't show off or brag...make fun of accents...criticise the food, beer or cigarettes and NEVER criticise the King and Queen!'

There was a certain resentment at first. The hackneyed cliche, 'over-paid, over-sexed and over here' obviously had some substance, and many locals complained that, 'The streets, pubs are crowded with Yanks, a state of social chaos exists in the town [Peterborough]'. The Bell Hotel in Cambridge became the first American Red Cross Club in the County and, in December 1942, before it had formally opened, a large party was held for the children in the area, the first of many to be held in American bases thoughout East Anglia. Slowly, the friendly and generous nature of the newcomers thawed much of the locals' reserve, and strong links of friendship were established, which have lasted down the years.

By November 1942 the tide of war had suddenly turned. At long last there was a victory to celebrate - El Alamein. Church bells were rung on the 15th as a celebration, though Churchill added a note of caution, 'This is not the end. It is not even the beginning of the end. But perhaps, the end of the beginning.' During the next twelve months there were positive signs in the County of the change of fortunes. More airfields opened and day and night the skies were filled with armadas of Allied aircraft leaving to bomb targets far and wide.

In May 1943 the Minister of Food was able to announce that, 'The country is now better fed than a year ago'. Much of this was a result of the vast increase in home food production, and because for the first time for several years no North Atlantic convoy had been attacked. But the improvement in the diet was also attributed to the number of works, office and school canteens which had opened and were not so restricted by the food rationing.

Another attributable factor was the introduction of 'communal feeding centres', or 'British Restaurants', as Churchill had insisted on naming them. They were non-profitmaking and Government-sponsored, providing a good, wholesome hot mid-day meal for one shilling per head. The first British Restaurant in Cambridge was sited in Pitt Club in Jesus Lane, which had once been a retreat for wealthy undergraduates. Well over 6,000 hot dinners were being served each week in the several British Restaurants in the city. For country areas, a Rural Pie Scheme had been introduced in 1942 to supply hot snacks (some one and a half million a week) to over 5,000 villages.

From now on, life on the Home Front improved. The country began to feel that it was only a matter of time before victory was achieved. The local press greeted 1944 with the message, 'There is one universal hope today. It is that the year upon which we are entering may see the end of the war.' D-Day was shortly followed by the V1 rocket onslaught. Although for the majority of people the flying bombs or doodle-bugs remained a mystery, rumours quickly spread of the vast damage in London. It was not until 6th July that the Government publicly admitted that '100 a day are falling'. The first V1 rocket in the County landed near Fowlmere on 28th June, and mercifully it was spared the worst of the attacks with only another nine falling, the last at Somersham in March 1945. The rocket attacks did bring about a second evacuation from London, and it was reckoned that by July over 10,000 women and children had arrived in Cambridge. There was an acute shortage of voluntary homes for them and compulsory billeting orders were used, which caused considerable local opposition. However, by the end of September the majority had returned to London.

During the autumn things began to get back to normal. Blackout restrictions were partially lifted and the gas lamps came back on to universal approval. On 1st November the Home Guard was stood down, and in December over 3,500 of them paraded in Cambridge for the last time. Even by Christmas there was still an acute shortage of goods and food. One pound of oranges were allocated per ration book, but the promised lemons did not arrive. And as for bananas, they had

*An almost intact Do 217M came down in allotments at Chesterton on the night of 23rd February 1944.*

not been seen since 1939. When the first supplies arrived post-war, the Attlee government was said to have issued one free to every person under the age of 18, but not many people (including the writer) remember this ever happening!

The war ended almost as it began, in a state of uncertainty. The first week of May 1945 was riven with rumours and counter rumours. When the news of Hitler's death was broadcast on the 2nd, everybody assumed that peace was at hand. However, for the next five days it was a matter of, 'It's peace. It isn't peace. They've surrendered. They haven't surrendered.' Finally the news came that Tuesday, 8th May 'will be treated as Victory-in-Europe Day, and will be regarded as a holiday.' The People's War had come to an end, and as Winston Churchill said, 'This is your victory.' Over 65,000 civilians had paid the ultimate price, with another 86,000 seriously wounded.

As he had done on the first day of the war, so HM The King addressed the Nation on 8th May: 'I ask you to join with me in that act of thanksgiving. Let us remember those who will not come back...the men and women in all the services who have laid down their lives. Then let us salute in proud gratitude the great host of the living who have brought us to victory. Armed or unarmed, men and women, you have fought, striven and endured to your utmost. Today we give thanks for our great deliverance.'

# BIBLIOGRAPHY

During my research I consulted various books. I list them below with my grateful thanks to the authors.

Air Ministry, *Bomber Command*, H.M.S.O, 1941.

Air Ministry The Battle of Britain, H.M.S.O, 1941.

Armitage, Michael, *The Royal Air Force: An Illustrated History*, Cassell, 1993.

Asworth, Chris, *RAF Bomber Command, 1936 - 1968*, Patrick Stephens, 1995.

Bennett, Don, *Pathfinder*, Frederick Muller, 1958.

Bowyer, Chaz, *Bomber Barons*, William Kimber, 1983.

Bowyer, Chaz, *Fighter Command: 1936 - 1968*, Dent, 1980.

Bowyer, Michael J.F., *Action Stations: 1. Military Airfields of East Anglia*, Patrick Stephens, 1990.

Bowyer, Michael J. F. & Sharp, C. Martin, *Mosquito*, Faber & Faber, 1967.

Calder, Angus, *The People's War; Britain 1939-45*, Pimlico, 1992

Chorley, W. R., *RAF Bomber Command Losses in the Second World War*, Vols 1 to 4, Midland Pubns., 1992-96.

Cooper, Alan, *Air Battle of the Ruhr*, Airlife, 1992.

Cooper, Alan, *Bombers over Berlin*, William Kimber, 1985.

Croall, Jonathan, *Don't You Know There's a War On?: the People's Voice*, Hutchinson, 1989.

Currie, Jack, *Mosquito Victory*, Goodall, 1996.

Deighton, Len, *Fighter: The True Story of the Battle of Britain*, J. Cape, 1977.

Delve, Ken, *D-Day: The Air Battle*, Arms & Armour, 1994.

Dundas, Hugh, *Flying Start*, Stanley Paul, 1988.

Embry, Sir Basil, *Mission Completed*, Methuen, 1957.

Franks, Norman, *Claims to Fame: Lancaster*, Arms & Armour, 1995.

Franks, Norman, *Forever Strong: The Story of No 75 Squadron RNZAF*, Random Century, 1991.

Freeman, Roger A, *The Mighty Eighth*, Arms & Armour, 1989.

Freeman, Roger A, *The Mighty Eighth War Manual*, Janes Publishing Co., 1984.

Hamlin, John F, *The RAF in Cambridgeshire, Part 2*, J. F. Hamlin, 1989.

Harris, Sir Arthur, *Bomber Offensive*, Collins, 1947.

Jackson, Robert, *Guinness Book of Air Warfare*, Guinness Publishing, 1993.

Jackson, Robert, *Storm from the Skies: The Strategic Bombing Offensive, 1943-5*, Arthur Barker, 1974.

James, John, *The Paladins*, Macdonald & Co., 1990.

Johnson, Johnnie, *Wing Leader*, Chatto & Windus, 1956.

Longmate, Norman, *The Bombers*, Hutchinson, 1983.

Longmate, Norman, *When We Won The War*, Hutchinson, 1977.

Maynard, John, *Bennett and the Pathfinders*, Arms & Armour, 1996.

Middlebrook, Martin, *The Battle of Hamburg*, Allen Lane, 1980.

Middlebrook, Martin, *The Berlin Raids*, Viking, 1988.

Middlebrook, Martin, *The Schweinfurt - Regensburg Mission: American Raids on 17th August 1943*, Allen Lane, 1983.

Middlebrook, Martin & Everitt, Charles, *The Bomber Command Diaries*, Viking, 1985.

Moyes, Philip J.R., *Bomber Squadrons of the RAF*, Hutchinson, 1981.

Musgrave, Gordon, *Pathfinder Force: The Story of No 8(PFF) Group*, Macdonald & Jane, 1976.

North, Peter, *Eagles High: The Battle of Britain*, Leo Cooper, 1993.

Price, Alfred, *The Spitfire Story*, Arms & Armour, 1982.

Rawlings, John, *Fighter Squadrons of the RAF*, Crecy Books, 1993.

Richards, Denis, *The Hardest Victory: RAF Bomber Command in the Second World War*, Hodder & Stoughton, 1994.

Richards, Denis, *The Royal Air Force, 1939-45*, H.M.S.O., 1953.

Robinson, Anthony, *RAF Fighter Squadrons in the Battle of Britain*, Arms & Armour, 1987.

Scutts, Terry, *Lions in the Sky*, Patrick Stephens, 1987.

Searby, John, *The Great Raid: Peenemunde - 17th August, 1943*, Nutshell Press, 1978.

Smith, David J., *Britain's Military Airfields, 1939-45*, P.S.L., 1989.

Townsend, Peter, *Duel of Eagles*, Weidenfeld & Nicholson, 1970.

Townsend, Peter, *Duel in the Dark*, Harrap, 1986.

Turner, John Frayn, *VCs of the Air*, Harrap, 1960.

Wadsworth, M. P., *They Led the Way: The Story of Pathfinder Squadron 156*, Highgate Publications (Beverley) Ltd., 1992.

Webster, Sir Charles & Frankland, Noble, *The Strategic Air Offensive against Germany, 1939-45*, H.M.S.O., 1961.

# INDEX